THE FEDERAL COURTS IN THE POLITICAL ORDER

Martin H. Redish

THE FEDERAL COURTS IN THE POLITICAL ORDER

Judicial Jurisdiction and American Political Theory

Carolina Academic Press

Jessica,
This One's For You

International Standard Book Number 0-89089-411-6
Library of Congress Catalog Number 90-85345
Manufactured in The United States of America

Carolina Academic Press
700 Kent Street
Durham, North Carolina 27701
919-489-7486

Contents

Preface

This book grew out of my recognition that the seemingly technical and legalistic doctrines of federal jurisdiction in reality have significant implications for the implementation of American political theory. An attempt was therefore made to articulate my understanding of that political theory, and to explore its implications for the shaping of jurisdictional doctrine.

The volume has its origins in two articles I authored in the mid-1980s. The first, "Abstention, Separation of Powers, and the Limits of the Judicial Function," 94 Yale L. J. 71 (1984), provided the basis for development of the "Representational" principle, as well as much of chapter 4. The second, "Judicial Review and the 'Political Question,'" 79 Nw. U. L. Rev. 1031 (1985), gave rise to the logic of the "Counter-Majoritarian" principle, and is largely incorporated in chapter 7. In addition, chapter 4 draws on a subsequent article, "Judicial Parity, Litigant Choice, and Democratic Theory: A Comment on Federal Jurisdiction and Constitutional Rights," 36 UCLA L. Rev. 329 (1988). Also, portions of other chapters, written initially for this book, have subsequently appeared in various articles.

Thanks are owed to the many individuals who contributed to the completion of this project. My colleagues at Northwestern Law School, Ron Allen, Bob Bennett, Gary Lawson, Larry Marshall, and Steve Presser, made extremely helpful contributions, both in their comments on written drafts of various chapters and in their numerous discussions with me about the ideas contained in the book. Also extremely helpful were discussions with two members of Northwestern's Political Science department, Jerry Goldman and Jane Mansbridge. In addition, scholars at other institutions—including Richard Fallon, William Marshall, and Gene Nichol—made valuable comments on earlier drafts. Of course, none of the views expressed in this volume should necessarily be attributed to any of these individuals.

A number of students at Northwestern also made substantial contributions. The fourteen members of my advanced Federal Courts seminar in the fall of 1988—the most intellectually and pedagogically stimulating class I have ever taught—constantly forced me to rearticulate or rethink many of the positions I ultimately take in this book. In addition, valuable individual research assistance was provided by Elizabeth Cisar, Mark Jaffe, and Michael Warner.

Once again, my secretary, Pat Goffer, performed her magic in the typing of the manuscript. The Northwestern University School of Law generously provided all the support services needed to complete the project. Finally, my wife, Caren, and my daughters, Jessica and Elisa, have made me aware that there is considerably more to life than writing books.

THE FEDERAL COURTS IN THE POLITICAL ORDER

ONE

INTRODUCTION: Federal Judicial Authority and the Principles of American Political Theory

Although constitutional theorists have, in recent years, expended significant effort in an attempt to link substantive constitutional doctrine to analysis of American political theory,[1] scholars have only very rarely engaged in similar efforts to apply such theoretical principles to the doctrines of federal jurisdiction.[2] Political theorists have apparently found this area of the law to consist for the most part of highly technical lawyers' doctrines, and therefore to be largely inappropriate for analysis from the perspective of political theory.

The premise of this book is that issues of constitutionalism, democratic theory, and interpretive analysis should be deemed as relevant to the law of federal jurisdiction as they have been to substantive constitutional law. This is because determination of the questions of *if* and *when* a federal court is to adjudicate an issue of constitutional or federal law—questions traditionally answered by the doctrines of federal jurisdiction—will implicate principles of American political theory as much as *how* those substantive legal issues are ultimately resolved. The goal of this book, then, is to explore how prevailing normative principles of political theory should affect the current law of federal jurisdiction.

The thesis expounded here is that there exist two fundamental, deceptively simple underlying normative principles of American political theory that should provide the political framework for the exercise of jurisdictional authority by the federal judiciary. These postulates may be labeled the "Representational" and "Counter-Majoritarian" principles. Although these precepts may seem largely noncontroversial when stated in the abstract, closer examination reveals their extremely controversial nature in the broader scheme of American political theory. Moreover, careful examination of current jurisdictional doctrine in the federal courts reveals significant problems in the translation of these principles into judicial analysis of jurisdictional structure.

Application of both principles to the law of federal jurisdiction turns on the single fact of the federal judiciary's unrepresentativeness—its formalized insulation from the direct influences of the political process.[3] This fact dictates a considerably greater judicial role than is presently authorized in certain situations, and a dramatically reduced role in other jurisdictional contexts. The following chapters provide both an explication and theoretical defense of these two postulates, as well as a detailed explanation of how their application should dramatically alter existing jurisdictional doctrine. At this point, however, it is appropriate to provide a brief summary of the two principles.

The Representational principle posits that, within constitutionally established boundaries, the representative branches of government may make policy decisions, free from judicial power to ignore or overrule them simply on grounds of social, political, or moral disagreement. This principle flows from the fundamental values underlying democratic systems in general and the American system in particular: the right of the populace to have basic policy choices made by representatives whom it has chosen and whom it may replace if, on balance, their policy choices do not coincide with the wishes of a majority of the electorate. Under this principle, the unrepresentative federal judiciary may not fashion jurisdictional doctrines that ignore or undermine the policies embodied in constitutionally valid jurisdictional statutes.

On the other hand, our system is far from a total or unlimited representative democracy. A carefully crafted, relatively detailed written Constitution defines the powers of and imposes limitations upon the representative branches of government. This document, which established the organization and structure of our modern political system and provides the legitimizing source of our government, is framed in mandatory, rather than advisory, form; and provides for alteration only through resort to a difficult, formalized process requiring the consent of a substantial super-majority.[4] Both practically and theoretically, then, the Constitution provides counter-majoritarian (at least counter-*simple* majoritarian) limitations on democratic government.

For much the same reason that the federal judiciary should evince deference to the jurisdictional policy choices of the representative branches when those choices go constitutionally unchallenged, the federal courts should avoid judge-made jurisdictional doctrines[5] that limit or preclude judicial authority to adjudicate constitutional challenges to the actions of those branches. This, in short, describes the Counter-Majoritarian principle. However, it does not rest, as has been suggested, on the theory that the text of the Constitution commands the exercise of this power[6] (though it is surely true that the judicial review power, though not constitutionally compelled, is neither extra- nor counter-constitutional).[7] Nor is it solely because—as has also been suggested[8]—it is necessary for the judiciary to enforce the constitutionally protected rights of the individual. Nor is it because, as Chief Justice Marshall disingenuously suggested in *Marbury v. Madison*,[9] the courts must decide the governing law as an incident to the resolution of individual disputes involving the adjudication of private rights. Rather, it is because both common sense and practical experience dictate that the provisions of the Constitution will effectively be deprived of all legal force and meaning if the very majoritarian branches regulated and controlled by that document are allowed to act as the final arbiters of the counter-majoritarian limitations which the document imposes upon them. It is, then, the basic, positivistic belief in the rule of law which dictates that the one branch of government formally insulated from majoritarian pressures must exercise the final interpretive and enforcement power over *all* the Constitution's provisions. Thus, the judiciary is no more authorized to pick and choose which constitutional provisions it will enforce on the basis of ideological compatibility than the representative branches are free to ignore constitutional commands which they find to be inconvenient.

To be sure, the procedural requirements imposed by Article III[10] make clear that the federal judiciary is to operate only in a judicial manner, as the resolver of live disputes. Presumably such limitations were imposed to prevent the unrepresentative judiciary from exercising political power in a manner similar to that exercised by the representative branches. But that fact should not be allowed to obscure the vital political role that the judiciary must play within our governmental framework, as the counter-majoritarian check on the representative branches and as the final arbiter of the provisions of the counter-majoritarian Constitution.

Serious practical and theoretical difficulties arise when the representative branches attempt to limit or exclude federal judicial authority to expound constitutional meaning. Although the language of Article III appears to vest broad authority in Congress to limit the jurisdictions of both the Supreme Court and lower federal courts,[11] the exercise of such power is thought by some to conflict with the spirit, if not the letter, of the Constitution. Such attempts give rise to delicate issues of political theory and textual analysis, to which I have given substantial attention in the past.[12] But one need not face these troubling issues when the question concerns what are, for the most part, self-imposed jurisdictional limitations on the power of the federal courts to adjudicate constitutional questions, such as the doctrines of standing, mootness, ripeness, and political question—what Alexander Bickel referred to as the "passive virtues."[13] Under the Counter-Majoritarian principle of American political theory, the federal courts should impose a strong presumption against the creation of jurisdictional doctrines impeding the performance of their important political function of interpreting and enforcing the counter-majoritarian Constitution. Such jurisdictional limitations should be tolerated only when clearly necessary to ensure the effective performance of the judicial role.[14]

It is important to emphasize that the Counter-Majoritarian principle concerns only the exercise of judicial *jurisdiction* to adjudicate constitutional challenges. It says absolutely nothing about how the judiciary is substantively to resolve those challenges. For example, it would not necessarily be inconsistent with the dictates of the Counter-Majoritarian principle for the federal judiciary, in adjudicating particular constitutional challenges, to construe the Constitution to authorize broad governmental power over the individual. Although as a matter of substantive constitutional analysis one may reasonably quarrel with such a result, the Counter-Majoritarian principle is agnostic on the matter. Thus, it is theoretically conceivable that a federal judiciary adhering strictly to the Counter-Majoritarian principle could nevertheless manifest significant restraint in ruling upon constitutional challenges to majoritarian action. Those are issues for a different day and a different debate. What the Counter-Majoritarian principle does command, however—as a matter of the logic of American political theory, if not constitutional directive[15]—is that the unrepresentative judicial branch not defer the final interpretation of constitutional provisions to the majoritarian branches, but rather itself decide those questions on their substantive merits. To the extent that the exercise of such an authority by the unrepresentative judiciary may be characterized as "undemocratic," it is so only to the extent that the American political structure is itself undemocratic.

The preceding discussion provides merely a bare-bones description of the thesis. A more complete theoretical analysis and defense will be made in subsequent chapters. For the present, it should be emphasized that, under my description of American political theory, it is impossible to characterize the projected role of the federal judiciary as exclusively either "activist" or "restrained." The theoretical structure is too complex for any such simplistic characterizations. When the representative branches enact constitutionally valid jurisdictional directives, pursuant to the Representational principle considerably greater restraint is called for on the part of the unrepresentative federal judiciary than it has generally manifested to date in the development of its jurisdictional doctrines—even if that restraint will at times dictate an increase in the scope and frequency of the exercise of federal judicial power.[16]

At the same time, the Counter-Majoritarian principle dictates the avoidance of virtually all judicially created limitations on the adjudication of constitutional challenges to majoritarian action. In this sense, I might be accused of suggesting an increase in judicial "activism" and a decrease in judicial "restraint," at least to the extent the latter term is defined solely as "reduc[ing] the power of the federal courts vis-à-vis the other organs of government."[17] But this is much too simplistic a definition, in light of the intricacies of American political theory. For example, a judicial decision authorizing congressional suppression of unpopular political views, despite the commands of the First Amendment's guarantee of free speech, because the judge, too, dislikes the substance of the views expressed, cannot rationally be characterized as "judicial restraint," even though the net result is of course a decrease in judicial control of the other branches. In such a case, the judge has abandoned her commitment to the Constitution, and instead has made a purely normative, ad hoc policy judgment, in disregard of the fact that it is only as interpreter of the Constitution that she is authorized to speak.

Consistent, unbending performance of the judiciary's important political role as expositor of the counter-majoritarian Constitution, then, does not—standing alone—constitute improper judicial "activism." Such activism will occur in two situations: (1) when the courts pick and choose among which constitutional provisions they will enforce on the basis of their agreement or disagreement with the social policy or political philosophy manifested in those provisions; and (2) when, in the course of making substantive constitutional decisions, the judges ignore the ways in which their role in the governmental system differs from that of the other branches by ignoring the institutional confines of past legal developments, the concern about future applications of the decisions, and the constraints of the governing documents being interpreted. The former problem is actually avoided by strict adherence to the Counter-Majoritarian principle, and rejection of that principle is too clumsy a device to avoid the latter because the Counter-Majoritarian principle operates solely at the jurisdictional level. If "restraint," in the proper sense of the term, is to be achieved, it is not by limiting or excluding the exercise of judicial jurisdiction over constitutional claims, but rather by crafting guidelines and limitations on the substantive exercise of that jurisdiction.

The remainder of this book is divided into two sections. The first, consisting of the following three chapters, examines the theory of the Representational principle in some detail, and then proceeds to analyze how various federal jurisdictional doctrines should be modified to reflect the values embodied in that principle. Specifically, I will consider the doctrines of federal common law and judge-made abstention. The second section initially examines the theoretical critiques and defenses of the Counter-Majoritarian principle, and then considers the impact of that underlying theoretical norm on the classic jurisdictional doctrines of judicial self-restraint: standing, ripeness, mootness, and the so-called "political question" doctrine.

TWO

THE "REPRESENTATIONAL" PRINCIPLE

Democratic Values and American Political Theory

In attempting to define fundamental precepts of American political theory, it is important to recall the division of authority among the branches of the federal government dictated by constitutional text, democratic theory, and our historical tradition. Ours is a system that, on both historical and philosophical levels, has generally focused upon the value of popular sovereignty and political accountability.[1] Basic policy judgments not derived from constitutional text or structure are, for the most part, to be made by the representative branches of government. Thus, the unrepresentative and unaccountable federal judiciary is not permitted to ignore, contradict, or overrule the constitutionally valid policy choices made by the representative branches in the form of legislation. Such usurpation would effectively remove the basic policymaking function from those branches that are accountable to the populace, and place it in the hands of the one branch purposely insulated from that populace. It is hard to imagine a more blatant undermining of the principle of representational democracy, on which our normative political framework is premised.[2]

To be sure, our society has on occasion chosen to prescribe specific substantive normative principles of governmental behavior beyond the reach of simple majoritarian processes—for example, the rejection of governmental discrimination on the basis of race.[3] Although it has been argued that all such specific normative principles, codified in the super-majoritarian Constitution, are themselves designed solely to foster broader process values,[4] one need not accept such a controversial proposition[5] in order to recognize the fact that, at least as a general matter, our political theory focuses the legitimation inquiry primarily on the source of a societal policy decision, rather than on what that decision ultimately is. Of course, it may be neither feasible nor advisable to expect individuals to have a direct say in every decision affecting their lives. But that is why a pragmatic, large-scale democracy must emphasize the notion of political accountability: the requirement that those who do make policy choices periodically present themselves to the populace for an accounting, so that the electorate may revoke their power if, on balance, their decisions have not been consistent with the populace's wishes.[6] This fundamental notion of modern democratic theory was described by Alexander Meiklejohn, who wrote that "[g]overnments . . . derive their just powers from the consent of the governed. If that consent be lacking, governments have no just powers."[7] It is this notion that, as a definitional matter, characterizes any democratic system and that distinguishes such systems from totalitarian forms of government.[8]

It is important to understand that a democratically based system may on occasion produce policy choices which, on a moral level, some would condemn and, on a social level, with which some would disagree. But it would run directly contrary to the essence of self-determination to judge the legitimacy of policy decisions by measuring them against a particular substantive value structure; the "freedom" to reach only those substantive decisions that have been determined on some external, objective basis is effectively no freedom at all. Thus, a representational democratic system will measure the legitimacy of governmental decisionmaking—at least of those decisions not constitutionally removed from simple majoritarian control—not by objective examination of the wisdom of the decision, but rather by determining how consistent the processes used to reach that decision are with the notion of "representationalism," as embodied in our constitutional structure. It is in part to preserve this democratic premise that our system provides for separation of powers between the judicial and representative branches of government. Short of a finding of constitutional invalidity, then, it is democratically illegitimate for an unrepresentative judiciary to overrule, circumvent, or ignore policy choices made by the majoritarian branches.

The Implications of Public Choice Theory and "Neo-Republicanism"

It might be thought that this emphasis on the fundamental principle of political accountability is, in modern American society, naive because it ignores the enormous political power and influence exercised by a small number of groups, who effectively shape legislative choices to meet their narrow private needs. Because decisions by the legislative branch do not in reality reflect the wishes of the majority, the argument has been made, little is lost—in terms of democratic values—by allowing the unrepresentative judiciary to limit legislative power.[9]

To a certain extent, these points reflect the findings and opinions of the so-called "public choice" theorists, who have shaped much of the recent political and legal debate. Although there is a risk in attempting to characterize the elements of public choice theory in a few sentences, given the truly staggering amount of work recently done in the area,[10] it is probably accurate to find as a common thread of one branch of the theory a concern over "the problems produced by the existence of interest groups . . . and their influence over the political process."[11] The public choice theorists' primary empirical insight in this area is that the legislative process is in reality not as democratic as we may have thought. Rather, "it allows powerful private organizations to block necessary government action,"[12] and, as a result, "the lawmaking process has been transformed into a series of accommodations among competing elites; and . . . the rise of a large bureaucracy exercising broad discretionary power has undermined original constitutional goals by circumventing the safeguards of . . . electoral accountability."[13] Politicians are portrayed as "wealth-maximizing egoists"[14] who, as legislators, "will produce too few laws that serve truly public ends, and too many laws that serve private ends."[15] In the words of one of its critics,

> [t]he 'public choice' tradition . . . expresses an unbending contempt for legislative and agency action that represents a quite radical departure from the centrist [Legal] Process tradition. . . . [T]he public choice literature . . . is an effort to demonstrate that . . . the democratic sphere is, at its core, an arena of theft, an unmitigated disaster that should be limited carefully, tolerated only if fundamentally powerless.[16]

If one were to accept the public choice characterization of the legislative process as highly undemocratic and not oriented toward enactment of legitimate public values, one could reasonably choose to shed few tears over the revelation that numerous judicially created doctrines of federal jurisdiction depart from unambiguous legislative directives. There is reason to believe, however, that modern public choice theory has seriously mischaracterized the essence of prevailing American political theory.

I do not pretend to be in a position to judge the accuracy of the public choice theorists' empirical findings, though my instinct is to agree with those critics who contend "that the motivations of politicians are far too mixed to be understood through the generalizations that . . . public choice theorists formulate about political behavior."[17] Even assuming their accuracy, however, I find problems in the inferences drawn by at least several theorists on the basis of public choice theory's empirical insights. This is especially true of the views of modern "neo-republican" scholars.[18] The neo-republican model begins with the empirical assumption, derived from the work of modern public choice theorists, about the nature of the legislative process: that all too often[19] this process acts, not out of a desire to achieve certain coherent goals fostering the public interest, but rather in response to narrow, selfishly motivated bargains struck among legislators and special interests.[20] But this insight, even if empirically accurate,[21] is, in and of itself, value neutral. Indeed, certain jurists have relied on this insight to justify a substantially reduced judicial role in demanding legislative rationality, for the very reason that the operation of our accepted legislative traditions should be expected to function by means of the political bargaining process.[22] Neo-republican scholars, however, have drawn the opposite normative conclusion: that failure of the legislative process to act in the public interest is a deplorable derogation of our republican value structure.[23]

Well established in the historical scholarly literature,[24] the theory of "civic republicanism" has recently undergone something of a boom in legal scholarship.[25] In its modern form as "modified" by legal scholars,[26] the theory of civic republicanism posits several foundational normative precepts of American government. Perhaps key among them is the "republican belief in the subordination of private interests to the public good. . . ."[27] To the neo-republicans, "[i]n the deliberative process, private interests are relevant inputs into politics; but they are not taken as pre-political and exogenous and are instead the object of critical scrutiny."[28] Intimately related to this principle is the neo-republicans' emphasis on the value of deliberation as the central element of the governmental decisionmaking process.[29] Linking these two values is the principle of "universalism, exemplified by the notion of a common good, and made possible by 'practical reason.' The republican commitment to universalism, or agreement as a regulative ideal, takes the form of a belief in the possibility of settling at least some normative disputes with substantively right answers."[30]

Because the neo-republicans see a dramatic disparity between their ideal of universally agreed upon legislative solutions furthering the common good, reached by careful deliberation largely insulated from the political pressures of narrow private interests on the one hand, and the realities of what is perceived to be the jungle of private interests that is our modern legislative process on the other,[31] they suggest a number of ways to make reality more closely comport with the ideal. Because the problems to be corrected are in the legislature itself, it is not surprising that for the most part neo-republican scholars urge a substantially increased role for the judiciary, which was purposely insulated from the majoritarian political pressures to which the legislature is subject.[32] This analysis, however, is fraught with both conceptual and practical difficulties.

One of the most troubling aspects of neo-republican theory is the artificial distinction drawn between so-called "public" values and "private" interests. The problems can be seen in Professor Cass Sunstein's analysis of the intended link between the republican process and so-called "public" values:

> The republican conception carries with it a particular view of human nature; it assumes that through discussion people can, in their capacities as citizens, escape private interests and engage in pursuit of the public good.... [T]his conception reflects a belief that debate and discussion help to reveal that some values are superior to others. Denying that decisions about values are merely matters of taste, the republican view assumes that "practical reason" can be used to settle social issues.[33]

If one accepts the precept that there exist objectively defined value choices which are morally preferable to other alternatives, it becomes quite easy to criticize the results of the democratic process when they depart from those choices. Such an analysis, however, confuses process with substantive result. As previously explained, all democratic theory, in its most basic state, turns on some principle of self-determination. To allow individuals to choose only what some external force determines is "rational" and "intelligent," therefore, is effectively to deprive them of self-rule. Thus, the authorization of a judicial veto of legislation on the sole ground that the laws fails to enforce some externally derived "public values" (so long as those values have not been constitutionalized) represents the epitome of anti-democratic thought.

Equally unpersuasive is the idea that "private" and "public" interests are somehow mutually exclusive under our democratic structure. As political scientist Jane Mansbridge has argued, the form of democracy adopted by the framers could properly be characterized as "adversary" democracy, "built on self-interest."[34] She writes:

> In current adversary theory there is no common good or public interest. Voters pursue their individual interests by making demands on the political system in proportion to the intensity of their feelings.... From the interchange between self-interested voters and self-interested brokers emerge decisions that come as close as possible to a balanced aggregation of individual interests.[35]

When, in the course of a political campaign, the candidates discuss alternative methods of controlling inflation, it is likely that the voters are interested primarily because of their own private economic interest. Yet could anyone seriously suggest that voters' concern about the effect of proposed governmental programs on their pocketbooks is somehow inconsistent with fundamental democratic theory? If we begin with the basic theoretical premise that "[d]emocratic participation . . . is a process in which persons formulate, discuss, and decide public issues that are important to them and directly affect their lives,"[36] it becomes clear that any proposed dichotomy, for purposes of democratic theory, between "public values" and "private interests" is a false one. Thus, to the extent that neo-republican theorists measure the legitimacy of substantive legislative choices by means of the private-public interest dichotomy, they are employing a measuring rod for which our system was simply not created.

Neo-republican scholars argue, however, that modern revisionist historical scholarship establishes that "[r]epublican thought played a central role in the framing period,"[37] and that "[i]t is no longer possible to see a Lockean consensus in the founding period, or to treat the framers as modern pluralists believing that self-interest is the inevitable motivating force behind political behavior."[38] But any historical claim of the dominance of civic republicanism in the thought of the framers would at best be overstated[39] and at worst subject to considerable doubt as to its accuracy.[40] Moreover, even if one were to concede that the framers' thought actually was dominated by precepts of civic republicanism, modern theorists point to no evidence to indicate that the framers contemplated an expansive role for the politically unaccountable judiciary as an enforcer of civic republican values, particularly on the level of statutory construction. At most, the framers appear to have imposed certain structural requirements on the legislative process, designed to reduce the dangers of powerful special interests.[41] Once the judiciary, in the exercise of its judicial review power, has assured that these formal structural prerequisites are met,[42] there is no apparent basis for believing the framers contemplated a further checking role (of course, other than compliance with the substantive requirements imposed by other provisions of the Constitution).

In any event, modern neo-republican scholars have openly rejected what they find to be the morally troubling elements of the classic republican theory supposedly adopted by the framers and earlier generations of political philosophers,[43] "which contained, and prominently displayed, militarist, elitist, religious, and sexist sentiments. . . ."[44] By rejecting these morally repugnant elements of classical civic republicanism, modern theorists have effectively gutted the key premises of the earlier theory, leaving them without any coherent tradition from which to draw historical support.[45] Even if modern neo-republicanism merely constituted a relatively limited "liberal"[46] modification of classical theory, however, the republican scholars' admitted willingness to pick and choose among the elements of that theory on the basis of modern moral precepts would undermine any claim to historical legitimacy, even in the unlikely event that modern generations should feel bound by all elements of the framers' political theory.[47] Once neo-republican scholars concede that *some* elements of classical theory may be abandoned on grounds of modern normative precepts, they logically must concede that *all* elements of the theory may be subjected to critical normative scrutiny on the basis of modern moral or political values, whatever the theory's historical pedigree. When tested on this basis, if no other, neo-republicanism must be rejected.

It is difficult to overstate how inconsistent the theory advocated by neo-republican scholars is with the fundamental concepts of both self-determination and the political accountability of the governors to the governed that characterize our system.[48] The neo-republicans have thrown out the baby with the bath water: in their attempt to curb what they perceive as the harms of self-interested politics, they have ultimately lost the overriding principle of popular sovereignty, and have thus failed to heed the warning Madison issued when he sought to curb the very same excesses attacked by the neo-republicans.[49]

In a certain sense, the value of deliberation emphasized by republican theorists is fully consistent with the ideals of classical democratic thought, which emphasized the benefits to the personal and intellectual development of the individual to be derived from active participation in the governmental decisionmaking process.[50] In the context in which neo-republicans employ the concept, however, deliberation becomes at best a device to insulate the governors from the will of the governed, and at worst a means to superimpose on the populace one particular externally derived substantive value system, whether the populace likes it or not.[51]

Although neo-republican scholars appear to have substantially rejected basic democratic values, many public choice theorists attempt to justify increased reliance on the judicial branch by pointing to the procedural flaws in the legislative process,[52] which render that process something considerably less than fully representational of public will. To the extent that these criticisms turn not on an external moral judgment on the substantive policy choice made by a legislative body but rather on the "undemocratic" influences brought to bear on the legislative process, they are at least prima facie consistent with our normative constitutional and political structure.

The most bizarre aspect of the public choice critique in this context, however, is the suggestion that the remedy lies in significantly expanding judicial authority to ignore or possibly even supersede legislative policy choices. If the problem is that the legislative process is insufficiently responsive to true public will, it hardly makes sense to attempt to correct that defect by placing expanded power in the hands of the one branch of the federal government subject to the direct electoral check of absolutely no one. No conceivable basis exists upon which to assume an ability of the wholly unrepresentative federal judiciary to tap majoritarian values and opinions. Indeed, such an assumption is counter-intuitive because it directly conflicts with the traditional democratic precept that representatives elected by the people are more likely to reflect public will than are unelected dictators, regardless of how benevolent such dictators might be. Whatever problems may exist, at the very least a public sufficiently unhappy with legislative judgments may vote legislators out of office; the same, of course, cannot be said of the federal judiciary. Thus, although several conceivable methods exist for rendering the legislative process more directly responsive to popular will,[53] it is only by means of a truly Orwellian form of double-speak that we can vest increased authority in a totally unrepresentative organ of government in the name of augmenting democratic principles.

An additional argument—premised on established principles of social choice and game theory—that has been made in response to the democratic critique of increased judicial power is that the concept of "public will" is for all practical purposes meaningless, and that a representational legislative system can never be certain to reflect accurately the aggregation of individual preferences of the constituents.[54] Conceding, for purposes of argument, the accuracy of the application of social choice and game theory to representationalism, one can only wonder whether these theorists have proven too much. If one took their logic to its extreme, presumably there would be no normative basis, from the premise of democratic theory, upon which to prefer representationalism to a wholly totalitarian system. Such a preposterous conclusion should provide a sufficient basis on which to cast serious doubt on the implications they draw from the perspective of game theory. There is no reason to adopt an "all-or-nothing" approach to the issue. Granting that the idea of a direct correlation between legislative choice and the preferences of a majority of the populace may be more fanciful than real does not necessarily imply that representationalism is no better than alternative political structures in reflecting the will of the electorate.[55]

It might be argued, however, that a focus on the importance of popular sovereignty within our political structure ignores the substantial amount of political decisionmaking today exercised by governmental officials, primarily administrative in nature, who are in no way directly responsive to the electorate. It is true that the enormous growth of the administrative state during the last two-thirds of this century has in many ways threatened the notion of representative government. However, two key factors distinguish the exercise of policymaking authority by administrators from the usurpation of legislative authority by the unrepresentative federal judiciary. Initially, although administrators are not directly accountable to the populace, they are accountable to those who are themselves so accountable.[56] Federal judges, on the other hand, are formally insulated from the pressures of elected officials by Article III's protections of their independence. Secondly, when administrators exercise policymaking authority, it is only as a result of a conscious delegation of that power by the representative branches. Although even such delegation might be thought to give rise to both constitutional and political difficulties,[57] those problems pale in comparison to an unauthorized usurpation of legislative power by the federal judiciary.

Although it would be absurd to suggest that our system, either by design[58] or in practice,[59] constitutes a pure representational democracy, the exercise of policymaking authority by the representative branches is the closest approximation we could reasonably expect to a structural implementation of the fundamental democratic values of self-determination and political accountability. An attempt by the federal judiciary to ignore, undermine, or contradict the constitutionally valid exercise of that legislative authority would therefore constitute a blatant departure from the political values that underlie our governmental structure.

The Representational Principle and the Law of Federal Jurisdiction

Although the point may not be self-evident to an observer unschooled in the law of federal jurisdiction, by considerations of tradition, constitutional text, and political theory the jurisdiction of the federal courts is deemed primarily a matter for legislative determination. Article III of the Constitution provides that there shall be such inferior federal courts "as the Congress may from time to time ordain and establish,"[60] and that the Supreme Court's appellate jurisdiction—by far the primary portion of its authority—shall exist "with such exceptions, and under such regulations as the Congress shall make."[61] Although both provisions remain the subject of scholarly controversy[62] and it is clear that both are subject to limitation by other constitutional provisions,[63] no one today seriously questions Congress's authority to direct the federal courts to adjudicate and enforce federal constitutional and statutory rights.

The existence of such congressional authority makes perfect sense, in light of the well-understood fact that judicial enforcement of a substantive legislative program is often intertwined with the success of the program itself.[64] Nor is there serious controversy over congressional authority to restrict federal court power, so long as no other constitutional provision is violated as a result.[65] Just as the federal courts may not, consistent with our political value structure, ignore or overrule congressional social legislation simply because of disagreement with its policies—at least without formally holding that legislation to be unconstitutional—so, too, are the federal courts prohibited from ignoring constitutionally valid jurisdictional legislation.

It is therefore surprising to see the number of judicial doctrines of federal jurisdiction—developed by the Supreme Court and accepted by commentators—based solely on the Court's own perceptions of the most appropriate policy choice, in total disregard of the pre-existing network of relevant substantive and jurisdictional statutes.[66] Professor Richard Fallon has underscored this point (albeit probably unintentionally) by characterizing modern federal courts scholarship in terms of two extreme ideological models: the "Federalist" model, under which "states emerge as sovereign entities against which federal courts should exercise only limited powers,"[67] and the "Nationalist" model, which "minimizes the significance of state sovereignty in comparison with national interests and posits a constitutional and statutory preference for federal over state courts as the guarantors of federal rights."[68] Although Professor Fallon concludes that neither ideological extreme adequately controls every issue of federal jurisdiction,[69] he generally refuses to reject the judiciary's ultimate authority to make such a decision.[70]

In light of accepted American political theory, making a choice between the two ideological models described by Professor Fallon should give rise to a reaction reminiscent of a Cub fan's emotive response to a Mets-Cardinals game: the fervent hope that somehow both will lose. This is not because, as Professor Fallon believes, both ideologies present too one-sided a portrait of the policy interests,[71] but rather because, in more instances than most courts or scholars recognize, the authority of the unrepresentative federal judiciary to choose between the "Federalist" and "Nationalist" models of jurisdictional allocation has been preempted by the legislative choices already made by the politically representative branches. Under the analytical model dictated by the Representational principle, a federal court, faced with a doctrinal issue of federal jurisdiction, is required initially to inquire whether resolution of that issue has already been made by the political branches in the form of legislation—in other words, whether the judiciary is the appropriate governmental *institution*, under the circumstances, to make that normative policy choice. Hence, this model is best characterized—in contrast to those described by Professor Fallon—as an "institutionalist" perspective on the law of federal jurisdiction.

Of course, it will often not be a simple task for the judiciary to determine congressional intent in the adoption of particular legislative provisions. Statutory construction implicates issues of political theory and interpretive analysis that are deserving of detailed attention, and therefore these issues form the basis for the following discussion.[72] The key precept to be underscored at this point, however, is the need for humility, dictated by the political value structure embodied in the Representational principle, which the unrepresentative federal judiciary should bring to issues of federal jurisdiction when those issues are regulated by constitutionally valid congressional statutes.

Political Legitimacy and Statutory Construction: The Implications of the Representational Principle

The most important insight of the "institutionalist" perspective, derived from the underlying normative premise of representational self-determination,[73] is that nonconstitutionally controlled issues—including those involving judicial jurisdiction—are to be resolved on the basis of judicial policy assessment only to the extent that the representative branches have not already made that policy choice through legislative action. Thus, when a constitutionally valid statute addresses a particular jurisdictional matter, under the Representational principle a federal court must initially determine the extent to which that statute actually resolves the issue.

To be sure, situations will arise in which a good-faith judicial effort to determine whether—and how—a statute resolves a specific question will, because of textual or historical ambiguity, be effectively fruitless. In such an event, judicial resolution on the basis of the court's own assessment of the competing social and political policies will probably be unavoidable, whether or not desirable. But, for reasons previously discussed,[74] the political theory underlying the "institutionalist" perspective morally and logically dictates that judicial resort to such a practice come only as a last resort—after the court has done all it reasonably can to ascertain whether the social policies and goals sought to be attained by the representative branches through enactment of specific legislation actually dictate a particular resolution of the question before the court.

Under this normative political framework, it is not enough that an interpreting court is somehow able, ex post, linguistically to rationalize its own policy choices with the statute's text. To the extent that such a statutory "interpretation" either contradicts the statute's reasonably ascertainable goals, or is made without a prior judicial attempt to determine whether a logical extrapolation of those purposes could be thought to dictate a conclusion in the particular case, the judicial effort is no more normatively defensible, under a separation-of-powers structure, than is a judicial policy choice that openly ignores the arguably applicable statute. For such statutory "interpretation" amounts to nothing more than thinly disguised judicial usurpation of power, granted to the unrepresentative judiciary by neither the Constitution[75] nor our governing political theory of representational democracy.

Rejecting Counter-Models of Statutory Construction

Adoption of this view of the judicial role in statutory construction necessarily entails rejection of four conceivable models of statutory construction that have recently received varying degrees of positive attention:[76] what I have chosen to label the "textual deconstructionist" model, the "political deconstructionist" model, the "functionalist" model, and the "neo-republican" model.[77]

The "Textual Deconstructionist" Model

The textual deconstructionist model is similar to the generally familiar arguments of linguistic deconstructionists,[78] which have been widely applied by certain legal commentators to constitutional analysis.[79] At the risk of oversimplifying, the principle posits that words are inherently subjective and thus texts are inherently capable of numerous—and perhaps infinite—meanings, none of which can be rationally preferred as "correct" over any of the others. Acceptance or rejection of this assertion turns on assessment of linguistic and philosophical arguments well beyond the scope of this book. If one accepts the abstract validity of linguistic deconstructionism—a judgment that will likely be made on the basis of factors having nothing to do with the issues of American political theory debated here—one would probably have to conclude that any judicial resolution of an issue of statutory construction would necessarily amount to the court's own assessment of social policy because the court is incapable of ascertaining, on the basis of an examination of the text, any objectively verifiable meaning. More important, perhaps, is the fact that an "interpreting" court could reasonably justify *any* construction on the basis of text, so no "interpretation" could be said to be "wrong."

Although it is no doubt true that words have no "objective" meaning, use of subjective albeit widely shared linguistic conventions can quite rationally render linguistically "wrong" textual constructions that indisputably depart from those conventions. The individual who leaves a note for his or her spouse to bring home two quarts of skim milk from the store would rightly be surprised if, in response to the note, the spouse brought home two apples and a peach. Although it is of course theoretically conceivable that there exists a special linguistic code between them, absent evidence to that effect it is reasonable to measure normal communication by the standards of widely shared conventions. Indeed, it has long been established in the law of contracts that people will be held to the reasonable implications of their words, based on widely shared understanding.[80] It is therefore difficult to comprehend why legislators should not be held to similar standards. Although this in no way means either that words may or should be construed outside of the context in which they are placed, or that even in context there will always—or even often—be one undisputed construction, it surely does not follow that we need to accept a principle of linguistic anarchy.[81]

Equally as troubling as abstract linguistic deconstructionism is what might be referred to as "selective, rationalizing deconstructionism," a version of deconstructionism designed specifically for the legal context of statutory construction. Unlike the pure linguistic deconstructionist, legal scholars advocating this view do not necessarily endorse the concept of "linguistic nihilism" in all uses of language, but rather rely on it selectively in the context of statutory construction, in order to rationalize an "interpreting" court's own ex ante policy assessment—one with which these scholars happen to concur.[82] In effect, jurists and scholars employing this model act as advocates. Like legal adversaries to a litigation, they urge statutory constructions that lead to the social policy choice they are advocating. Implicit in this position is the assumption that, with at most rare exception, statutory language is sufficiently malleable to rationalize just about any conceivable social policy choice.

Such a model of statutory construction, however, places undue policy making authority in the hands of the unrepresentative judiciary, and is thus inconsistent with the underlying Representational principle, which, at least in its fundamental sense, is inherent in any variant of accepted American political theory. Even if one were willing to accept the essential deconstructionist premise that statutory language is inherently malleable—a questionable assumption in and of itself—the fallacy of this model is the improper leap from this assumption of unlimited *linguistically* permissible constructions to the assumption of unlimited permissible constructions of *legislative intent*. In numerous instances, a good-faith judicial attempt to ascertain an overriding, coherent legislative purpose will reveal that a linguistically conceivable construction may not properly reflect that overriding purpose.

The "Political Deconstructionist" Model

It is possible to argue that, even if one rejects a pure linguistic deconstruction model, it is nevertheless naive to believe that a coherent overriding legislative purpose can accurately be ascertained.[83] This is because, as modern "public choice" theorists tell us,[84] rarely is legislation adopted in order to achieve a single "public purpose." Rather, legislators are merely responding to "rent seeking," anti-majoritarian private "special interests." Because of the complex intertwining of special interest influences and political favors, the argument proceeds, it is impossible for an interpreting court to construe any coherent overriding legislative purpose that the court can extrapolate to resolve specific issues of statutory application.[85] If this analysis is accurate, a reviewing court might be freed from the control of an overriding legislative policy judgment, for the simple reason that no such coherent policy judgment actually exists.

Even if one were to accept the extremely cynical factual premises of the public choice literature, however, it does not necessarily follow that legislation is devoid of any coherent purpose—even if that "purpose" is simply to benefit a specific private interest.[86] In this context, it is important to distinguish between an individual legislator's *motive* and the concept of legislative *purpose*. The legislator may be motivated by a variety of complex factors: currying favor with special interests, responding to constituent pressures, repaying a fellow legislator who had supported the legislator's own proposed legislation, or attempting to foster broad social or moral policies. But the fact that individual legislators have distinct—and often cryptic—personal motivations for supporting legislation does not necessarily mean that it lacks an overriding goal or desired social impact—or "purpose." In other words, though determination of a legislator's *motive*—his or her personal motivation for voting for particular legislation—may be all but impossible to decipher, the legislation's *purpose*—how the law is designed to alter the existing social or political topography—is considerably easier to ascertain.

The "Functionalist" Model

A third alternative which, if accepted, could authorize substantial judicial power to ignore legislative action I have labeled the "functionalist" model. Although grouped here are a number of theorists, some more extreme than others,[87] linking them is the belief that the enacters of legislation are often unable to foresee changing circumstances that will dictate the need for modification or repeal. Although presumably future legislatures retain the authority to undertake such action, the inertia inherent in the legislative process[88] reduces the likelihood that such action will take place. Therefore, it is appropriate for the judiciary, the governmental organ in the best position both to assess the need for such legislative alteration and to respond to that need, to undertake such action.[89]

The functionalist model is fraught with both conceptual and practical difficulties. Vesting the authority to repeal legislative enactments in the unrepresentative judiciary runs directly counter to the essence of American democratic theory, embodied in the Representational principle: that basic social policy choices are to be made by those governmental organs ultimately responsible to the voters.[90]

The functionalist model suffers from two major fallacies: first, that the inertia inherent in the legislative process renders the judiciary a preferable organ to assess statutory obsolescence; and second, that statutory obsolescence is somehow objectively determinable. As to the first fallacy, the functionalist model, at least when applied to the federal government, ignores the fact that the difficulty of achieving legislative action is not merely a necessary but unwanted by-product of the legislative process, but rather represents a conscious choice by the Constitution's framers. As the Supreme Court recognized when it invalidated the one-house legislative veto in *INS v. Chadha*,[91] the bicameralism and presentment requirements of Article I[92] serve an important function as a part of the system of checks and balances. Moreover, the constitutionally imposed obstacles to federal legislative action can also be viewed as a protection of federalism values. By imposing barriers to the adoption of federal legislation, the framers attempted to reduce the risk that federal legislation would consume state legislative authority.[93] Thus, rather than a difficulty to be overcome, as it is viewed by advocates of the functionalist model, the inertia inherent in the federal legislative process is actually a carefully crafted protection of both separation of powers and federalism.

Even with these barriers to action, however, Congress nevertheless remains a viable resource to remedy social problems that have evolved in enforcement of a particular statute. Although legislative revision is not always swift or certain, it is surely a more than negligible possibility. Hence, if circumstances have in fact changed dramatically, justifying change in pre-existing legislation, it is fallacious to assume that only the judiciary may perform that function.

More importantly, from the perspective of democratic theory, it is usually impossible to determine—objectively and without controversy—that circumstances have changed in such a way as to justify legislative revision. Such a judgment will often be infused with ideological implications or reasonable differences of opinion over an assessment of complex social circumstances. Thus, a type of anti-democratic arrogance pervades the functionalist model, in its assumption that obsolescence is an objectively verifiable fact. It is impossible, ex ante, to provide objective criteria to determine statutory obsolescence. Hence, it will be both conceptually and practically impossible to distinguish simple judicial disagreement with the legislative policy choice from a true judicial finding of statutory obsolescence. Because the issue of obsolescence itself is so often subject to reasonable debate, the question whether the originally adopted decision of the elected branches should be reversed cannot be resolved by some externally verifiable standard. Thus, a finding of obsolescence by the unrepresentative judiciary amounts to a usurpation of political authority reserved, in a democratic system, for the representative branches of government.

Although the functionalist model's use of obsolescence must be rejected as a violation of basic democratic principles, it is important to distinguish this usurpation from judicial performance of certain functionally dictated tasks that are less offensive to the norms of American political theory. For example, the "common-sense" judicial authority not to apply a statute to a situation obviously not intended to be reached by the legislature, despite its inclusion within a literal definition of the text,[94] is a necessary element of any successful government. Although situations will no doubt arise in which uncertainties exist in the application of this principle, that in no way distinguishes the power from any other form of statutory construction. If exercised reasonably, this judicial power will ultimately *foster* democratic principles, by making day-to-day applications more consistent with the legislature's actual understanding. This is a far cry, however, from a judicial authority to ignore or invalidate what was concededly the legislature's purpose at the time of enactment because of the judicial judgment that, in light of changed circumstances, that purpose is no longer socially or politically appropriate.[95] The former judicial power effectively fulfills the enacting legislature's desires; the latter power effectively guts them.

The "Neo-Republican" Model

The fourth alternative model of statutory construction, drawing on elements of both the political deconstructionist and functionalist models, is the neo-republican model, premised on the theories of the group of scholars described previously.[96] They have suggested several methods by which judicial involvement in the legislative process should be increased.

One is in the form of an expanded scope of constitutional review, imposing a constitutional requirement of both meaningful legislative deliberation and the attempt to attain a public-regarding purpose for the enactment of legislation.[97] Another is through the sub-constitutional process of statutory construction. Although neo-republican scholars do not appear to go so far as to vest in the judiciary a direct power to ignore or overrule an unambiguous statutory directive,[98] they are clearly willing to imbue the process of interpretation with canons of construction that will often enable the judiciary to ignore or alter legislative enactments that are likely to have been the product of something other than rational deliberation in the public interest.[99]

An ambiguity exists in neo-republican thought on the role that the politically unaccountable judiciary is intended to play in assuring that the legislature engaged in true "deliberation" prior to enactment. If the prerequisite is meant simply as a procedural requirement, presumably the judiciary would have to accept a legislative judgment with which it substantively disagreed, so long as the specified processes had been followed by the legislature. Even in this limited form, the deliberation requirement would undermine the value of political accountability to the governed because it is inherently designed to insulate the decisionmakers from the influences of those whom they represent.[100] As one commentator has correctly noted, however, the mere fact that rational processes are employed in the decisionmaking in no way ensures that the decision reached will necessarily be consistent with the neo-republican concept of "civic virtue."[101] It is therefore not surprising that on several occasions Professor Sunstein—the leading neo-republican theorist—has suggested that there may well exist substantively "correct" solutions—presumably ones that comport with his notion of the "common good."[102] Thus, it is quite conceivable that, when they suggest imposition of the procedural requirement of legislative "deliberation," neo-republican scholars actually intend imposition of their own substantive value structure. For if it is true, as Professor Sunstein asserts, that there actually does exist a substantively correct solution to the question of the common good, then by definition any legislative process reaching something other than the "correct" conclusion could not have been sufficiently "deliberative." If, in the neo-republican scheme, the unaccountable judiciary is directed to overrule the legislative judgment any time that judgment reaches a result that does not conform to the judge's (or Professor Sunstein's) perception of the common good—unfortunately not an unreasonable construction of neo-republican thought[103]—then the fundamental precepts of self-determination and political accountability will have been totally abandoned.

Fashioning "Institutionalist" Canons of Statutory Construction

Because I have concluded that none of the conceivable alternative models of statutory analysis is consistent with our overriding representational democratic structure,[104] it is necessary to fashion specific canons of statutory construction that flow from the relative roles of enacting legislature and interpreting judiciary dictated by both the Representational principle and the "institutionalist" perspective.

"Institutionalist" canons of statutory construction must reflect the fact that basic value choices are to be made, for the most part, by the representative branches of government. The initial canon, then, must be that the very first task to be undertaken by an interpreting court is to ascertain, as best it can, the coherent social purpose or purposes embodied in the statute—in other words, to determine what the legislature was attempting to accomplish by enactment of the statute—in what manner the legislature intended to alter the social or political status quo. Absent performance of this initial task, the statutory construction process would at best amount to an empty exercise and at worst to a guise for judicial usurpation of legislative authority.

It should be noted that to underscore the importance of this judicial task as a matter of political legitimacy is in no way to suggest the ease of its accomplishment. Generally, the judiciary may perform its duty by examining a combination of statutory text, specific legislative history, surrounding political context, and, where necessary, a certain degree of common sense. Because of the difficulty of the task, however, it is important for the judiciary to approach it with a degree of humility dictated by its role as an unrepresentative organ within our representational democratic structure.[105] Although performance of the task is not the impossibility suggested by the linguistic or political deconstructionist models,[106] its complexity may on occasion mean that the judiciary cannot be totally secure in its ascertainment of overriding purpose. But absence of perfect knowledge cannot justify abandonment of the task, given the serious harm to democratic values caused by such an alternative. Hence, the most one can expect of an interpreting court is a good-faith, diligent effort. As part of that effort, the court must make every attempt to avoid making judgments—explicit or implicit—on the morality or wisdom of the legislative choice (at least short of a finding of constitutional invalidity), and allowing those judgments to influence its ascertainment of legislative purpose.

Secondly, the "institutionalist" canons of construction dictate that an interpreting court not fashion a construction of statutory text that effectively renders the statute a nullity. Basic principles of rationality dictate the assumption that a legislature does not go through the enactment process to accomplish absolutely nothing. One might initially react to this suggested canon by noting its obviousness. But, if one were to accept one or more of the alternative models of statutory construction, it is by no means clear that this canon would be recognized.

The final "institutionalist" canon concerns the proper judicial role in applying a statute to specific situations not directly covered by the statute's text. Given the inherent nature of statutory directives, it is not uncommon for an interpreting court to face specific situations where either the statute's text does not clearly indicate how—or even if—it should be applied, or where a literal application of the statute's language might appear to lead to anomalous results.[107] Necessarily, in such situations, an interpreting court must retain a certain degree of case-by-case flexibility. However, it is important, even in this context, for the court not to employ the statutory construction process as a mere guise for substitution of its own policy choices, in derogation of those made by the representative branches.

In establishing the appropriate contours of the judicial power in performance of this function, it is important to distinguish situations in which broad statutory language could, at least linguistically, conceivably apply, and those in which the statute's text indisputably fails to reach the particular circumstances before the court. In the latter case, the court cannot properly reason that, though the statute's language does not concern itself with the specific fact situations, had the legislators thought about this possibility they would have chosen to apply the statute. Once the court acknowledges that the statute's text, by its terms, is inapplicable, to extend the statute's reasoning to apply to the specific situation amounts to purely judge-made law;[108] for whatever reason, the legislators did not choose to deal with that particular instance. It is therefore inaccurate to characterize such an extension of the statute's unambiguous language as "statutory construction."

In certain instances, though a statute clearly applies, its text is silent on a collateral issue that must be resolved in some manner, one way or the other.[109] In such cases, it is incumbent upon an interpreting court to resolve the issue in the manner most consistent with attainment of the policies sought to be achieved by the statute. Here, too, the court properly performs its "gap-filling" function. But, if the judiciary is not to exceed its bounds as interpreter, it is important not to confuse these cases with those in which a statute is, by its terms, simply inapplicable, even though a compelling moral or practical argument might be fashioned that the legislation should have reached such a situation. If the court possesses legitimate authority to apply the policies of the statute to such situations, it can do so only to the extent that it is authorized to establish its own common law principles; it cannot properly shield its lawmaking with the democratically protective mantle of statutory construction.

This chapter has described the theoretical framework of the Representational principle, and has explored its implications for general issues of statutory construction. The following two chapters examine how that theoretical analysis should affect specific areas of the law of federal jurisdiction.

THREE

Applying the Representational Principle, I: The Power of the Federal Courts to Fashion Common Law

Introduction: Federal Common Law as a Function of the Democratic Process

Every first-year law student is well aware that in *Erie R. Co. v. Tompkins*[1] the Supreme Court, for a variety of reasons, rejected the authority of the federal courts to develop so-called general federal common law. Nevertheless, to this very day the Court has, not infrequently, demonstrated a willingness to fashion discrete areas of purely judge-made federal law.[2]

As is all too often true in the law of federal jurisdiction, the Supreme Court has developed the concept of federal common law while largely ignoring the overriding institutional questions posed by prevailing principles of American political and constitutional theory, examined in the preceding chapters.[3] In the creation and development of federal common law, the judicial focus has been all but exclusively on what policy choices—in the judgment of the Court—would give rise to the optimum allocation of political authority between state and federal systems, in almost total disregard of the appropriateness of its exercise of this function within the broader political context of a carefully structured system of separation of powers.

With rare and only limited exception, the work of the commentators has not represented significant improvement. Often, they, like the Court, have simply ignored the issue of the institutional appropriateness of the entire enterprise of federal common lawmaking, and have instead focused solely on the wisdom of the particular judicial choices in the fashioning of substantive doctrine.[4] Although more recent commentators have at least recognized the relevance of the initial question of political legitimacy, they have either raised it simply to circumvent it[5] or have ignored important theoretical distinctions that flow from the separation-of-powers concept.[6]

The extent to which the problem of political legitimacy facing the creation of federal common law is constitutionally derived is subject to debate.[7] One need not resolve this difficult constitutional issue, however, in order to find the judicial creation of federal common law inconsistent with our democratic structure. The primary difficulty is statutory in nature. Finding its origins in the very first Judiciary Act in 1789,[8] the Rules of Decision Act currently provides:

> The laws of the several states, except where the Constitution or treaties of the United States or Acts of Congress otherwise require or provide, shall be regarded as rules of decision in civil actions in the courts of the United States where they apply.[9]

Although, as is true of most statutes, the Act is not free from ambiguity in either language or history, use of any legitimate technique of statutory construction will reveal that the Act's fundamental purposes are to reduce the pervasive reach of federal substantive law or, at the very least, to limit the situations in which federal substantive law displaces state law to those specific instances in which Congress—rather than the federal judiciary—chooses to do so. By limiting federal judicial lawmaking power in this manner, Congress has assured that state substantive law will be supplanted only when (1) the inherent inertia of the federal legislative process has been overcome; and (2) the branch of the federal government historically considered most responsive to state interests and concerns—the Congress—will have deemed such action necessary.[10]

If the Rules of Decision Act is construed in this manner, as I believe it must be,[11] all federal "common law"—at least in the literal sense of that phrase[12]—constitutes an illegitimate judicial rejection of that legislative goal.[13] Equally important, from the "institutionalist" perspective described in the previous chapter,[14] is that judicial recognition of the power to create substantive federal common law—again, at least in the literal sense—violates the inescapable textual command of the Act,[15] and effectively renders the Act a nullity,[16] results that are wholly unacceptable under the separation-of-powers analysis dictating the "institutionalist" perspective.[17]

Thus, it is incorrect to suggest, as at least one commentator has,[18] that the issue of federal common law gives rise primarily to problems of federalism, rather than to those of separation of powers. In this context, the two structural political values are inextricably intertwined: the political branches of the federal government, traditionally deemed more responsive to state concerns than the federal judiciary, have chosen to protect federalism interests by legislatively limiting federal judicial power to supplant state law. In light of the existence of the Rules of Decision Act, then, whether or not a ban on judicial common lawmaking power is politically advisable[19] is not, within our structure of separation of powers, a matter for judicial resolution.

Applying the "Institutionalist" Canons to the Rules of Decision Act: Implications for the Creation of Federal Common Law

The Lessons of Textual Analysis

If one were to apply the "institutionalist" canons, developed in chapter 2,[20] to the Rules of Decision Act, it is likely that a picture of judicial authority to fashion federal common law would be obtained that is considerably different from the existing doctrinal structure.[21] At least on a prima facie level, the statute's language appears to recognize only three exceptions to its directive that state law shall supply the rule of decision: where otherwise provided by the Constitution, treaties, or Acts of Congress.[22] Common lawmaking authority is not included. Thus, it might be argued that we need not delve into issues of legislative purpose and history; the text unambiguously precludes the judiciary's authority to establish federal common law.

As one might suspect, however, such a narrow textual analysis fails to dispose of all conceivable arguments to legitimize the creation of federal common law.[23] Nevertheless, this simple linguistic analysis does effectively dispose of at least certain arguments employed by commentators to rationalize the common lawmaking power. Professors Peter Westen and Jeffrey Lehman, for example, have asserted that, for all practical purposes, the Rules of Decision Act should be construed in the following manner:

> The laws of the several states, except where the Constitution or treaties of the United States or Acts of Congress *or federal common law* otherwise require or provide, shall be regarded as rules of decision in civil actions in the courts of the United States, in cases where they apply.[24]

Although Professors Westen and Lehman believe that a federal court may choose to adopt state law as its federal rule of decision, they emphasize that in such cases state law is not applied of its own force as a result of the dictates of the Rules of Decision Act, but rather is merely incorporated by reference as the federal standard.[25]

The most striking flaw in this "construction" of the Rules of Decision Act—other than that it directly contradicts the Act's terms—is that it effectively renders the Act a nullity, an illegitimate mode of statutory interpretation under the "institutionalist" canons of construction.[26] When the words "federal common law" are inserted into the statute, the Act effectively provides: "*Except for every situation*, state law supplies the rule of decision." For one might reasonably ask, what is left, after the Act is construed to except cases controlled by Acts of Congress, the Constitution, treaties, *and* federal common law?[27]

Where, it might be asked, do Westen and Lehman find the authority effectively to amend the text of the Rules of Decision Act?[28] They argue that they are not amending the Act, but simply construing the statutory term "Acts of Congress":

> The difference between "common law" and "statutory interpretation" is a difference in emphasis rather than a difference in kind. The more definite and explicit the prevailing legislative policy, the more likely a court will describe its lawmaking as statutory interpretation; the less precise and less explicit the perceived legislative policy the more likely a court will speak of common law. The distinction, however, is entirely one of degree.[29]

Commentators have not been kind to this reasoning,[30] and with good reason. Initially, one might suggest that, even if the assertion that "[t]he distinction . . . [between common law and statutory interpretation] is entirely one of degree" is assumed to be accurate, it is unclear why that necessarily implies that "common law" somehow *is* statutory interpretation. That the two differ only in degree does not alter the fact that they do, in fact, differ.

Equally important is the fact that usually the differences between common law and statutory interpretation are, both conceptually and politically, qualitatively distinct. It would be difficult to argue, for example, that the processes that the common law judges have employed over the years in fashioning the doctrine of contributory negligence or establishing the elements of the tort of battery bore any substantial resemblance to their approach to interpretation of a legislative enactment.[31] To be sure, on occasion the legislature would enact a statute bearing on or even preempting a particular common law doctrine, and in such an instance the judiciary would face the task of reconciling common law development with statutory interpretation. But such a practice surely does not render the common law doctrine an "interpretation" of that statute. Moreover, in the numerous instances in which there was no relevant legislative action, judicial development of the common law resembled very little the process of statutory interpretation.

The most obvious difference between the two judicial processes is the fundamental question the court answers when it decides a case. In developing common law principles free from legislative restriction, the court, in the context of relevant precedent (which itself represents merely policy choices made by earlier judges)[32] makes its own social, moral, and political determination of policy. It is the judiciary itself that makes the ultimate normative judgment in fashioning social policy. It is in this manner that courts have, for centuries, developed various common law doctrines. In contrast, when they engage in the process of statutory interpretation, their ultimate question—at least if they are performing their function correctly[33]—is not, "What is the best social policy?" but rather, "What social impact did the legislature intend by adoption of this legislation?" As a matter of American political theory, it is difficult to imagine a more fundamental distinction in the nature of the judicial function in nonconstitutional cases.[34]

Professors Westen and Lehman may have been confused by the existence of what appear to be "hybrid" situations—what Professor Thomas Merrill refers to as instances of "delegated lawmaking."[35] An example relied on by Westen and Lehman to support their link of common law development and statutory interpretation is section 1 of the Sherman Act.[36] It is widely accepted today that the language of that provision was intentionally drawn broadly so that the judiciary could mold federal antitrust policy in ways it deems advisable, in order to meet changing needs and conditions.[37] In a sense, then, Congress has chosen statutorily to delegate policy making authority to the judiciary. As a result, judicial decisions that technically constitute "statutory interpretation" appear in many respects similar to the product of the common law developmental processes. Of course, even here the legislature has set out certain conditions and guidelines that an interpreting court is not authorized to ignore. If, for example, it chose to apply section 1 of the Sherman Act to cases in which there was concededly only individual, rather than concerted, action, its decision would not represent a legitimate "construction" of the terms of the statute.

A more extreme example than section 1 of the Sherman Act is section 301(a) of the Labor Management Relations Act,[38] which, as construed,[39] vests unlimited authority in the hands of the federal judiciary to fashion a common law of labor agreements.[40] Such cases will look, smell, and taste like common law decisions, but may nevertheless be appropriately characterized as "statutory interpretation." Hence, such cases properly fall within the exception to the Rules of Decision Act's required use of state law for "Acts of Congress." It surely does not follow, however, that parallel judicial lawmaking, unauthorized by federal statute, should likewise be deemed to fall within the same exception to the dictate of the Rules of Decision Act.[41]

In fact, it ultimately matters little whether one conceptualizes cases brought under section 301(a) as "statutory interpretation" cases or "common law" cases because the terms of the Rules of Decision Act do not require that the particular cases actually involve statutory interpretation. Rather, the Act creates an exception when "provide[d]" by Act of Congress. Even if one were to conceptualize cases arising under section 301(a) as "common law decisions," this would not alter the key fact that an Act of Congress "provided" for the federal judicial power to create common law in such instances. Thus, in light of the clear words of the text of the Rules of Decision Act, the fact that the Act fails to bar federal common lawmaking authorized by congressional legislation does not legitimize federal common lawmaking when no such legislative delegation can be found.[42]

Ascertaining Legislative Purpose

Although a facial examination of statutory text may suffice to dispose of such dubious suggested constructions as those discussed in the last section, it cannot resolve all uncertainties of application and construction. Before delving into those issues more specifically, it is necessary—in accordance with the "institutionalist" canons fashioned in the previous chapter[43]—to ascertain one or more coherent underlying purposes sought to be served by the legislation. Prior to undertaking this task, however, it must again be emphasized that such purposes need not be so-called "public-oriented" purposes; rather, they may be more narrowly focused, less commendable goals. Unless the moral repugnance of the statute rises (or sinks, depending upon your perspective) to the level of constitutional violation, however, it is not for the interpreting court to reject that purpose on grounds of moral or social disagreement.[44] Of course, if one were to hypothesize a case in which there can be discerned two conceivable, mutually exclusive purposes, and it is truly impossible for the interpreting court, on the basis of the available evidence, to determine which of the two Congress actually intended, it may not be illegitimate for the court to choose the purpose it finds morally more acceptable. But, if the interpreting court approaches the question of legislative purpose in good faith, with the degree of political humility dictated by its place within the democratic structure in nonconstitutional adjudication, it is likely that such instances will be relatively rare.

Performance of this task for statutes as ancient as the Rules of Decision Act is of course complicated by the "archaeological"[45] efforts that the interpreting court is called upon to undertake. Unfortunately, there appears to exist no "smoking gun" in American political history that unambiguously reveals the drafters' purposes in adopting the Act.[46] However, certain contemporaneous data do exist that may reasonably be drawn upon for instruction as to the Act's likely political and social focus.

The history of the Constitution's drafting reveals on numerous occasions a tension between those who desired a strong federal judiciary on the one hand and those who feared substantial federal encroachment into state sovereignty on the other.[47] Although states' rights' advocates generally expressed few concerns about the threat to federalism posed by Congress, where states possessed substantial structurally assured influence,[48] their fear of the unrepresentative, insulated federal judiciary was widely known.[49] This special relationship between the states and Congress continues to receive attention from both the Supreme Court[50] and leading constitutional scholars.[51] Indeed, it is largely because of the disparity in the quality of the relationship with the states between the Congress and the federal courts that modern scholars have suggested that *Erie*'s[52] constitutional federalism component today limits only the federal judiciary, rather than Congress.[53]

Moreover, it surely was no secret, at the time of the framing, that proposed federal legislation faced severe obstacles before it could be enacted. Indeed, many of those obstacles—such as the bicameralism and presentment requirements[54]—clearly had as their inescapable effect, if not their primary purpose,[55] making enactment of congressional legislation that much more difficult. In contrast, federal courts, if left to their own devices, could conceivably fashion substantive law every time they adjudicated a private dispute.

For a variety of reasons, then, those concerned with undue federal incursions into state power would have quite reasonably preferred to entrust the federal substantive lawmaking power to Congress rather than to the federal judiciary. Although the extent to which this dichotomy in federal power was constitutionalized is debatable,[56] there can be little question that many of the founding fathers were motivated by such considerations, purely as a matter of social and political philosophy. When viewed in this historical light, the underlying legislative purpose intended to be served by the Rules of Decision Act, originally enacted by the very first Congress, becomes relatively clear. In enacting that legislation, Congress was attempting to preserve the political values of federalism by curbing the one branch of the federal government most feared as a threat to state power.

The Doctrine of Federal Common Law in Light of the Representational Principle: Distinguishing the Creative and Interpretive Processes

In light of the application of the Representational principle to construction of the Rules of Decision Act, it is clear that there can be no such thing as "federal common law," at least to the extent that it is used to provide a "rule of decision" and to the extent that the phrase "common law" is construed as a category of lawmaking distinct from constitutional or statutory "interpretation." The development of such "common law" by the federal courts runs directly contrary both to the plain meaning of the Rules of Decision Act's text[57] and to the most likely social-political purpose the Act was intended to serve: namely, to protect the interests of federalism by (1) reducing the likelihood of the exercise of federal lawmaking power to supplant otherwise governing state law; and (2) ensuring that whatever substantive lawmaking that does emanate from the federal government will come largely from the branch most closely tied to state interests.[58]

Professor Martha Field has fashioned an argument that challenges the force of the Rules of Decision Act as a meaningful limitation on federal common law. Although she concedes that, to be consistent with the Rules of Decision Act, a decision must at least technically be characterizable as "statutory interpretation,"[59] she asserts that this presents no real barrier to the judicial lawmaking power because virtually every substantive lawmaking decision of the federal courts can be tied back to *some* background federal statute, regardless of how remote that statute actually is from the specific issue before the court.[60]

If the view is adopted that the courts should act as primary policy determiners, one could feel comfortable with a decision to allow the courts to strain the concept of "statutory interpretation" to the linguistic and conceptual breaking point by characterizing the unabashed exercise of judicial lawmaking power as falling within the category of "interpretation" every time a court can find a statute even remotely relevant to the matter at hand.[61] Such an analytical mode is an illustration of what I have labeled "selective, rationalizing deconstructionism."[62] But such a cynical judicial usurpation in the interpretation of the Rules of Decision Act is both inappropriate and harmful in a democratic society, for two reasons. First, and most important, use of such statutory analysis directly undermines the almost certain social-political policy sought to be achieved by adoption of the Rules of Decision Act.[63] By adopting this analytical approach, then, the unrepresentative judiciary will effectively be overruling the choice of the representative branches. Thus, such a mode of statutory "construction" improperly inverts the hierarchy of policy decisionmaking authority established by our representational democratic structure. Second, the Supreme Court undermines its own credibility when it engages in such an obviously disingenuous and unprincipled form of analysis.

It might nevertheless be argued that even a good-faith attempt to separate the *creative* process of common lawmaking from the *interpretive* process of textual construction would face possibly insurmountable obstacles because it is generally impossible, in construing a text, to separate the interpreter's perception of the authors' intention from his or her own normative creative judgments.[64] But, although of course gray areas will appear,[65] it should not be all that difficult, at least in a general sense, to distinguish permissible true statutory "interpretation" from prohibited creative judicial lawmaking.

For a court properly to engage in the process of "statutory interpretation"—for purposes of the Rules of Decision Act or any other purpose—it must be performing at least one of three functions: (1) attempting to apply specific language of the statute's text to a set of facts; (2) deciding a legal question that, though not explicitly covered by the text, must be resolved, one way or another, before the statute may be applied to a specific set of facts to which the text concededly applies; or (3) engaging in creative lawmaking pursuant to a clear legislative delegation. If the court cannot reasonably claim to be engaging in one or more of these three functions, it is difficult to understand how judicial decisionmaking could rationally be deemed "interpretation" of an Act of Congress or one of the other texts expressly exempted from the Rules of Decision Act's directive to employ state substantive law. If the court is not engaged in one of these three tasks in the lawmaking process, it is necessarily engaged in naked legal creation, unguided and unauthorized by legislative directive.

It is debatable whether such a practice is, in the abstract, either undemocratic or inconsistent with our constitutionally dictated system of separation of powers. It is clearly rendered undemocratic, however, when the practice has been legislatively prohibited, as it has been for the federal courts by the Rules of Decision Act. Under this circumstance, then, the practice of unauthorized legal creation by the federal judiciary effectively amounts to a form of judicial civil disobedience to legislative will.

A word of elaboration is necessary to understand completely the three functions I have characterized as elements of the interpretive process in our legal and political context. When I include the attempt to apply specific portions of the text to a set of facts, I do not intend to include only those situations where the nature of the application will be unambiguous or free from difficulty. Indeed, these cases will often present the most difficult and controversial issues of statutory interpretation. But the key is that, difficult or not, it is *still* "statutory interpretation": the court is deciding how best to apply operative textual language, formally enacted by the representative branches, to a narrower fact situation. It is essential that the court be focusing on some word or words of the text to determine its meaning. In this sense, the prerequisite appears to be a rather modest limitation, and in many ways it is. It is interesting to note, however, the many examples of existing "federal common law" doctrine that do not meet even this modest limitation: judge-made abstention from enforcement of the civil rights laws;[66] "implied" statutory damage remedies;[67] matters involving foreign affairs,[68] and virtually all the so-called federal "proprietary interest" cases.[69] In none of these situations has the decision emanated from any real attempt by the court to apply the test of a specific federal statute to a particular fact situation.

Of course, recognition of the existence of the two other methods for qualifying as statutory interpretation makes clear that failure to fall within the first category is not necessarily fatal. The second category describes the venerable practice of "gap-filling": judicially resolving issues not foreseen by the legislature and therefore not expressly dealt with—even ambiguously—in the statutory text.[70] It is presumably this category that most advocates of modern federal common law would argue provides political legitimacy to such a doctrine.[71]

It is for the very reason that the gap-filling process provides the legitimizing mantle of statutory construction to judicial policy choices nowhere even arguably covered in the statute's text that it must be carefully confined, lest it effectively legitimize the very common law creation clearly prohibited by the Rules of Decision Act. Thus, a key prerequisite should be imposed before judicial action may be thought to constitute legitimate gap-filling: the issue being judicially resolved must be one that *must* be resolved before the statute may be applied—in other words, where not to decide the issue is effectively to decide it. For example, where a statute imposing a civil or criminal penalty fails to mention a statute of limitations, the interpreting court must resolve the question of whether a statute of limitations is to be imposed at all and if so what it will be. The court cannot logically conclude that it simply will not resolve the issue; so to decide effectively does resolve the issue, by concluding that no statute of limitations is to be imposed. A similar situation involves the application of res judicata or collateral estoppel to the enforcement of the federal civil rights laws.[72] Although the civil rights laws themselves says nothing about the issue, a court cannot logically apply the statute without first resolving the res judicata issue; to reach such a conclusion is effectively to resolve the issue against the use of res judicata. Finally, take the relatively common case of a statute, creating a federal cause of action, that is silent on the jurisdiction of the state courts to enforce the statutory claim.[73] In a suit challenging the state court's jurisdiction, the court cannot logically conclude that, because of the statute's silence, it will not resolve it: either the state court in which the federal claim has been brought possesses jurisdiction, or it does not; the question must be resolved before the statute may be applied to the factual situations to which it was intended to apply. Hence, "gap-filling," properly circumscribed, includes only those intermediate or "ancillary" issues not covered by the text, which must be resolved before the statute can be applied to matters concededly within its realm.

Such examples should be contrasted to matters simply not reached by the statute's text. In such situations, the court is neither applying the words of the text nor resolving an intermediate issue necessary to the statute's conceded application. For example, where a statute prescribes a standard of conduct and expressly imposes administrative and/or criminal penalties for violation of that standard, judicial "implication" of a private damage remedy cannot properly be viewed as an element of "statutory construction," and therefore must be deemed federal common lawmaking, proscribed by the Rules of Decision Act. The facts that the damage remedy may be thought to foster the beneficial purposes served by the statute[74] or that the legislature may have not foreseen the severity of the problem[75] matter little because the damage remedy was not subjected to the formal requirements of the legislative process,[76] and the statute may be easily applied to situations of conceded application without reaching this external issue. Nor would a finding in the legislative history of a legislative intent to create a damage remedy be sufficient, absent even an arguable reference to such a remedy in the statutory text because it was the text, not arguably self-serving legislative history, that was subjected to the enactment process and by which the legislators will be judged by the voting public.[77]

It is important to note, however, that the same may not necessarily be true of implied *constitutional* remedies.[78] Initially, the two might be distinguished on the basis of the appropriate judicial role in the constitutional democratic system, derived from the dichotomy drawn between the Representational and Counter-Majoritarian principles.[79] Although the unrepresentativeness of the federal judiciary dictates a substantial degree of humility in usurping nonconstitutional policy choices from the representative branches,[80] the very same factor imposes a political obligation on the judiciary to enforce the counter-majoritarian norms of the Constitution against those same representative branches.[81] Although it is therefore consistent with constitutional democratic theory to entrust to the judiciary the final say as to how best to enforce and protect basic constitutional rights and interests, the same is not true for sub-constitutional interests. Thus, even though most commentators appear to view the issues surrounding implied remedy analysis in statutory and constitutional cases as fungible,[82] fundamental distinctions in American political theory justify a significant difference in approach in the two situations.

Secondly, a much stronger case can be made that implied constitutional remedies better fit the mold of what Professor Merrill refers to as "delegated lawmaking" than can implied statutory remedies.[83] Delegated lawmaking applies when the operative text is so broadly phrased that it can reasonably be construed to constitute a delegation to the judiciary to create substantive principles. Many constitutional provisions fit this standard, but the same cannot be said for most statutes. This is particularly true of the remedies question. Constitutional provisions, though generally phrased in mandatory terms, do not explicitly provide specific remedies to enforce their directives. Because most people would agree that the Constitution was intended to be more than merely advisory, it would be difficult to assume that absolutely no enforcement mechanisms were contemplated—if only the equitable power to enjoin constitutional violations. Once this authority is conceded to the judiciary, it is logically difficult to deny to it the power also to recognize a damage remedy when it deems it necessary to enforce constitutionally protected interests.[84] By contrast, federal statutes almost always include at least *some* enforcement mechanism, whether administrative, criminal, or compensatory. On the other hand, Congress virtually never explicitly *prohibits* a particular enforcement mechanism. Hence, it would be difficult to construe congressional failure expressly to prohibit judicial creation of a damage remedy in a statute as an implied delegation to the judiciary to create one.

In fact, a strong argument might be fashioned that not only do implied statutory remedies constitute *extra*-statutory common law, but are also actually *counter*-statutory—that is, violative of Congress's intent in that particular statute. This is because a legislative choice to provide one remedy and not another may well represent Congress's judgment that the other remedy is inappropriate, either because it would overdeter, it would unduly burden the judiciary's dockets, or for a variety of other reasons. The likelihood becomes even greater if one accepts the empirical assumptions of public choice theory because under this analysis it is quite conceivable that the final legislative solution—with the inclusion of one remedy and the failure to include another—represents a compromise of competing private interests.[85]

The fact that implied damages remedies may be more appropriate for constitutional provisions than for statutes does not end the matter, however. For, even if the concept of implied constitutional remedies is accepted, the question remains whether they should be received as pure constitutional pronouncements, or as what has oxymoronically been referred to as "constitutional common law," subject to congressional reversal.[86] Such a concept, however, turns the principle of separation of powers—under which the unrepresentative judiciary acts as a countermajoritarian check on the representative branches by enforcing the Constitution—on its head, by effectively vesting in the representative branches authority to overrule the judiciary's constitutional judgments.[87]

One who adopts a strict originalist view of constitutional interpretation may be more disposed to view an implied remedy, nowhere found explicitly in the text or legislative history, as having only common law status.[88] However, a strict originalist should logically *reject* recognition of such remedies, rather than merely relegate them to common law status. By way of analogy, the fact that today it is believed that the Court's interpretation of the equal protection clause[89] in *Plessy v. Ferguson*[90] is incorrect does not mean that *Plessy* is viewed as a "common law" decision. Rather, it continues to be regarded as an interpretation of the Constitution itself, albeit an incorrect one.

The final category of legitimate statutory construction consists of those statutes in which the legislature has effectively or formally delegated to the judiciary the power to create substantive law—in other words, to make fundamental policy judgments. Although at least under current constitutional standards such a practice is legitimate,[91] it is nevertheless important to understand its inherent limitations. It is in this area—and only this area[92]—that the distinction between common law-like creative power and interpretive power becomes one of degree. Thus, certain statutes may delegate more lawmaking power than others,[93] and it is important for the court not to exceed the limitations inherent in the outer confines set out by the statute's text. But the fact that in such a case the difference is one of degree is irrelevant for Rules of Decision Act purposes because, wherever it falls on the continuum, such judicial lawmaking is "provide[d]" for by an Act of Congress. Most important for present purposes, however, is the fact that here, as in the other legitimate categories of statutory construction, it is not politically legitimate for the court simply to invoke the delegation concept merely as a shield for the legislatively unauthorized exercise of lawmaking authority. Unless the court, after careful examination of all of the proper factors,[94] finds that Congress actually understood and intended that the court would exercise the creative lawmaking power, the prerequisites for the exception to the Rules of Decision Act for situations provided by Act of Congress is not met. Absent such a finding, pure judicial lawmaking violates the plain meaning of the statute's text and undermines the coherent, underlying social-political purpose the Act was intended to serve.[95]

The Case of "Agent Orange": A Study in the Creation of Federal Common Law from the Perspective of the Representational Principle

One of the more dramatic illustrations of how reliance on the Representational principle would affect the scope of the federal courts' common lawmaking power is its application to the controversial "Agent Orange" decision in the Second Circuit.[96] "Agent Orange" is a privately manufactured chemical defoliant that was used in Vietnam. In the late 1970s a number of veterans who had been exposed to it there during the war developed various forms of cancer. They filed a major products liability class action against the manufacturers in the Eastern District of New York. One important preliminary issue that the federal court had to resolve was whether, in the absence of a controlling federal statute,[97] the suit was to be governed by federal common law or by the products liability law of the states.[98]

Although the district court declined to find an implied private right of action in any of the arguably relevant federal pesticide statutes,[99] it nevertheless held that an as yet undefined federal common law controlled. It reached this conclusion by finding "the existence of a substantial federal interest in the outcome of [the] litigation":

> Soldiers serving in the armed forces are government charges, entitled to government protection. Torts committed by war contractors against soldiers in action constitute "harms inflicted" on the soldiers and "interference" with the relationship between soldiers and the government....
>
> [T]his litigation... involves suits by many veterans against five war contractors who supplied a product used for some nine years in military operations across large portions of Vietnam.... As the number of veterans and the size of the claims against the war contractors increase so the federal interest in this litigation expands.[100]

The Second Circuit, over the vigorous dissent of Chief Judge Wilfred Feinberg,[101] reversed the finding that federal common law controlled.[102] Accepting the district court's "interest analysis" model, at least for purposes of argument, the court nevertheless disagreed with the district court's application of that model to reach a finding that federal common law controlled.[103]

Thoughtful commentators have vigorously attacked the court of appeals decision,[104] and it is true that, if one assumes the validity of the courts' interest analysis, it is difficult to dispute the district court's perception of a strong federal interest in the case. To reason, as did the court of appeals, that "[s]ince this litigation is between private parties and no substantial rights or duties of the government hinge on its outcome, there is no federal interest in uniformity for its own sake"[105] is to view the concept of "federal interest" from an artificially narrow perspective. The reason that the district court's conclusion was wrong and that of the court of appeals was right, however—from the perspective of democratic theory and separation of powers, if not Supreme Court precedent[106]—is that the Rules of Decision Act does not authorize a federal court to fashion a common law rule simply on the basis of a finding of an overriding federal interest. On the contrary, it quite explicitly prohibits the federal courts from creating their own free-standing substantive common law principles. Thus, once the court concluded that it could not reasonably find the directive for a federal substantive rule in the text, purposes, or properly confined gaps of a federal statute,[107] the clear command of the Rules of Decision Act prohibited judicial creation of a distinct federal standard.

The conclusion that federal substantive law does not control the outcome of a suit so permeated with strong federal, moral, and social interests may seem intuitively incorrect to many. But this is the very reason why I have chosen the Agent Orange case to illustrate operation of the Representational principle. In a democratic society, the unrepresentative federal judiciary is not automatically authorized to make sub-constitutional policy choices on the basis of its perception of social and moral dictates, *no matter how correct one believes those policy choices to be*. Indeed, irrelevance of that factor is the key premise of the Representational principle: if one disagrees with the social policy choices made by the legislature (in this case, the choice made in the Rules of Decision Act to prohibit federal common law creation not directly authorized by statute and the choice not to provide a uniform federal standard of products liability in cases affecting the armed forces), the appropriate body to remedy that deficiency is the legislature itself. In a representational democracy, it is neither morally nor politically legitimate for the federal judiciary, in a manner reminiscent of Platonic philosopher kings, simply to reverse or ignore the congressional choice. Thus, it is unresponsive to argue such policy issues solely on the basis of normative judgments. Unless the representative branches have authorized such creative lawmaking, the federal court is confined, in its application of substantive law, to an appropriate analysis of legislative action and intention. If not the product of a legitimate interpretive process of a governing federal statute, the substantive law to be applied in a federal court is the state's. If this directive is to change, it must emanate from the same source that produced the directive in the first place: the branches of the federal government most responsible to the will of the governed.

The Stare Decisis Problem

Assume that everything I have said to this point about the illegitimacy of federal common law—and therefore of most existing federal common law doctrine[108]—is found persuasive. If we conclude that, if we were writing on a clean slate, we would reject the concept of federal common law, untied directly to the interpretation or application of a specific federal statute or statutes, does it necessarily follow that the Supreme Court should dramatically alter existing doctrine? The answer basically comes down to one's assessment of the overriding importance of doctrinal stare decisis, for its own sake. To put the issue most starkly, should the value of stare decisis overwhelm a concededly valid normative attack on established judicial doctrine?

In a sense, one could reason that legal scholars need not directly deal with that question. It would be absurd to assume that they are somehow confined by some conception of narrow, doctrinal "court positivism."[109] If this were the case, their role would effectively be reduced to the limited task of pointing out internal doctrinal inconsistency, without making any philosophical, moral, social, or political normative judgment or critique of the doctrine itself. Under such an analysis, presumably legal scholars, writing in 1953, would have been precluded from criticizing *Plessy v. Ferguson*,[110] for the simple reason that at that time it represented Supreme Court precedent. Surely, the task of scholars cannot be so narrowly confined. Thus, they might reasonably suggest that their task includes only the obligation to provide a persuasive critique; how a court persuaded by that critique is to finesse the problem of stare decisis is an entirely separate matter.

Although of course lower courts may not act on the basis of such critiques in the face of contrary Supreme Court precedent, to the extent that the Supreme Court itself is seen as the scholar's intended audience, the stare decisis problem is, in many cases at least, hardly a problem at all. It is either naive or disingenuous for scholars or jurists to shield themselves behind the concept of stare decisis, in light of the Court's obvious inclination to reexamine its own precedent.[111] One might argue that it should not in fact be that way, but it is difficult to deny that it *is* that way. Thus, unless scholars are themselves focusing on the very issue of the legitimacy of stare decisis,[112] it is not unreasonable to take as a given the Court's flexible—if not free-wheeling—approach to its own precedent.

One conceivable complication in the present context is the position, articulated by some,[113] that stare decisis has special force in the case of statutory interpretation. Whether this should be so as a matter of legal process is open to debate, at least when the reason offered for overriding stare decisis is the desire to have judicial interpretive doctrine more accurately reflect legislative goals. After all, if stare decisis is itself seen as a manifestation of the value of judicial restraint, it is a strange concept of judicial restraint that ties a court to a statutory interpretation conceded to represent a departure from or abrogation of legislative will.

In any event, in the present context one may question the extent to which modern federal common law doctrine even purports to represent an "interpretation" of the text or purposes of the Rules of Decision Act. Other than an occasional, weak expression of consistency with the Act in the early post-*Erie* period,[114] the Justices have largely ignored the Act in fashioning federal common law. Thus, rather than representing an *interpretation* of the Rules of Decision Act, modern federal common law constitutes an overt, judicially created *circumvention*, or *contradiction*, of the statute. It is difficult to understand how the prevailing notions of American democratic theory could be thought to dictate a rigid adherence to stare decisis in such a situation.

Conclusion

Application of the Representational principle to the issue of statutory construction dictates a considerably narrower policymaking role for the judiciary than most courts and commentators today envision. Of course, an interpreting court requires a certain degree of flexibility in applying statutes to unforeseen circumstances. But nothing in American democratic theory or modern practicality justifies the unrepresentative judiciary's usurpation of the legislature's basic policymaking function, in situations in which the legislature has already spoken. Because reasonable people will so often differ over the wisest course, entrusting to the unrepresentative judiciary the authority to second-guess basic legislative policy choices seriously threatens our fundamental theoretical premise of governmental responsiveness to public will through the electoral process.

One might today seriously question whether the Rules of Decision Act's unbending prohibition of direct substantive lawmaking by the federal judiciary properly reflects the optimum allocation of lawmaking authority within the federal system. But once the legitimacy of the judiciary's ability to ignore the Act's directive on such grounds is accepted, it is logically difficult to reject similar judicial authority to ignore such legislation as the 1964 or 1965 Civil Rights Acts,[115] or the National Environmental Policy Act,[116] purely on grounds of a judicial social policy choice opposite to the one sought to be attained by the legislature. The point is that it is no more legitimate, in a representational democracy, for the unrepresentative judiciary to ignore, circumvent, or overrule constitutionally valid legislation with which one disagrees than it is for it to ignore legislation with which one agrees. Because our system implicitly recognizes a wide variety of policy choices that can reasonably be made, it has placed the policymaking authority primarily in the hands of the bodies most directly responsive to popular will. Short of a finding of unconstitutionality, or at the very least a finding of a serious constitutional question,[117] the federal judiciary may not legitimately modify or overrule that choice. Hence, if the clear directive of the Rules of Decision Act is to be amended, it is Congress, not the federal courts, which must make that judgment.

FOUR

Applying the Representational Principle, II: Judge-Made Abstention

The federal courts have long assumed the authority to decline to exercise jurisdiction explicitly vested in them by Congress. These courts have also assumed that they may decline to enforce certain substantive federal rights, usually those protecting individual civil liberties against state invasion. These presumptions of authority are manifested in the various "abstention" doctrines, developed by the federal courts largely within the last fifty years.[1] Although these doctrines have most often been applied in cases invoking only the federal courts' civil rights jurisdiction, in certain instances they sweep both civil rights and other forms of jurisdiction within their reach.[2]

The federal courts have assumed this authority, even in the absence of legislative history or statutory language authorizing such a refusal to act. Surprisingly, few have questioned whether the federal judiciary's authority to take such action violates the separation of governmental powers. To be sure, both scholars and jurists have criticized the efficacy and wisdom of the various abstention doctrines.[3] But they have left largely untouched the important question of the federal judiciary's authority to ignore the dictates of valid jurisdictional and civil rights statutes.[4]

Under the Representational principle, a federal court cannot legitimately invalidate a federal statute solely because of its unwise policies, or because it would make judges work harder than they believe they should, or because the judges themselves would not have enacted such legislation.[5] Such behavior by the judiciary would amount to a blatant—and indefensible—usurpation of legislative authority. At most, the judiciary possesses authority to overturn federal legislation because it is unconstitutional, not because the judiciary considers it unwise. Yet, in a sense, the abstention doctrines amount to such usurpation.

The questionable logic underlying traditional abstention has been taken to an extreme in recent years by members of the judiciary who argue that state court adjudication of federal rights against the states is generally to be preferred to federal court adjudication.[6] These "total abstention" theories would effectively prohibit the federal courts from enforcing federal civil rights laws, in particular section 1983,[7] and from exercising their congressionally vested jurisdiction to enforce those laws.[8] The term "total abstention" may be technically inaccurate, for these theories usually purport to preserve some jurisdiction for the federal courts to exercise.[9] But, as a practical matter, the abstention is total, and this seems to be the goal of the theories' supporters.

The burden of production in the abstention debate has been improperly reversed. The primary battleground has generally concerned the debate over whether state courts could protect federal rights as effectively as federal courts. Those who argue for either the adoption of "total abstention" or for the continuation or expansion of existing "partial abstention" raise various arguments founded in either social policy,[10] federalism,[11] or judicial efficiency.[12] They usually develop their arguments as if they were attempting to establish, on a totally clean slate, the wisest system of judicial federalism, in total disregard of the detailed and carefully balanced existing statutory network. Even more surprising, perhaps, is that many who oppose this argument have been willing to approach the problem on these terms, constantly seeking to demonstrate that federal courts are in fact superior to state courts as enforcers of federal rights.[13] In my opinion, the arguments that federal courts are superior are overwhelming.[14] But that should not be the point of contention, nor is it the point of this chapter.

The central difficulty with the argument for abstention is the forum to which it has been directed. Nothing, of course, prevents those who believe in the fungibility of state and federal courts as protectors of federal rights from attempting to convince Congress to repeal or substantially modify the broad jurisdiction it has vested in the federal courts. Generally, however, the arguments have not been directed to the legislative arena, but instead to the judicial forum, which is somehow believed to possess authority to alter or overrule the legislative directives.

Democratic principles clearly prohibit the judiciary from effectively repealing the statutory structure through "total abstention." Yet it is doubtful that the "partial abstention" model is substantially more consistent with American political theory. One could persuasively argue that whatever social harms may flow from federal judicial enforcement of federal rights against state entities cannot—short of a finding of unconstitutionality—justify judicial abandonment of federal legislation.

This chapter argues that neither total nor partial judge-made abstention is acceptable as a matter of legal process and separation of powers, wholly apart from the practical advisability of either form of the doctrine. Even if we were to conclude that unwavering judicial enforcement of this legislation actually would cause serious social harm, the recourse certainly should not be to the equivalent of judicial civil disobedience, but rather to the democratically ordained legislative process.

The Partial Abstention Model as a Judicial Usurpation of Legislative Authority

The various forms of partial abstention[15] arise regularly in federal litigation, primarily (though not exclusively) in cases under the federal civil rights jurisdiction. Perhaps the best known type is so-called *Pullman* abstention, developed in *Railroad Commission of Texas v. Pullman*,[16] under which a federal court will delay the exercise of its jurisdiction to allow a state court to interpret an ambiguous state statute subjected to a constitutional challenge. The doctrine is invoked only when the challenged statute is capable of at least two constructions, one that would render the law unconstitutional and one that would not. The case may ultimately return to the federal court for adjudication of the constitutional claim,[17] but only after the state courts have definitively interpreted the statute.[18]

The *Younger v. Harris*[19] abstention doctrine provides that a federal court may not enjoin an ongoing state criminal proceeding, even to protect federal constitutional rights. The Supreme Court has also applied the doctrine to the issuance of declaratory relief[20] and to certain state civil proceedings that implicate important state concerns.[21]

In *Burford v. Sun Oil Co.*,[22] the Supreme Court ordered abstention in order to prevent federal judicial interference in complex state administrative schemes. The Court also found abstention appropriate in *Louisiana Power & Light Co. v. City of Thibodaux*,[23] a case concerning the validity of state expropriation of property. Finally, though the presence of a parallel proceeding in a state court generally does not justify the dismissal of a federal suit, in *Colorado River Water Conservation District v. United States*[24] the Court held that "exceptional" circumstances may justify a stay.

Each of these variants of the partial abstention model could be characterized as a judicial usurpation of legislative authority, in violation of the Representational principle. The principle of separation of powers between the judicial and legislative branches derives from the fundamental democratic principle of electoral accountability.[25] The separation-of-powers critique of the partial abstention model begins with an analysis of the judiciary's proper role in a democratic society. Under the

Representational principle, the essential element of any democratic society is at least some level of majoritarian self-determination.[26] In our form of constitutional democracy, we have chosen to vest in a largely unrepresentative judiciary the power to invalidate laws adopted by a majoritarian legislature when those laws are deemed to violate constitutional protections.[27] But it would be directly contrary to the essence of American political theory for the judiciary to ignore a legislative judgment on any grounds other than unconstitutionality. Although the Supreme Court has reiterated this reasoning on a number of occasions,[28] its statement in *TVA v. Hill*[29] describes the principle as well as any:

> Our system of government is, after all, a tripartite one, with each branch having certain defined functions delegated to it by the Constitution. While "[i]t is emphatically the province and duty of the judicial department to say what the law is," ... it is equally—and emphatically—the exclusive province of the Congress not only to formulate legislative policies and mandate programs and projects, but also to establish their relative priority for the Nation. Once Congress, exercising its delegated powers, has decided the order of priorities in a given area, it is for the Executive to administer the laws and for the courts to enforce them when enforcement is sought.[30]

Thus, where Congress, exercising its power under section 5 of the Fourteenth Amendment,[31] has established a network of federally protected substantive rights and simultaneously vested the federal courts with jurisdiction to enforce those laws, the Supreme Court lacks the authority to ignore or invalidate those statutes merely because of disagreement with their substance. Viewed in the light of the Representational principle, then, virtually all of the debate over the relative competence of federal and state courts as enforcers of federal rights becomes logically irrelevant, except to the extent that it is directed exclusively to a call for legislative revision.

Conceptually, at least as a prima facie matter, there is little difference in this context between total and partial abstention. If Congress intended that the federal courts exercise a particular jurisdiction, either to achieve substantive legislative ends or to provide a constitutionally contemplated jurisdictional advantage, a court may not, absent constitutional objections, repeal those jurisdictional grants. But one may question why, if the courts do not possess the institutional authority to repeal the legislature's jurisdictional scheme, they possess any greater authority to modify the scheme in a manner not contemplated by the legislative body. In either repealing or modifying the legislation, the court would be altering a legislative scheme because of disagreement with the social policy choices that the scheme manifests. Thus, if a judge-made form of partial abstention is inconsistent with congressional intent to leave federal court jurisdiction unlimited, the fact that the abstention leaves intact a portion of the jurisdictional grant will not insulate it from a separation-of-powers attack.[32]

The foundation of the separation-of-powers critique of judge-made abstention is the assumption that judge-made partial abstention conflicts with congressional goals embodied in the seemingly unlimited grants of jurisdiction. It is the validity of this assumption that arguably separates the total and partial abstention models as departures from separation-of-powers principles. Various models of implied congressional authorization may be employed to justify partial abstention, but they are incapable of supporting total abstention. Although it is at least conceivable that Congress would implicitly delegate to the judiciary the authority to modify or limit a substantive statutory right or a jurisdictional grant,[33] it is absurd to imagine that Congress would implicitly grant the courts authority effectively to repeal such legislation. The exercise of such authority would render pointless the entire legislative process.

The fact that Congress theoretically *could* delegate to the courts the power to modify otherwise unlimited legislation, however, does not mean that Congress has actually done so. It is this improper leap from theoretical possibility to assumed fact that ultimately undermines any defense of the partial abstention model from a separation-of-powers attack. At the very least, the Representational principle should be deemed to impose a heavy burden of proof on one who would assert that a legislative body implicitly intended to allow the judiciary to amend unlimited legislation.[34] There is no reasonable basis, in terms of either democratic theory or the realities of the legislative process, for reversing the presumption and concluding that the partial abstention model should fall only if an affirmative case can be made that Congress did *not* intend such a power to be exercised. When a legislative body enacts legislation, one must assume, absent strong countervailing evidence, that it intended the courts to perform neither more nor less than their traditional function in a constitutional democracy—to interpret the language and intent of the statute, to enforce it as so construed, and to invalidate or ignore it only when they find that the law is unconstitutional. Although several conceivable separation-of-powers defenses exist for some or all elements of the partial abstention model, all of which derive ultimately from some concept of implied legislative authorization, none of them meets the heavy burden of proof that the Representational principle demands.

Defenses of the Partial Abstention Model

Before detailing and critiquing the conceivable justification for partial abstention, it is important to clarify the distinctions among the variations of the model. Two forms of partial abstention, *Pullman* and *Younger*,[35] are limited in their application to cases involving a federal constitutional challenge to state action. But, beyond this link, these two variants differ in several respects. Most important for a separation-of-powers analysis is that *Pullman* abstention, unlike *Younger* abstention, does not preclude the exercise of lower federal court jurisdiction; it merely delays it.[36] For this reason, *Pullman* abstention might be deemed less of a judicial undermining of the congressional jurisdictional structure. On the other hand, because the Court has traditionally limited *Younger* to situations in which a federal court is asked to disrupt an ongoing state judicial proceeding,[37] this form of abstention may arguably be justified by the long tradition of congressional disdain for federal court disruption of state judicial proceedings,[38] a justification not available for *Pullman* abstention. Some forms of partial abstention, such as *Colorado River* abstention for parallel state proceedings, may apply to any type of federal jurisdiction, and still others apply only to the diversity grant.

Although advocates of partial abstention have not attempted to categorize and synthesize the defenses of partial abstention, that task is an important one. Certain conceivable justifications are limited to a particular form of abstention, and others may apply to all forms. One category of arguments has been used to justify one or more of the forms of partial abstention in cases presenting a constitutional challenge to state action. This category includes (1) the general implied delegation argument (employed to justify any and all forms of partial abstention in such cases); (2) the argument from equity (a specific subset of an implied delegation rationale); and (3) the non-preclusive nature of *Pullman* abstention.

Ultimately, none of these rationales successfully defends the partial abstention model against a separation-of-powers attack. As the following discussion will demonstrate, no rationale overcomes the strong presumption against the concept of implied delegation dictated by the Representational principle.

The Implied Delegation Rationale in Constitutional Challenges to State Action

One might argue that federal court jurisdiction to enforce federal constitutional rights contains an implied authority to modify or limit the exercise of that jurisdiction in order to avoid friction within the federal system. Congress cannot foresee all conceivable federalism tensions that might arise in specific exercises of federal jurisdiction, the argument would proceed, and therefore it is reasonable to assume that Congress would allow the federal courts to modify or limit their jurisdiction when they find such dangers. It is indeed not uncommon for Congress to provide broad delegations of authority to the federal judiciary to make law. In *Textile Workers Union v. Lincoln Mills*,[39] for example, the Supreme Court held that what seemed to be merely a broad jurisdictional statute[40] vested in the federal courts the power to develop—wholly without congressional guidance—a substantive federal common law of labor relations. Similarly, the broad language of section 1 of the Sherman Act[41] has been construed as an effective delegation of legislative authority to the judiciary to develop a common law of restraint of trade.[42] Moreover, the implied delegation argument asserts, if Congress were unhappy with any existing form of partial abstention, it would legislatively revoke it. The failure to do so, combined with reenactment of the relevant substantive and jurisdictional legislation,[43] the argument posits, reveals an implicit congressional acceptance and ratification of such judge-made limitations.

This argument fails for several reasons. In light of the long history of congressional interest in the tensions of judicial federalism, the basic premise of implied delegation is dubious. Since the nation's beginning, Congress has statutorily dictated federal court abstention whenever it has found federal judicial action to present a danger to the federal system. The Anti-Injunction Act,[44] the Three-Judge Court Act,[45] the statutory branch of the habeas corpus exhaustion requirement,[46] the Tax Injunction Act,[47] and the Johnson Act[48] constitute a statutory network of legislatively directed limitations on the exercise of federal court power to disrupt state proceedings or interfere unduly with state policies.

It is true that the existence of this program of statutorily dictated abstention does not necessarily preclude Congress from vesting in the federal judiciary the authority to extend abstention beyond these legislative limitations. But it does establish that federal court abstention is not an area in which Congress has traditionally deferred to judicial discretion: Congress has long manifested concern with the issue, ordering abstention when it deemed abstention appropriate.

More importantly, the general implied delegation argument suffers from a fatal lack of evidentiary support. No supporter of partial abstention has pointed to anything approaching hard evidence in the legislative history of either the original enactment or the more recent reenactments of the substantive and jurisdictional civil rights statutes, which suggests that Congress intended that the federal courts possess authority to modify or limit otherwise unlimited legislation. This failure is not surprising because there were virtually no references made, in either the debates or committee reports of the 1948 revision of the judicial code, to the scope of jurisdiction under section 1343,[49] the statutory authorization for jurisdiction in cases brought under section 1983.

It is true that Congress has never overruled any judge-made form of abstention, but the argument that a legislative failure to reverse judicial action necessarily implies tacit legislative authorization for that practice is neither theoretically legitimate nor practically realistic. On a theoretical level, it is improper to transform a congressional failure to legislate into the equivalent of legislation. Before legislation is enacted, it must proceed through a detailed and rigorous substantive inquiry, investigation, debate, and formal review in both houses of Congress. This process is, in large part, mandated by the Constitution. The same cannot be said of a failure to legislate.

Moreover, reliance on a congressional failure to overrule a limiting judge-made doctrine, even in a recodification, effectively condones through legislative inertia what was initially an improper and unauthorized judicial usurpation of legislative authority. This breach of separation of powers is thus improperly transformed into the status of legislation. Such an approach, which effectively rewards past and encourages future judicial encroachments upon the legislative province, must be rejected. If Congress intends to condone such judicial action, it should be required to say so expressly in the recodification. At the very least, one should require a clear showing in the legislative history of congressional awareness and acceptance of the judicial action. No such evidence has been cited for the forms of partial abstention.[50]

On a more practical level, as my colleague Thomas Merrill has argued:

> The argument based on the possibility of congressional override ignores the institutional reality that, given its crowded agenda, Congress is far more likely not to act than to act with respect to any particular issue presented for its attention. Thus, the theoretical possibility of congressional override cannot disguise the fact that lawmaking by federal courts would in most cases result in the federal courts, rather than Congress, having the last say. In practice, therefore, institutionalization of the practice of lawmaking by federal courts would represent a major shift in policymaking power away from Congress toward the federal judiciary—in violation of the constitutional scheme.[51]

Ironically, one of the best known of the Supreme Court's opinions expressing a separation-of-powers concern about federal judicial lawmaking was written by a staunch advocate of judge-made abstention, Chief Justice Rehnquist. In *Milwaukee v. Illinois*,[52] he wrote:

> Nothing in this process [of formulating federal common law] suggests that courts are better suited to develop national policy in areas governed by federal common law than they are in other areas, or that the usual and important concerns of an appropriate division of functions between the Congress and the federal judiciary are inapplicable.[53]

Although the Court in general and Chief Justice Rehnquist in particular have expressed serious concern about federal judicial encroachment upon the legislative province by the creation of federal common law and have been hesitant to find an implied congressional delegation of lawmaking power,[54] neither has seen precisely the same dangers inherent in the development of judge-made abstention.

To the extent that there are differences between judge-made abstention and judicial creation of federal common law, the former will usually constitute a greater departure from accepted separation-of-powers principles. To be sure, when a federal court provides a private cause of action for a legislative violation where Congress has intended no such result, there are arguably serious separation-of-powers problems raised.[55] But a far greater judicial encroachment upon the legislative prerogative takes place when the federal courts directly undermine enforcement of an existing legislative program by declining to enforce federal rights in situations not authorized by Congress. Judge-made abstention, then, constitutes judicial lawmaking of the most sweeping nature. The principle of separation of powers would be better protected by the Court's application of the same cautious scrutiny used to review the creation of implied private remedies to the development of judge-made abstention.

Professor Bator contended that "[t]he Supreme Court has, quite correctly, always taken the position that the post-Civil War jurisdictional and remedial statutes, with their generative language and their complex and multifaceted legislative histories, are essentially open-textured, leaving much to interpretation in light of contexts and postulates not always visible on their surface."[56] Bator's view is both puzzling and vague. Why should these jurisdictional and remedial statutes be deemed any more "open-textured" than any other? The language of the relevant statutes leaves no room for judicial limitation or modification—certainly no more so than the language of other jurisdictional statutes.[57] Moreover, the very purpose of this legislation was to interpose the federal judiciary between the state and individual, largely because of concern about the functioning of state judiciaries.[58] If an implied delegation argument is to survive a separation-of-powers challenge, then, it must have a firmer basis in fact than Professor Bator has provided.

The Argument from Equity

An implied delegation argument based on equity has been suggested as justification for both *Younger* and *Pullman* abstention. However, the argument fails to support either.

In one of the rare instances in which a supporter of judge-made abstention even acknowledged the possibility of a separation-of-powers problem, Professor Bator argued that development of such abstention

> is the correct enterprise not only because this is institutionally the "correct" or "best" solution, but also because it seems to me to be the proper interpretation of the governing authoritative statutes. . . . Statutes such as § 1983 and the Habeas Corpus Act use language which, if woodenly and anachronistically read, can be interpreted to provide an "absolute" right of access to the federal courts. But these statutes were themselves passed against the background of a large body of standing law on matters of substance, remedy, and jurisdiction. . . . The fact that a given remedial doctrine is not explicitly mentioned therefore does not automatically mean that the new statute was intended wholly to supersede it. Thus, to give an example, it seems to me implausible to assume that the cause of action created by and the jurisdiction granted in the Civil Rights Act of 1871 were meant wholly to supersede the preexisting equity doctrine that a good faith criminal prosecution will not ordinarily be enjoined simply because the plaintiff asserts that he has a valid defense to it.[59]

This is a form of an implied delegation argument, but it is, in theory at least, a considerably more disciplined and defensible one than the general implied delegation theory. Section 1983 provides that culpable defendants "shall be liable to the party injured in an action at law, *suit in equity*, or other proper proceedings for redress."[60] Thus, the statute presumably incorporates pre-existing limitations on the use of equitable power. One could plausibly argue that *Younger* abstention accords with legislative will because equity would not traditionally enjoin a good-faith criminal prosecution where the defendant had an adequate remedy at law.

There are significant problems with Professor Bator's analysis, however. The accepted limitation on equitable relief against a criminal prosecution derived from an English unitary system, and therefore the limit on federal equitable power was traditionally confined to prosecutions in the *federal* courts.[61] The principle did not extend to preclude federal interference with state court proceedings. In light of this, it is unreasonable to impute to the enacting Congress the understanding that the equitable relief that they were providing would not be used against ongoing state prosecutions. Moreover, because the drafters of section 1983 were especially concerned with the good faith of the state courts, it is unlikely that they assumed that the ability to raise a federal defense in state court constituted an adequate remedy.

Analysis of the inconsistency of the equity argument with congressional intent underscores a broader theoretical danger from this form of argument. If we accept that the statutory provision of equitable relief inherently authorizes judicial discretionary authority to refuse to act on the basis of factors unrelated to traditional equitable discretion—for example, the doctrine of unclean hands or the adequacy of the remedy at law—we will have effectively provided the unrepresentative judiciary with the power to veto legislative policy judgments. Under such a framework, nothing logically precludes the judiciary from relying on simple disagreement with the statutory judgment as a basis for refusing to act. After all, if the concept of equity inherently implied total judicial discretion not to act on the basis of grounds previously unknown, how can such a result be avoided? Indeed, this is exactly what has taken place in the context of judge-made abstention. Hence, even in the unlikely event that one could establish the historical validity of such unlimited judicial discretion as an inherent element of equity, its recognition, at least to allow judicial second-guessing of a congressional judgment, is so inconsistent with fundamental notions of representational democratic theory that it must be rejected as part of American jurisprudence. Although it is conceivable that Congress could choose to vest such a veto power in the judiciary, surely more evidence of congressional intent must exist to support such a conclusion than the simple legislative authorization of equitable relief.

The assertion that the statutory provision of equitable relief incorporates traditional equitable limitations logically implies that a federal court may decline to issue a preliminary injunction if it fails to find a likelihood of success on the merits or may deny permanent injunctive relief if a damage remedy adequately protects the plaintiff's interests. But it does not follow that a federal court may appropriately decline to award equitable relief on grounds unrelated to traditional equitable concepts. *Younger* abstention is based more on considerations of comity and federalism than on traditional grounds of equity.[62] Because these considerations represent merely the Supreme Court's social judgment about the relative competence of state and federal courts or about the harm caused by federal review of state policies, they are illegitimate judicial incursions into an area where Congress has already spoken.

The Anti-Injunction Act[63] complicates the equity argument employed to justify *Younger* abstention. That statute provides: "A court of the United States may not grant an injunction to stay proceedings in a State court except as expressly authorized by Act of Congress, or where necessary in aid of its jurisdiction, or to protect or effectuate its judgments." A federal court may not enjoin a state proceeding unless the injunction falls within one of the three exceptions. The statute does not, however, resolve the separation-of-powers problems posed by *Younger*, and the Court's explicit analysis in *Younger* demonstrates that it did not rely on the Act.

In *Younger*, the Court found the injunction improper, purely as a matter of judge-made principles. It expressly declined to consider whether the injunction was barred by the Anti-Injunction Act. One year later in *Mitchum v. Foster*,[64] the Court, in a highly questionable opinion,[65] found that section 1983 constituted an implied yet "expressly authorized" congressional exception to the Anti-Injunction Act. It nevertheless continued to adhere to the terms of *Younger*'s judge-made abstention doctrine.[66] In what may be one of the most bizarre contortions of Supreme Court analysis, the Court in *Mitchum* found section 1983 to be an "implied" express exception (an oxymoron if ever there was one) because of the grave mistrust of the state judiciaries expressed by the drafters of the statute.[67] Yet *Younger* rests largely on the desire to avoid insulting state judiciaries by questioning their competence or good faith.[68]

One could reasonably reject *Mitchum* as a poorly reasoned construction of the "expressly authorized" exception to the Anti-Injunction Act. *Younger* abstention, at least to the extent that it is applied to bar injunctions of *ongoing* state proceedings,[69] could conceivably then be viewed as an application of the Anti-Injunction Act. Such a conclusion would logically lead to the abolition of the narrow exceptions to *Younger* abstention,[70] but as so modified (in fact, expanded) the doctrine would be insulated from a separation-of-powers critique. Even if the *Mitchum* analysis were rejected, however, there remains at least an arguable construction of the Anti-Injunction Act that could justify most of the injunctions that *Younger* bars.[71]

If, on the other hand, one accepts the logic of the *Mitchum* holding—as the Court presumably does when it expands the reach of *Younger* abstention[72]—then the equity argument fails to justify *Younger* abstention. The primary purpose of the Anti-Injunction Act is to limit potential friction between state and federal courts.[73] If Congress intended section 1983 to be an exception to the statute's bar, then presumably Congress decided that the dangers of increased federal-state friction are outweighed by the need to enforce the federal rights guaranteed by section 1983. It is inconceivable that Congress would vest in the federal judiciary total discretion to overrule the product of the congressional balancing process.

One might counter that Congress decided to grant the federal judiciary the discretion to reach a different result in individual cases not foreseen by Congress. But *Younger* represents considerably more than judicial discretion to restrike the balance in individual cases. Qualified only by a narrow set of rarely used exceptions,[74] *Younger* abstention is all but total.[75] Thus, if *Mitchum* is assumed to be valid, *Younger* abstention represents an effective reversal of the congressional decision to make section 1983 an exception to the Anti-Injunction Act. In any event, even if *Younger* abstention were to take the form of an individualized, case-by-case analysis, in light of *Mitchum* a separation-of-powers analysis of judicial lawmaking requires that such a practice be justified by convincing evidence in the legislative history (of *either* the Anti-Injunction Act or section 1983). No one has ever suggested that such evidence exists.

In sum, the combined effect—if not the motivation—of the Court's decisions in *Younger* and *Mitchum* is that the federal judiciary has arrogated to itself the authority to decide when to enjoin state court proceedings. It is difficult to imagine a starker illustration of judicial usurpation of legislative authority. To the extent that *Younger* is viewed as a judge-made doctrine, then, it cannot be rationalized on the basis of traditional equitable principles.[76]

In *Pullman*, Justice Frankfurter attempted to rationalize that form of judge-made abstention as a traditional exercise of the judiciary's equitable powers:

> In this situation a federal court of equity is asked to decide an issue by making a tentative answer which may be displaced tomorrow by a state adjudication.... The resources of equity are equal to an adjustment that will avoid the waste of a tentative decision as well as the friction of a premature constitutional adjudication.
>
> An appeal to the chancellor... is an appeal to the "exercise of the sound discretion, which guides the determination of courts of equity."... The history of equity jurisdiction is the history of regard for public consequences in employing the extraordinary remedy of the injunction.... Few public interests have a higher claim upon the discretion of a federal chancellor than the avoidance of needless friction with state policies.... This use of equitable powers is a contribution of the courts in furthering the harmonious relation between state and federal authority without the need of rigorous congressional restriction of those powers.[77]

This resort to equity fails to rationalize *Pullman* abstention. Initially, the doctrine has never been limited to cases in which equitable relief is sought.[78] More importantly, Justice Frankfurter's reliance on equitable principles as a means of avoiding friction within the federal system amounts to an historical non sequitur. As previously noted,[79] the doctrine of equity was developed in England, which knows no federal structure. One may reasonably wonder, then, how Justice Frankfurter could assert that the doctrine of equity can serve as a vehicle for the judicial accommodation of federalism concerns.

The most puzzling aspect of his analysis is the assertion that a federal court's equity powers allow it to take account of federalism concerns "without the need of rigorous congressional restriction of those powers."[80] He seems to imply that Congress has silently chosen to allow the federal courts to limit themselves, so that Congress need not do so. But, as already noted, Congress has limited federal judicial power when it deemed such limitation necessary to protect federalism interests. The Anti-Injunction Act is one example. There is thus no basis for inferring such an implied delegation of congressional authority to the federal courts.[81]

The Unique Impact of Pullman *Abstention*

The unique nature of *Pullman* abstention suggests an arguable means of rationalizing it with separation of powers. Although all other forms of partial abstention in some sense preclude, or at least have the potential of precluding, federal court adjudication, *Pullman* abstention does nothing more in theory than delay federal adjudication. Under the terms of this form of abstention, the federal court simply gives the state courts an opportunity to provide a definitive construction of an ambiguous state statute's meaning. However, if the plaintiff so indicates, he or she may reserve the opportunity to return to federal court for the adjudication of the federal issue once the state court has definitively construed the state law.[82] In a sense, then, *Pullman* abstention may be deemed not to undermine separation-of-powers principles because it does not actually preclude the exercise of federal court jurisdiction.

But even a delay in the exercise of federal jurisdiction may be considered a violation of separation of powers if it has not been contemplated by Congress.[83] Conceptually, a delay of federal adjudication constitutes a modification of the statutory structure, much as a preclusion under narrowly defined circumstances may. The difference is merely one of degree. Moreover, invocation of *Pullman* abstention may, as a practical matter, so severely delay the exercise of federal jurisdiction that it acts as a significant deterrent to the resort to federal court.[84]

The Argument from Substantive Legislative Analysis: Two Wrongs Don't Make a Right

Professor Michael Wells has suggested that my separation-of-powers attack on judge-made abstention is "fundamentally mistaken"[85] because of its "faulty premise" that "Congress is responsible for the modern federal cause of action under 42 U.S.C. § 1983 against state actors to redress constitutional violations."[86] "The problem with the institutional argument," he continues, "is that the statute was never intended to create such a broad cause of action. It was directed at a specific problem, the Ku Klux Klan terror in the South against blacks and their supporters in the aftermath of the Civil War."[87] Thus, the judicial reading of section 1983 "to provide a general federal cause of action" in *Monroe v. Pape*[88] "cannot be credibly defended as the result of a successful search for the intent of the framers of the statute,"[89] and as a result "[a]bstention is more accurately viewed as a judge-made forum rule for a judge-made cause of action."[90]

Professor Wells's analysis is highly questionable on many levels. First, although the tone of his writing suggests the absence of any conceivable debate on the correctness of the Supreme Court's expansive construction of the section 1983 cause of action as a matter of congressional intent, that issue is by no means so simply resolved as Professor Wells implies. In fact, though reaching a firm conclusion about the proper scope of the section 1983 cause of action is unnecessary to the rejection of Professor Wells's attack on the separation-of-powers critique, it is highly likely that he is wrong on the point. The statute's text clearly points to a broadly conceived substantive cause of action. The Act imposes liability upon any state actor who "subjects . . . any citizen of the United States . . . to the deprivation of any rights, privileges, or immunities secured by the Constitution and laws."[91] At least without examining the legislative history, one would find it difficult to believe that rational individuals who had intended to define the cause of action as narrowly as Professor Wells suggests would have chosen such broadly phrased language. Indeed, when the post-Civil War Congress intended to confine civil rights statutes to the protection of the recently freed black race, the text of the statute clearly reflects that fact.[92] Moreover, it is unlikely that the fact that section 1983 is today construed to provide a remedy for violations of constitutional rights unknown at the time of the Act's original passage in 1871 in any way undermines the conclusion that judicial interpretation is consistent with congressional intent. It is not unreasonable for Congress to conclude that there should exist both a substantive federal remedy for and federal judicial enforcement of whatever federal or constitutional rights may be found to exist, for the simple reason that those rights, whatever their substantive content, are wholly federal in nature.

In any event, much exists in the Act's legislative history to support a broad scope for the section 1983 cause of action.[93] The fact that the problems of the Ku Klux Klan served as the impetus for congressional consideration in the first place does not mean that, once it chooses to deal with the issue, Congress must confine its legislative solution to the contours of that narrow problem.

Thus, Professor Wells's analysis of section 1983's substantive scope is probably inaccurate. Even if one were ultimately persuaded by his evidence and arguments, however, it is difficult to believe that the Court's interpretation of the statutory scope is so devoid of even colorable support that it amounts to little more than a ruse for naked judicial lawmaking. The mere fact that one can persuasively criticize a court's statutory interpretation does not render its decisions devoid of the status of statutory interpretation.

Assume, however, that we concede the extreme of Professor Wells's analysis—namely, that (1) the Court's interpretation of section 1983 is incorrect; (2) it is so incorrect as to be not even arguable; and (3) it is therefore characterizable only as disguised judge-made law. Professor Wells's resulting response to the separation-of-powers critique of judge-made abstention seems to turn on the long-invalidated premise that two wrongs make a right. He initially concedes that, if the Court's construction of section 1983 is valid, judge-made abstention is institutionally impermissible.[94] Under Professor Wells's argument the illegitimate status of the latter is somehow purified by the inaccuracy of the former. In other words, the Court is wrong to abstain, but, because it was also wrong to interpret section 1983 the way it did, abstention somehow becomes proper.

The point ignored in Professor Wells's analysis is that the Court's expansive construction of the substantive civil rights cause of action, whether right or wrong, does not purport to be purely judge-made law, but rather assumes the democratically protective mantel of statutory interpretation. In the unlikely event that Professor Wells is correct in his critique of substantive section 1983 law, the remedy is not to compound judicial usurpation on top of judicial usurpation, but simply to correct the initial usurpation—in other words, to reinterpret section 1983 correctly, and perhaps openly refashion as judge-made law what was previously characterized as statutory construction, with all of the political and legal complications to which such an approach would likely give rise.[95] Until such action is taken, it is difficult to understand how an institutionally dubious judge-made abstention doctrine can be purified by recognition of the inaccurate characterization of the substantive law as statutory construction.

My separation-of-powers critique of judge-made abstention takes as a given the validity of whatever substantive section 1983 interpretation the courts have made. To the extent that this interpretation is inaccurate, it should be corrected by subsequent judicial reinterpretation,[96] not by a compounding of the judiciary's excesses.

The Argument from Tradition: Recognizing the Need to Separate the Normative from the Descriptive

Somewhat more compelling than Professor Wells's critique is the argument presented by Professor David Shapiro.[97] Professor Shapiro asserts that the separation-of-powers critique of judge-made abstention is

> far too grudging in [its] recognition of judicial discretion in matters of jurisdiction ... [partly because] the existence of this discretion is much

> more pervasive than is generally realized, and . . . it has ancient and honorable roots at common law as well as in equity. Thus, far from amounting to judicial usurpation, open acknowledgement of reasoned discretion is wholly consistent with the Anglo-American legal tradition.[98]

Furthermore, he argues "that the continued exercise of discretion in these matters has much to contribute to the easing of interbranch and intergovernmental tensions in our complex system of government."[99] Professor Shapiro thus suggests both empirical and normative responses to the separation-of-powers critique. Although the two must be considered separately, ultimately neither proves persuasive.

Initially, even prior to an examination of Professor Shapiro's data to support his descriptive argument, one might seriously question any such empirical appeal. Such an approach amounts to little more than "proof by adverse possession":[100] it may be wrong, but it has been done this way so long it now assumes a patina of legitimacy. In discussing our national traditions, it is important to distinguish between our descriptive tradition and our normative tradition. After all, ours is a nation that for almost half of its existence authorized slavery; committed near-genocide on native Americans; and, in the lifetime of many living today, placed individuals in concentration camps solely on the basis of their ethnic origin.[101] Although it is unfortunately difficult to dispute these incidents as part of our descriptive tradition, it is much easier to reject all of them as part of our normative tradition—the values to which our nation aspires as a democratic society. The point, in other words, is that in discussing our national traditions, it is both dangerous and fallacious to infer an "ought" from an "is."

Admittedly, Professor Shapiro's empirical argument is intended to do much more than simply demonstrate the existence of judge-made abstention. He is arguing that similar forms of judicial discretion are recognized in numerous other contexts. However, even if I were to concede the validity of his analogies,[102] I fail to see how his empirical argument responds to my normative critique. I simply reply that, to the extent that the practices he points to are in fact analogous to judge-made abstention, they are subject to the very same normative attack, and should likewise be rejected.

In any event, I do not find most or all of the situations to which he points to be analogous to judge-made abstention in its essential element of clear judicial disregard of a substantive statutory scheme. In fact, as I shall subsequently demonstrate,[103] established practice in other contexts is actually inconsistent with recognition of such broad judicial discretion in the abstention area. Professor Shapiro points to eight examples[104] of well-established judicial discretion that he deems similar to judge-made abstention: justiciability doctrines, forum non conveniens, exhaustion of remedies, pendent and ancillary jurisdiction, Supreme Court original jurisdiction, a federal court's ability to determine its jurisdiction, the Supreme Court's discretionary appellate jurisdiction, and "the common law tradition."

Justiciability Doctrines. Professor Shapiro correctly notes that the Supreme Court has recognized limitations of standing, ripeness, and mootness on the exercise of federal court power.[105] Of course, to the extent that these doctrines are derived from Article III, they fail to support an analogy to abstention. Even if Congress in its jurisdictional grants had intended the federal courts to hear such cases, the Court would effectively be saying that legislative extension of federal jurisdiction in contravention of these limitations is unconstitutional. Professor Shapiro also correctly notes, however, that to a certain extent the Court has characterized these doctrines as prudentially, rather than constitutionally, based, though exactly how it derives this distinction from the cryptic word "case" in Article III has always remained a mystery. To that extent, at least a partial analogy to the abstention context exists: the court, for non-constitutionally based reasons, declines to exercise jurisdiction Congress intended it to have.[106] As already noted, however, to the extent that the analogy actually holds, such prudentially based refusals to exercise jurisdiction likewise violate properly recognized separation-of-powers principles. Their previously unchallenged existence is no more normatively persuasive than was the similar status of judge-made abstention.

Ultimately, however, the analogy fails. Initially, one might argue that the inconsistency between the judicial doctrine on the one hand and the textually manifested congressional intent on the other are substantially different in the two contexts. With the one possible limited exception of equity, which I have ultimately rejected,[107] there exists absolutely no textual basis upon which to infer congressional recognition of a judicial power to veto the legislatively directed exercise of federal jurisdiction in the abstention context.[108] On the other hand, one could reasonably argue that the term "civil actions" in the general federal question statute, with which Congress has extended federal court jurisdiction, is ambiguous, and that, in the absence of standing or ripeness or in the presence of mootness, the federal court is not presented with a true "civil action."

A better analogy to judge-made abstention is the well-established doctrine of *Testa v. Katt*[109] that state courts are not permitted to refuse congressionally directed adjudication of federal causes of action absent a valid excuse that is neutrally based and unrelated to a judgment on the policy of the congressional scheme.[110] In this context, we have long recognized that a judicial refusal to adjudicate may be just as disruptive to democratic processes as overly aggressive judicial action. It is puzzling that we have failed to recognize the same principle in the case of judge-made abstention.

Forum Non Conveniens. The doctrine of forum non conveniens, in the words of Justice Jackson, "is simply that a court may resist imposition upon its jurisdiction even when jurisdiction is authorized by the letter of a general venue statute."[111] Unlike abstention, however, this doctrine is largely geographically, rather than systemically, based.[112] Thus, one state court may indicate that another state forum is more appropriate, or one federal court may reach a similar conclusion about another federal forum. Moreover, where the doctrine is employed by a state court to decline jurisdiction over a cause of action specifically created by the state legislature, which had simultaneously enacted a jurisdictional statute to enforce that cause of action, as is the situation in sections 1983 and 1343, there can be little doubt that the invocation of the doctrine would constitute a violation of legislative supremacy.

Finally, it is interesting to note that, in the federal system, Congress has expressly codified the doctrine of forum non conveniens.[113] The existence of such an express congressional delegation of discretion not only distinguishes the doctrine from judge-made abstention, it also underscores the point that, when Congress wishes the federal judiciary to exercise such broad-based discretion, it does so by means of an express statutory grant. This fact, if anything, renders more significant the absence of any such congressional authorization of federal judicial discretion to abstain in section 1983 cases.

Exhaustion of Remedies. Most puzzling is Professor Shapiro's citation of the doctrine of exhaustion of remedies as an analogy to the abstention practice. In fact, the practice of the Supreme Court concerning exhaustion of remedies in the section 1983 context renders its willingness to invoke abstention extremely awkward. In *Patsy v. Board of Regents,*[114] the Court expressly rejected a judge-made doctrine of exhaustion of state administrative remedies for section 1983 suits, for the very reason that the statute did not direct such exhaustion and, in fact, exhaustion undermined the substantive congressional scheme.[115] Thus, much like the example of forum non conveniens, Professor Shapiro's citation of this example actually renders more dubious the existence of abstention doctrines, not expressly authorized by statute, which have the effect of interfering with congressionally directed federal judicial enforcement of the substantive legislative scheme.

Pendent and Ancillary Jurisdiction. Professor Shapiro correctly notes that "[m]ore often than not, the existence of [the] authority [to exercise pendent or ancillary jurisdiction] is, at most, implicit in a legislative grant of jurisdiction."[116] He therefore points to the existence of such forms of judge-made jurisdiction as yet another example of judicial discretion.

The pendent and ancillary forms of jurisdiction, at least as a prima facie matter, seem to exceed the confines of congressional jurisdictional statutes. Although several attempts have been made—by commentators, rather than the Supreme Court—to defend pendent and ancillary jurisdiction from a separation-of-powers attack,[117] the doctrines might ultimately suffer from the same separation-of-powers defect as judge-made abstention. If this is so, employing my normative-descriptive dichotomy,[118] that conclusion should more appropriately undermine the normative validity of pendent and ancillary jurisdiction than shore up the theoretical defects in abstention.

Even if pendent and ancillary jurisdiction were found to exceed legislatively imposed limitations, however, it is hard to view the resultant undermining of separation-of-powers principles as being as egregious as the corresponding impact of judge-made abstention in the civil rights context. First, the language of the relevant jurisdictional statutes refers to "civil actions," which is at least arguably an ambiguous term. Congress might conceivably have intended this language to include the entire constitutional "case" for Article III purposes, as defined by Chief Justice Marshall in *Osborn v. Bank of the United States*.[119] In any event, there exists no substantive legislative scheme that is undermined by the judicial exercise of pendent and ancillary jurisdiction. Although that fact may not ultimately save those doctrines from separation-of-powers attack, at the very least, it reduces the severity of the breach. This is an ameliorating factor unavailable to support judge-made abstention.

The Determination of Original and Appellate Jurisdiction. Professor Shapiro's reliance on the ability of the federal courts to determine the scope of their original jurisdiction need not give us pause because all of those decisions represent constructions of broadly phrased jurisdictional statutes,[120] and thus are distinguishable from purely judge-made abstention doctrines, which are nothing more than contradictory appendages to the relevant statutes. Traditionally, Supreme Court appellate jurisdiction has been more problematic because the Court has always treated as discretionary its mandatory jurisdiction.[121] In a certain sense, the practice has always constituted indefensible judicial abrogation of a congressional directive and is thus as politically tenuous as abstention. This problem appears to have recently been mooted by congressional action abolishing the Supreme Court's pre-existing mandatory appellate jurisdiction.[122] Even prior to this legislation, however, the Court had not totally ignored the congressional directive because it always recognized, consistent with the concept of mandatory jurisdiction, that dismissals or affirmances of cases within its mandatory appeal jurisdiction constituted decisions on the merits and therefore binding precedent for the lower courts.[123]

"The Common Law Tradition." Professor Shapiro argues that the tradition of England during the development of the common law included an important discretionary component.[124] With the possible exception of traditional equity analysis,[125] however, it is largely irrelevant whether in seventeenth-century England courts were deemed to have discretionary authority to decline jurisdiction. That country has never measured itself by the standards of the American political theory of separation of powers. This example, like all the others Shapiro cites, fails to provide any real analogy on which to support judge-made abstention.

Defining the Contours of Judicial Discretion. Professor Shapiro cautions that "the discretion I urge is not an uncontrolled or whimsical power to decide like cases differently, but a power that carries with it an obligation of reasoned and articulated decision, and that can therefore exist within a regime of law."[126] Although such restraint is surely commendable from a practical standpoint, it is difficult to understand how he derives this normative limitation as a matter of political theory. Once it is conceded that the unrepresentative judiciary has authority to decline to exercise congressionally directed jurisdiction, designed to enforce a substantive legislative program, on grounds unrelated to a construction of specific statutory language or ascertainment of congressional intent, from the perspective of the separation of powers, at least, no particular exercise of such discretion is logically more defensible than any other.

The Total Abstention Model: Justifications and Critique

To my knowledge, no scholar or judge has ever expressly called upon the federal courts to ignore the congressional grant of jurisdiction to adjudicate suits against persons acting under color of state law for violations of federal rights.[127] However, several legal doctrines developed by the Justices, if accepted by a majority of the Court, could effectively exclude the lower federal courts from the exercise of their jurisdictional authority to enforce section 1983. In the discussion that follows, I describe the several theories and legal devices that make up the total abstention model.

The State Judicial "Exhaustion" Theory

Ironically, one finds the seeds of the most sweeping aspect of the total abstention model in the opinion that revitalized the section 1983 action after many years of dormancy. In *Monroe v. Pape*,[128] the Court recognized a cause of action under section 1983 in a suit seeking damages from local police officers who allegedly violated plaintiffs' Fourth and Fourteenth Amendment rights against unreasonable search and seizure.[129] The decision was widely perceived as marking a new age in federal judicial activism against unconstitutional state conduct.[130] The Court, per Justice Douglas, emphasized that plaintiffs need not exhaust their state judicial remedies,[131] a conclusion that suggested expansive federal judicial authority to enforce section 1983. Discussing the history and purpose of the 1871 Civil Rights Act, however, Justice Douglas noted that "it provided a remedy where state law was inadequate,"[132] and that its aim "was to provide a federal remedy where the state remedy, though adequate in theory, was not available in practice."[133] Chief Justice Rehnquist—the leading architect of the total abstention model—has pointed to these statements in *Monroe* in urging a "reconsideration" of *Monroe*'s no-judicial-exhaustion rule. The statutory purposes cited in *Monroe*, he argues, "need not bar exhaustion where the State can demonstrate that there is an available and adequate state remedy."[134]

An obvious difficulty with Justice Douglas's conclusion is that neither the substantive nor the jurisdictional statutes provide a federal remedy only "when state law was inadequate." The absence of such language quite probably reflects a congressional decision to allow plaintiffs to make that determination for themselves. Indeed, at another point in *Monroe*, Justice Douglas seems to contradict his earlier purpose analysis by noting that "[a]lthough the legislation was enacted because of the conditions that existed in the South at that time, it is cast in general language and is as applicable to Illinois as it is to the States whose names were mentioned over and again in the debates."[135]

It may, at first, appear inaccurate to characterize Chief Justice Rehnquist's statement as urging a form of "total" abstention. Initially, he suggests merely exhaustion of state judicial remedies, which one might reasonably believe would only delay federal adjudication, not preclude it. Secondly, he purports to leave open the possibility of federal court adjudication where the state is unable to demonstrate the existence of an adequate remedy. As a practical matter, however, acceptance of Rehnquist's suggestion would amount to total federal abstention. The reason for such a conclusion is that the term "exhaustion" in this context is a euphemism. In situations not involving section 1983, a requirement of exhaustion of state remedies, whether administrative[136] or judicial,[137] would result simply in a delay of federal court adjudication. When, and only when, the required state remedies had been sought, the plaintiff could return to federal court for adjudication of a federal claim. Such a practice has its disadvantages, but at least at some point a federal court may exercise its jurisdiction to adjudicate the federal claim. A requirement of state *judicial* exhaustion, on the other hand, would have no such result. We could, I suppose, structure our system so that a plaintiff who completed the state judicial adjudication of state remedies could return to federal court. This is, in fact, exactly what happens under habeas corpus[138]—a device that Professor Cover described as "diachronic or sequential redundancy."[139] But, outside the expressly contemplated exception in the habeas corpus model, this jurisdictional route is unavailable to plaintiffs, as Chief Justice Rehnquist was no doubt aware when he urged reconsideration of the use of "exhaustion" of state judicial remedies in section 1983 actions.

The Supreme Court held in *Allen v. McCurry*[140] that the doctrine of collateral estoppel—the binding effect of a finding of fact or of a mixed question of law and fact in a previous state judicial action on a subsequent federal action—barred section 1983 plaintiffs. Under the Full Faith and Credit Act,[141] a federal court must employ the broader doctrine of res judicata, which bars litigation of any aspect of the same cause of action or any claim arising out of the same operative facts *which might have been brought.*[142] Because it is well established that state and federal courts have concurrent jurisdiction over section 1983 suits,[143] a failure to raise a section 1983 claim in the course of the state judicial action would bar a subsequent federal suit.

Perhaps Chief Justice Rehnquist intended to imply that, if the Court were to impose a state judicial exhaustion requirement, the doctrines of collateral estoppel and res judicata would be abandoned. However, he gave no such indication, and it is highly unlikely that he would intend this result; not surprisingly, those who call for one or another form of state judicial exhaustion generally endorse the *Allen* decision.[144] This is because much the same philosophy lies behind both: a belief in the extensive use of state courts as the forum for the adjudication of federal constitutional challenges to state action.[145] Hence, one must assume that Chief Justice Rehnquist did not intend to abandon the dictates either of *Allen* or of the Full Faith and Credit Act when he called for reconsideration of the exhaustion of state judicial remedies in section 1983 actions. Thus structured, the so-called exhaustion requirement does considerably more than delay lower federal court adjudication; it effectively precludes it, leaving section 1343—the jurisdictional component of section 1983—a null set.

It is probably safe to assume that Chief Justice Rehnquist did not intend a probing case-by-case inquiry into the adequacy of the state remedy.[146] It is true that, in theory, his analysis still leaves room for federal judicial action where state remedies are found inadequate. However, a detailed, probing, case-by-case federal judicial inquiry into the adequacy of substantive and procedural state remedies would necessarily entail a significant increase in both the federal courts' workload and in the frictions of judicial federalism. Indeed, it is the fear of these very dangers that has caused the Supreme Court to render all but useless the Civil Rights Removal Statute,[147] even though the statutory language expressly calls for such a case-by-case inquiry.[148]

How an "adequacy" analysis would work in practice was candidly illustrated by Professor Bator, who endorsed a similar approach (albeit in a somewhat more limited context):

> [T]he "full and fair opportunity" formula leaves untouched the more subtle and invisible aspects of comparative competence. Indeed, it does not purport to be a technique for measuring the state judge's competence and sensitivity at all. If we are fundamentally suspicious of the state court system—if the central problem continues to be the problem of mistrust—then the "full and fair opportunity" formula will not do. I realize, too, that much will turn on the spirit in which the "full and fair opportunity" formula is interpreted in the various specific contexts to which it is relevant. Nevertheless, it is a virtue of this formula that it asks a question about the hospitable nature of the state courts rather than starting with an adverse presumption about it.[149]

Most states will provide theoretically adequate tort remedies for any conduct that amounts to a substantive violation of section 1983.[150] Because neither Chief Justice Rehnquist nor Professor Bator accepted the traditional institutional arguments for state court inadequacy,[151] only in those rare cases in which the entire state judicial process is glaringly inadequate would either of them be willing to find that state procedural remedies did not provide a plaintiff with a "full and fair opportunity" to litigate. Thus, although purists might quibble with my characterization of Chief Justice Rehnquist's call for a state judicial exhaustion requirement as a form of *total* abstention in section 1983 suits, in reality that is exactly what he seeks.

Expansion of Pullman *Abstention into Total Abstention*

As originally structured, *Pullman* abstention itself could not be deemed an element in the total abstention model because it is used only in the relatively rare situations in which the challenged state law is ambiguous. A minor modification of the doctrine, however, could easily shift it toward the total abstention model.

There are two ways effectively to transform *Pullman* abstention into total abstention. One alternative, suggested by Chief Justice Burger's dissent in *Wisconsin v. Constantineau*,[152] is to expand the doctrine into the equivalent of a state judicial exhaustion requirement. Traditionally, *Pullman* abstention applies only when the challenged state law presents the ambiguity. On rare occasions, however, the Court has employed the doctrine when the state constitution contains a provision that might invalidate the state law without a federal constitutional challenge.[153] In *Constantineau*, the Court appeared to have limited this branch of the doctrine to situations in which the state constitution provides a unique and specialized form of protection.[154] Chief Justice Burger, however, was unwilling to limit resort to state constitutional remedies to such special cases.[155] Because virtually every state constitution contains a protection similar or identical to the Fourteenth Amendment's due process and equal protection clauses, it would be a rare case indeed in which Chief Justice Burger would not have ordered federal abstention[156] in a case challenging the constitutionality of a state statute.

The second alternative, articulated by Chief Justice Rehnquist, represents an equally clear modification of the doctrine into a type of total abstention. In a decision in which *Pullman* abstention was not at issue,[157] his opinion for the Court suggested that "[a]lmost every constitutional challenge . . . offers the opportunity for narrowing constructions that might obviate the constitutional problem and intelligently mediate federal constitutional concerns and state interests."[158] The Chief Justice did not take this totally unsupported assertion to its logical conclusion[159]—that a federal court should abstain in every federal constitutional challenge to a state statute. However, when combined with a logical interpretation of Chief Justice Rehnquist's suggested "reconsideration" of a state judicial exhaustion requirement, this analysis provides the final piece to the total abstention model, creating a structure that effectively precludes the exercise of federal court jurisdiction under section 1343 to adjudicate federal constitutional challenges to *any* form of state action, and that instead places primary, if not exclusive, responsibility for the protection of federal rights in the state judiciaries.

Critique of the Total Abstention Model under the Representational Principle

The separation-of-powers attack on the total abstention model is, at least prima facie, a relatively simple and seemingly irrebuttable one. In a constitutional democracy, the unrepresentative judiciary may overrule the policy judgments of an electorally accountable legislative body only when those judgments violate the Constitution. The courts may not ignore or overrule congressional policy decisions because of simple disagreement with their wisdom.

Although the concept of partial abstention might conceivably be justified through some notion of implied congressional delegation,[160] total abstention has no such defense available. For it is all but inconceivable that Congress would impliedly delegate to the courts the authority in effect to repeal an entire substantive or jurisdictional legislative scheme. Nevertheless, three arguments could conceivably be advanced in support of the total abstention model. None of these, however, can adequately support the existence of the sweeping incursion on the legislative prerogative contemplated by the total abstention model.

The Social Policy Argument in Favor of State Adjudication. A proponent of total abstention might defend the model by contending that adoption of the principle in no way represents a repeal of section 1983 because the concept simply makes the state judiciaries the primary enforcers of the substantive federal rights—a power that they are constitutionally competent to exercise. This argument fails for two reasons. First, it disregards the primary motivating force behind the legislation. The legislative intent—which has been well documented by both commentators[161] and the Court itself[162]—was to interpose the *federal* judiciary between the individual and the state, largely because of the failure of the state courts adequately to protect the individual. Second, the total abstention model conflicts not so much with the *substantive* directive of section 1983 as with the *jurisdictional* directive of section 1343. Although section 1983 could conceivably coexist with a scheme supplementing federal judicial enforcement by state adjudication, it is logically inconceivable that section 1343 could survive such a move. If, as a practical matter, the federal courts completely forego their jurisdiction to enforce section 1983, the jurisdictional statute is inescapably rendered a nullity.

The response that the status of the state courts in the 1870s is irrelevant to their status in the 1990s must be directed to the legislative body rather than the judiciary. As Justice Douglas noted in *Monroe*,[163] the legislation as it currently stands is absolute in its terms: It does not limit the federal cause of action only to the southern states, or only to situations where the state remedy is found to be inadequate. Indeed, when the post-Civil War Congress intended federal jurisdiction to turn upon the adequacy of the state court remedy, it explicitly stated its intention, as it did in the Civil Rights Removal Statute.[164] The contrast between such contingent, case-by-case application of federal jurisdiction to protect federal rights and the unqualified, all-encompassing directive for enforcement of section 1983 underscores the clear congressional intent to avoid having the exercise of federal jurisdiction turn on the viability of the state remedy in the individual case. In the Civil Rights Removal Statute, Congress made access to federal courts contingent upon an objective judicial finding of the state judiciary's inadequacy in the particular case. In the precursor to section 1343, Congress made access contingent on a purely subjective choice, to be made by individuals seeking to vindicate their federal rights against state intrusion. Therefore, the commonly employed argument that abstention is justified because of the fungibility of state and federal courts is unacceptable.

The Jurisdictional Discretion Rationale. Even accepting the questionable supposition that the substantive directive of section 1983 is not undermined by exclusive state judicial enforcement, the total abstention model cannot be defended from the separation-of-powers attack on the ground that the judiciary would be departing only from a jurisdictional directive, rather than a substantive congressional program. Indeed, Chief Justice Rehnquist himself—the primary architect of the incremental total abstention model—has often expressed an overriding concern with congressional intent in the fashioning of jurisdictional allocations, at least when the result has been to decrease the reach of federal court power.[165]

The Supreme Court has recognized the important interrelations between congressional jurisdictional allocations and substantive congressional programs when the *state* courts have refused to obey a jurisdictional directive, even when such refusals theoretically would not have rendered the substantive legislation a nullity.[166] Although the normative institutional principle may be different (separation of powers, rather than federalism), one could apply the same logic to a federal court's refusal to adhere to the congressional allocation of jurisdiction. Thus, an argument that construes a jurisdictional statute as somehow vesting a power in the federal courts to adjudicate the relevant claims without a corresponding duty to do so is unacceptable. Although federal jurisdictional statutes have traditionally been framed in terms that might conceivably lead to such a construction,[167] the absurd results that would flow from that construction make it clear that Congress could not have intended such an interpretation. Under such a structure, every substantive right created by Congress would effectively be subject to a practical veto by the federal judiciary: If a jurisdictional grant is merely an invitation to exercise jurisdiction, there is no logical reason why a federal court could not choose to disregard a particular federal statute—or a particular suit arising under a federal statute—that the Court deemed inadvisable. Surely, then, a congressional provision of jurisdiction must mean more than simply the option for the federal court to act. Although perhaps Congress could constitutionally delegate such discretionary authority to the federal judiciary, absent a much clearer legislative directive we must assume that Congress did not intend such a dubious result.

Conclusion

Judge-made abstention constitutes judicial lawmaking of the most sweeping nature. Although a federal court's decision to infer a private cause of action undermines the Representational principle, judge-made abstention presents a considerably greater risk of judicial usurpation. Judicial creation of private rights of action can undermine a carefully structured statutory goal only indirectly. Judicial lawmaking through abstention, on the other hand, can very directly undermine that goal.

Recognition that abstention amounts to judicial lawmaking should shift the focus of the abstention debate away from the comparative merits of the policies for and against the various forms of abstention and toward the issue of the institutional legitimacy of such action on the part of the judiciary. Well-accepted principles of separation of powers mandate that an electorally accountable legislature make the basic policy decisions concerning how the nation is to be governed. The authority to make these policy decisions necessarily includes the authority to employ the federal judiciary to enforce the substantive statutory programs adopted by Congress. Absent a finding of unconstitutionality, the Representational principle dictates that it is not the judiciary's function to modify or repeal a congressional enforcement network unless Congress has clearly delegated such authority to the judiciary. No court or commentator has presented persuasive evidence of any congressional intent to delegate such authority. Indeed, throughout the nation's history, Congress has retained for itself the authority to decide when federal courts should decline to exercise their jurisdiction.

It may well be that, if Congress were to consider the matter today, it would choose to structure abstention much as the federal courts have. But the comparative arguments for and against such forms of abstention are by no means so one-sided as to make that conclusion inescapable. In a constitutional democracy, in any event, such decisions are most appropriately rendered by the legislature, not the judiciary.

FIVE

THE "COUNTER-MAJORITARIAN" PRINCIPLE

The Representational principle examined in the preceding chapters focuses upon the limitations that American political theory places on federal judicial authority to fashion jurisdictional doctrines, resulting from the fact of the federal courts' unrepresentativeness. Yet, the concept of a constitutional democracy imposes significant obligations on the federal judiciary to act, for the very reason that the judiciary is unrepresentative. The concept of a formalized, written, counter-majoritarian constitution logically requires, for its continued viability, interpretation and enforcement by some governmental organ independent of the majoritarian branches. This principle dictates a moral and political obligation on the judiciary to provide a forum for adjudication of constitutional claims.

Of course, one might reasonably suggest that it is too late in the day to require a defense of the concept of judicial review. Rightly or wrongly, we have accepted that principle, at least in its essence, since the decision in *Marbury v. Madison*.[1] Therefore, the argument proceeds, we need not continually reinvent the wheel; we may reasonably take the judicial review concept as a political and constitutional given, and fashion jurisdictional doctrine on that premise. To a certain extent, the point is valid, and, as will be seen, portions of my critique of existing jurisdictional doctrine are based on its logical inconsistency with the generally accepted premise of judicial review.[2]

Nevertheless, an attempt to rationalize the concept of judicial review with American political theory is by no means a wasted effort, for two reasons. Initially, there are a number of conceivable theoretical rationales for judicial review within the American political framework, and subsequent analysis will demonstrate that which rationale one adopts may dramatically influence the structuring of jurisdictional doctrine in constitutional cases.[3] Secondly, to perhaps a surprising extent, respected constitutional scholars have raised serious doubts about the theoretical viability of the entire concept.[4]

An earlier chapter has already set forth the basic elements of the Counter-Majoritarian principle.[5] By examining and critiquing both the arguments against judicial review and the alternative theoretical rationales for the concept, this chapter will flesh out the arguments in support of the Counter-Majoritarian principle's defense of the judicial power—and obligation—to enforce the Constitution against the majoritarian branches.

The "Democratic Character" of Judicial Review

"The root difficulty," Alexander Bickel wrote, "is that judicial review is a counter-majoritarian force in our system."[6] To put the point in its most simple form, he argued that, "when the Supreme Court declares unconstitutional a legislative act or the action of an elected executive, it thwarts the will of representatives of the actual people of the here and now; it exercises control, not in behalf of the prevailing majority, but against it." That, Bickel noted, "is the reason the charge can be made that judicial review is undemocratic."[7] To be sure, Bickel ultimately accepted some form of the principle of judicial review.[8] But both his substantive constitutional analysis and his proposed jurisdictional structure appear to have been substantially influenced by what he called "the essential reality that judicial review is a deviant institution in the American democracy,"[9] based on the assumption that "[j]udicial review works counter to" the "distinguishing characteristic" of a democratic system—"the policy-making power of representative institutions, born of the electoral process. . . . "[10]

When policy issues are not claimed to be controlled by the Constitution, Professor Bickel's concern about the undemocratic character of judicial action is most certainly a legitimate one. Indeed, a similar insight guides the framing of the Representational principle, described in the previous chapters. But it is both puzzling and disturbing that Bickel could seriously raise these concerns in the context of *constitutional* adjudication. The doubts he raised about the democratic character of the federal courts[11] effectively beg the question when raised in the constitutional context. For by its nature the Constitution is unambiguously *not* a democratic document. Although of course its content ordains and establishes a form of representative democracy, the limitations it imposes on the authority of the various branches are profoundly undemocratic.

If those who created our political system had intended an unfettered majoritarian system, they could easily have adopted a governing document that did nothing more than establish the procedural mechanisms for the operation of such a structure. Then, the only policy choice removed from the will of a simple majority would have been the very fact of majority rule itself. Alternatively, they could simply have chosen not to adopt any single governing document at all, and instead to allow the government to function on the basis of accepted tradition and periodic written edicts of fundamental values—much as the British system has.

Those who founded our system chose neither of these courses. Although they wisely declined to adopt a highly detailed and extended code in a manner that would have been disturbingly similar to today's Internal Revenue Code, they did adopt a governing document that went considerably beyond either a simple declaration of basic values or a mere procedural structure designed to ensure majority rule. In addition to both of these, the Constitution provides a moderately detailed political blueprint, establishing both the mechanics of day-to-day governmental operation and the boundaries inside of which that government and its particular branches were to exercise power. We may debate the exact motivations for the various structural and political limitations imposed by the document. But two key points are beyond dispute: (1) these limitations—whether on the structure of the federal government, on the scope of its powers, or on its authority to restrict individual liberty—are framed in mandatory, rather than advisory, terminology; and (2) they are all subject to the stringent, super-majoritarian protections of Article V's amendment process. Thus, there can be no doubt that by its terms the Constitution imposes substantial limitations on the outer reaches of the governmental power that it created, and that those limitations were placed beyond the power of a simple majority to modify or repeal. In its essence, then, the Constitution is very much a counter-majoritarian document.

It is, then, nonsensical to attack judicial review, as Bickel and others have done, as "counter-majoritarian" or a "deviant" element within a democratic society. Ours is not now—and never was—a total or unlimited democratic system. Democratic theorists have made clear, however, that a limited (or "constitutional") form of democracy is no less properly classifiable as "democratic," merely because it is limited.[12] In point of fact, historians agree that many of those who formulated the Constitution were far from radical democrats.[13] Although the framers obviously chose as their underlying political value a concept of fundamental popular sovereignty and self-determination—the necessary condition of any democratic system[14]—they often expressed concern over the dangers of unlimited democracy.[15] More importantly, there can be little doubt that the political system they embodied in the Constitution—with its delicate structure of checks and balances,[16] its imposition of numerous hurdles to the enactment of legislation,[17] its dilutions of a direct representational system,[18] its formal insulation of the judiciary from majoritarian pressures,[19] and, in the Bill of Rights, its creation of extensive enclaves of individual liberty protected from governmental invasion[20]—was far from either a pure democracy or a system of simple majoritarianism. Hence, just as the neo-republican scholars, criticized earlier,[21] have incorrectly ignored the noun in the phrase "constitutional democracy," so, too, have commentators such as Bickel incorrectly ignored the adjective in the very same phrase.

Ironically, in the development of his own ultimate rationale for judicial review in light of the straw man of a mythical pure American democracy that he erected, Bickel himself seriously endangered the very majoritarian values he had initially exalted. He rightly began his analysis with a "search ... for a function which might (indeed, must) involve the making of policy, yet which differs from the legislative and executive functions; which will not likely be performed elsewhere if the courts do not assume it ... and whose discharge by the courts will not lower the quality of the other departments' performance by denuding them of the dignity and burden of their own responsibility."[22] His answer is that "courts have certain capacities for dealing with matters of principle that legislatures and executives do not possess."[23] Thus, according to Bickel, to the extent that an issue may be decided on the basis of "principle"—in other words, by means of an analysis of long-range values[24]—it is appropriate for final judicial resolution, despite the inherent tensions between judicial review and democratic theory. At no point, however, does Bickel appear to limit this judicial authority to the expounding of principles and values gleaned from the text, structure, or history of the Constitution. Because in a constitutional democracy the only justification for judicial review by an unrepresentative governmental organ is to ensure that the majoritarian branches adhere to the counter-majoritarian limitations imposed by the Constitution, judicial invalidation of the exercise of majoritarian will on any other grounds erodes fundamental democratic principles. Yet, in view of his unwarranted concern over the "deviant" nature of judicial review as an element of American democratic theory, Bickel would have significantly confined the judiciary's jurisdictional and substantive power in constitutional cases. Thus, his approach to judicial review somehow manages to be simultaneously over- and under-inclusive.

The Political Necessity of Judicial Review

The fact that judicial review may not be inherently inconsistent with American political theory does not, of course, necessarily establish the logical validity of the mirror image proposition, namely, that the *absence* of judicial review is necessarily inconsistent with our prevailing political precepts. In other words, the fact that we logically *can* vest in the judiciary the final say as to the Constitution's meaning does not mean that we logically *must* vest such authority in the courts. Bickel, for example, raised the possibility that each branch be deemed the final arbiter of the meaning of the constitutional provisions governing its behavior.[25] Professor William Van Alstyne, in critiquing John Marshall's reasoning in *Marbury*, argued:

> That the Constitution is a "written" one yields little or nothing as to whether acts of Congress may be given the force of positive law notwithstanding the opinions of judges, the executive, a minority or majority of the population or even of Congress itself . . . that such Acts are repugnant to the Constitution. That this is so is clear enough simply from the fact that even in Marshall's time (and to a great extent today), a number of nations maintained written constitutions and yet gave national legislative acts the full force of positive law without providing any constitutional check to guarantee the compatibility of those acts with their constitutions.[26]

Close analysis demonstrates, however, that both Bickel's suggestion and Van Alstyne's critique are wrong. We could not, as Bickel suggests, logically vest in each branch the final say as to the meaning of the constitutional provisions governing their authority—that is, at least if we still intend to maintain a meaningful constitutional system. Nor should we be persuaded by Van Alstyne's argument that judicial review is not logically inherent in a constitutional system because other nations possessing written constitutions fail to provide for judicial review. No one, to my knowledge, has ever suggested that judicial review is a *physical* necessity of a constitutional system, only that it is a *logical* or *practical* necessity. That other nations decline to provide for judicial review at most establishes the former proposition; it says absolutely nothing about the latter. To the extent that other nations with written constitutions fail to adopt a system of judicial review, they could simply be wrong—at least to the extent that those nations either desire, or believe they possess, a meaningful constitutional system. Certainly, since the time of the framers, our nation, in shaping its governmental structure, has never considered itself logically or normatively bound by the practices of other nations. In any event, many nations governed by a written constitution have, in fact, erected detailed systems of judicial review.[27]

Also, contrary to Professor Van Alstyne's assertion, the fact that the Constitution is in written form is by no means irrelevant to the logical necessity of judicial review. It is, rather, a necessary—though not sufficient—element of the argument. If the Constitution were not written but rather came in the unwritten form of consensus and tradition, it would have to be assumed that the "constitution" was subject to regular modification, to the extent deemed warranted by those in political authority. This must be so, at least as a practical matter, because no one could point to either a specific, concrete legal limitation that those in power had violated or a directive, possessing the positivistic force of law, not subject to modification by those in power. Of course, the failure of those people to adhere to well-accepted political traditions might ultimately lead to their downfall, but if so it would simply be as a result of political factors, such as the belief of the people in the wisdom of the violated traditions. It would not be because their conduct was illegal as a violation of a concrete limitation on their power.

In short, a system that adopts an *unwritten* constitution is placing ultimate confidence in those in political power to act in good faith. Because both the existence and meaning of unwritten traditions are so uncertain, it would not be difficult for political leaders to argue persuasively that no such applicable tradition actually exists. Moreover, even an understood tradition could be abandoned, so long as a simple majority deemed it advisable to do so. This, of course, does not mean that a system premised on an unwritten constitution would necessarily degenerate into a political state of nature, but only that the system could not reasonably be deemed to be governed by a counter-majoritarian constitution.

When a constitution assumes a *written* form, however, those establishing the government are manifesting considerably less trust of those who will exercise political power. This is particularly so when the constitution—as is true of ours—speaks in mandatory terms. It is even more true when that constitution—again, as does ours—in both its history and text expressly manifests profound mistrust of those in power.[28] This mistrust, it should be noted, extends well beyond the political leaders themselves. Those who drafted our Constitution often expressed serious concern over the power of the electorate who put the leaders in power.[29] That our Constitution was not structured merely as a means of protecting the interests of the electorate from abuse by those in power can be seen in Article V, the amendment provision. If that had been the sole goal of a written constitution, presumably amendments could have been authorized by a vote of a simple majority of the electorate. Instead, the framers adopted an amendatory structure under which it had to be obvious to all concerned that situations could easily arise in which both political leaders and a simple majority of the electorate wish to ignore or change a constitutional dictate, but they would nevertheless be deprived of the legal authority to do so.

In light of these considerations, let us examine Bickel's suggestion (one to which he was not necessarily committing himself, it should be noted)[30] that each branch retain final say as to the meaning of the provisions regulating its own authority. It should not be difficult to determine that when the majoritarian branch is allowed to act as the final arbiter of the counter-majoritarian constitutional limitations on its authority, at least as a practical matter there are no limitations at all. Indeed, one should need to draw only on common sense and generic experience to make this realization. Whether one conjures up Lord Coke's principle "Nemo Judex in re sua"[31]—no man is to be a judge in his own cause—or merely the commonly accepted wisdom that one does not rely on the fox to guard the chicken coop, it would require the height of naivete to believe that the majoritarian branches could, as a general matter, be trusted to sit objectively in final judgment on the constitutionality of their own actions. All one need do to grasp the point is to imagine a litigation between two parties, where the final decision is to be made by one of those parties. Just as it would be absurd to suppose that the resolution of such a case could be deemed fair, so, too, is it absurd to imagine that one majoritarian branch could be universally trusted to make a fair assessment of a constitutional challenge to its actions.

It is conceivable that one majoritarian branch could be placed as the final arbiter of the constitutionality of the actions of the *other* majoritarian branch. In such an event, we would not be left with the absurd situation of a party finally resolving the legality of its own actions. But, it should be recalled, the Constitution is by nature a counter-majoritarian document, as can be seen from the mandatory nature of its language and its extreme super-majoritarian amendment process. If one majoritarian branch were to sit in final judgment on the constitutionality of the actions of the other majoritarian branch, we would still be left with a situation in which a simple majority could, as a practical matter, effect an amendment of the Constitution. It is not by happenstance that, in structuring a largely representational democratic system, the framers formally insulated the members of one of the three co-equal branches of government from direct majoritarian pressure. It should, then, not require tremendous insight to see an inherent link between a counter-majoritarian governing document on the one hand, and a counter-majoritarian branch of government, expressly vested in Article III with authority to adjudicate cases "arising under this Constitution," on the other.

The obvious problem with this analysis is that the judiciary, as much as the other two branches, is itself created, regulated, and controlled by the Constitution.[32] If, as I have argued, it is absurd to suggest that one branch could effectively sit as final arbiter of the constitutional provisions governing its conduct, one might reasonably ask how the federal judiciary may be allowed to sit as the final arbiter of the entire Constitution, including the provisions governing its own behavior.

At most, acceptance of this argument would mean that the judiciary should be deprived of its final authority to sit in judgment on its own actions; it in no way logically requires that the judicial branch cede to the other branches the power to determine the constitutionality of their own actions. Under such a system, Congress and the executive, through the legislative process, would sit as the final arbiter of the limitations and powers imposed on or granted to the federal judiciary by Article III.

It is possible, however, to suggest a rationale for reconciling the logic of the Counter-Majoritarian principle with the judicial power finally to resolve the constitutional limits of its own authority. It is well established in the law of due process that, despite the enormous importance of a disinterested and independent adjudicator, existence of an overwhelming and compelling interest—bordering on actual necessity—can justify reliance on an adjudicator who is not completely neutral.[33] If the majoritarian branches retained final authority to determine the constitutional contours of the judicial power, those branches could easily employ that authority to undermine judicial enforcement of the constitutional limitations imposed upon them. When one realizes the potentially ominous consequences of entrusting to the majoritarian branches final say as to the constitutional limitations on the judicial power, then, it is not difficult to find that the vesting of such final say in the judicial branch itself rather easily fits within the contours of such a "necessity" exception. Thus, the seeming anomaly of allowing the judiciary to sit as final judge of its own powers becomes not only reasonable but actually essential in an instrumental sense, as a means of ensuring the judiciary's effective performance of its central role within our political framework.

The constitutional system our nation adopted was neither handed down from on high, nor was it the only form a democratic government need assume. It is, however, the system upon which our whole governmental structure has been both established and legitimized. The Constitution continues to retain the positivistic force of law; therefore, if the rule of law is to be valued, the directives of the Constitution must be obeyed, unless and until modified in the manner prescribed in Article V, or until the system is openly rejected in favor of a new governing structure. If the counter-majoritarian limitations imposed by the Constitution are to retain meaning, their final interpretation and enforcement must come from the counter-majoritarian judicial branch.

At this point, it is necessary to make clear exactly what arguments I am *not* making in support of the Counter-Majoritarian principle:

1. I am not arguing that a representational democracy necessarily cannot flourish without either a binding, written, counter-majoritarian constitution or the practice of judicial review. The point, rather, is that a *limited constitutional* democracy cannot exist without a binding, written

constitution, as a definitional matter, or without judicial review by an independent judiciary, as a practical matter. To the extent that a democracy lacking these features is considered "limited," it is only as a result of the good faith and self-imposed limitations of both those in political power and a majority of the electorate.

2. I am not arguing that judicial review is compelled by either the text or history of the Constitution. Although Herbert Wechsler attempted to ground a requirement of judicial review in the constitutional text,[34] he has rightly been criticized for this attempt.[35] It is important to note, however, that, though the Constitution's text may not *compel* judicial review, neither is the practice in any way extra- or counter-constitutional, as Article III's extensions of the federal judicial power to cases arising under the Constitution make clear.[36] Moreover, even though there is substantial historical evidence to support the framers' assumption of the existence of a judicial review power[37]—not the least of which is Hamilton's direct and eloquent statement in support of the concept in Federalist No. 78[38]—my arguments in no way require such a historical foundation. I argue, rather, that, to the extent the framers did not actually contemplate judicial review, they should have because without it there is no way that the constitutional system they adopted could realistically be expected to function in the manner they so obviously contemplated that it would. Thus, although it might be difficult to declare at least certain attempts by the majoritarian branches to exclude judicial review to be unconstitutional,[39] my argument is merely that the concept is dictated by the logic of American political theory, not—at least as a general matter[40]—by the text of the Constitution. As such, it should guide and limit the decisions of the majoritarian branches to exclude the practice. More importantly, as the next two chapters will demonstrate, it should prevent the judiciary from erecting self-imposed barriers to the performance of its essential political role within the constitutional system.

3. I am not arguing, as have several respected scholars, that the concept of judicial review derives from the premise that "the final aim of [our constitutional democratic] society is as much freedom as possible for the individual human being."[41] Similar logic has led Dean Jesse Choper to urge judicial abstention on issues of both federalism and separation of powers in order to preserve the Supreme Court's preciously limited "institutional capital" for cases concerning individual constitutional liberties, where, he argued, performance of the judicial review function is crucial.[42] I in no way intend to derogate the vital role played by individual liberty within our political structure.[43] But the fact remains that nothing in the constitutional text suggests that the provisions protecting individual liberty were the only provisions meant to bind the ma-

joritarian branches, and the structural provisions, concerning federalism and separation of powers, were intended to be merely advisory. Indeed, when the framers simultaneously protected judicial independence and extended power to the courts over cases arising under the Constitution, the document included precious few protections of individual liberty.[44] Most of those protections were, of course, added in the Bill of Rights, which amended the original text. Thus, to the extent that the constitutional structure contemplated judicial review, that power was apparently directed primarily at the very types of constitutional issues Dean Choper wishes to exclude from the Court's province.

If the structural provisions of the Constitution were deemed merely advisory, it would be difficult to discern any textual basis for finding the provisions protecting individual liberty any less advisory. Although scholars may argue that individual liberty protections are somehow more fundamental to our system, the alternative argument could be—and has been—made that in reality it is the constitutional protections of federalism, not those concerning liberty, that are central.[45] Moreover, it has been persuasively argued that the constitutional dictates concerning separation of powers were themselves fashioned in order to prevent tyranny.[46] Thus, it is difficult to discover any basis in either constitutional text or political theory to justify the distinctions in the exercise of judicial review urged by Dean Choper. Most importantly, the judiciary's function in our governmental system is to enforce and interpret the Constitution, not effectively to repeal provisions it views as unwise or outmoded. And there can be little doubt that, by abdicating its function of reviewing the actions of the majoritarian branches to ensure compliance with constitutional dictates, the Court would effectively repeal the constitutional provision in question; the majoritarian branches would be left to ignore constitutional restrictions any time they so desired.[47]

4. In arguing for recognition of a political obligation on the judiciary to exercise its jurisdiction in cases arising under the Constitution, I am saying nothing about how, as a substantive matter, those cases should be resolved. Thus, it is theoretically conceivable that the judiciary could meet the obligation of the Counter-Majoritarian principle and still find against the constitutional challenge to governmental action in virtually every case. It would therefore be inaccurate to characterize the Counter-Majoritarian principle as necessarily a form of "judicial activism," at least to the extent that the concept is defined as ultimate judicial interference with the functioning of the majoritarian branches.[48] But, although limited in its reach, the importance of the jurisdictional implications of the Counter-Majoritarian principle should not be discounted. For by exercising judicial review, at least in all constitutional cases in which its jurisdiction has not been validly precluded by Congress, the federal ju-

diciary will be assuring both the legitimacy of the rule of law and the continued vitality of our constitutional system.

It is true, of course, that the principle of judicial review has received considerable support in the scholarly literature[49] and has gained wide acceptance as an element of American political practice. However, the following chapters will demonstrate how acceptance of the logic of the Counter-Majoritarian principle should drastically alter well-established Supreme Court jurisdictional doctrines that have dangerously undermined or ignored the judiciary's essential role in our constitutional system dictated by that principle.

SIX

Applying the Counter-Majoritarian Principle, I: The "Passive Virtues" and the "Judicial-Political" Model of Constitutional Adjudication

There have long existed several doctrines of federal court jurisdiction "whose chief content," in Professor Bickel's words, "is a generalization on the timing and limits of the judicial function."[1] By individual name, they are referred to as the doctrines of standing, mootness, ripeness, and political question. Collectively, Bickel referred to them as "the passive virtues"[2]—judge-made doctrines that, if employed properly, Bickel believed could be utilized carefully to circumscribe the political reach of the Court's role.[3] Although all these doctrines involve complex legal technicalities, each has enormous implications for the role played by the federal judiciary within the framework of American political theory. It is therefore advisable to test these doctrines in terms of the Counter-Majoritarian principle described in the previous chapter.

The political question doctrine, by far the most substantively oriented of these jurisdictional devices, provides the exclusive focus of the next chapter. The present chapter explores the theoretical implications of the Counter-Majoritarian principle for the remaining jurisdictional doctrines, with a primary focus on the law of standing. This analysis will demonstrate that, as currently structured, these doctrines are, to varying degrees, premised on a misunderstanding of the judiciary's vital political role within our constitutional system. Instead, they are grounded in a perception of the adjudicatory function that, at least in constitutional cases, is largely fictional.

The Supreme Court's current doctrine measures the judicial role in constitutional litigation in terms of the traditionally accepted "private rights" adjudicatory model, which posits that the judiciary's primary role is to resolve disputes between individuals, and to enforce and protect individuals' rights and interests. Under this model, any judicial exposition of constitutional principles is merely incidental to the performance of this dispute resolution function. Although the dispute resolution function should of course never be ignored, when viewed as the exclusive or even primary judicial role in constitutional litigation such an analysis effectively mischaracterizes the federal judiciary's proper role. As a result, the doctrines evolving from this adjudicatory model seriously undermine the performance of the judiciary's political function, derived from the Counter-Majoritarian principle, of expounding and enforcing the counter-majoritarian Constitution and thereby assuring adherence to its dictates by the majoritarian branches.[4]

It is true that neither constitutional text nor accepted political theory authorizes the federal judiciary to act in a purely legislative or executive fashion. Article III expressly confines the exercise of the federal judicial power to the adjudication of "cases" or "controversies," lest the unrepresentative judiciary be allowed to exercise the type of power reserved, in a constitutional democracy, to the representative branches of government. Yet it is possible, both linguistically and conceptually, to fashion a reasonable definition of "case-or-controversy" that takes into account the frankly political nature of the federal judiciary's role in constitutional adjudication while at the same time confining the courts to what is for the most part a traditionally judicial manner of operation. The synthesis of these two fundamental yet potentially conflicting roles may be labeled the "judicial-political" model of adjudication. After critiquing the origins and asserted functional and political rationales for use of the "private rights" adjudicatory model in the law of standing, this chapter will examine how the "judicial-political" model should be structured. The chapter will then explore the implications of the "judicial-political" model for the existing doctrines of standing, ripeness, and mootness.

Standing, Injury-in-Fact, and the Political Theory of the Judicial Role in Constitutional Adjudication

No individual may resort to the federal courts unless she possesses the requisite standing to sue. According to Supreme Court precedent,[5] the standing doctrine contains both "constitutional" and "prudential" elements. In other words, certain requirements of standing have been held to flow out of Article III's "case-or-controversy" requirement, and are thus not subject to congressional repeal; other requirements are deemed merely "prudential," and thus have no constitutional status.[6] Although the exact definition of the standing concept in Supreme Court decisions has varied at the margins,[7] since early in the century the Court has steadfastly adhered to the principle that the constitutional "case-or-controversy" requirement demands that at the very least a plaintiff have suffered some "injury-in-fact."[8] Although the Court has been somewhat flexible in its definition of this concept,[9] at no point has it suggested that the doors of the federal courts will be open to one who does not even purport to have suffered concrete injury in some real sense.[10]

Several modern rationales have been proferred for the injury-in-fact prerequisite.[11] Initially, commentators have rationalized the requirement on historical grounds, claiming to derive it from Chief Justice Marshall's asserted rationale to justify the concept of judicial review in *Marbury v. Madison*.[12] Secondly, injury-in-fact has been grounded by both Court and commentators in principles of separation of powers and judicial restraint.[13] Finally, the requirement has been justified on instrumental grounds, as a means of ensuring a full, fair, and accurate litigation process.[14]

Application of the Counter-Majoritarian principle demonstrates that none of these asserted rationales justifies the injury-in-fact requirement as an element of standing doctrine in constitutional cases. Close examination reveals that its historical origins are, at best, suspect.[15] Moreover, the requirement is a particularly clumsy means of preserving separation-of-powers principles; it neither precludes excess judicial activism nor assures proper performance of the judicial function.[16] Finally, injury-in-fact is neither a necessary nor sufficient condition for the attainment of a fair or efficient litigation process.[17]

Most importantly, the injury-in-fact requirement is fundamentally inconsistent with recognition of the judiciary's important political role in providing a constitutional check on the majoritiarian branches, as dictated by the Counter-Majoritarian principle.[18] By superimposing a "private rights" model of adjudication[19] on constitutional litigation, use of the injury-in-fact requirement effectively undermines judicial performance of that role.

It should be emphasized that abandonment of the injury-in-fact requirement should not be taken to imply abandonment of the constitutionally dictated "case-or-controversy" requirement, but merely that injury-in-fact should not be deemed to be an essential element of that requirement. The "case-or-controversy" prerequisite was presumably designed to ensure that the unrepresentative branch would not function in a manner identical to that of the representative branches. By confining the judiciary's operation to the adjudication of live, adversary disputes capable of being resolved and whose resolution may be enforced, Article III ensures that the judicial branch will neither be able to initiate or enact wholly generalized legislative edicts, nor carry out the day-to-day executive or administrative tasks of government.[20] Article III, then, requires that the judiciary perform its essential political role in a manner unique among the branches. As will be seen, however, imposition on the litigants of the injury-in-fact prerequisite is not an essential element of the "judicial" aspects of the federal judiciary's function, and may well undermine performance of its important "political" function.[21]

Marbury and the "Private Rights" Model of Constitutional Adjudication

In one of the most dazzling political maneuvers in American history, Chief Justice John Marshall in *Marbury v. Madison* established the principle of judicial review.[22] Leading commentators[23] have seen in that decision the seeds of what has been referred to as the "private rights" model of adjudication—the theory that "the power of constitutional exposition [is] an incident of the Court's obligation to decide the particular 'case or controversy' before it."[24] What Marshall said to give rise to this theory was the following:

> It is emphatically the province and duty of the judicial department to say what the law is. Those who apply the rule to particular cases, must of necessity expound and interpret that rule. If two laws conflict with each other, the courts must decide on the operation of each.
>
> So if a law be in opposition to the constitution; if both the law and the constitution apply to a particular case, so that the court must either decide the case conformably to the law, disregarding the constitution; or conformably to the constitution, disregarding the law; the court must determine which of these conflicting rules governs the case. This is of the very essence of judicial duty.[25]

At another point, in response to the suggestion that the exercise of judicial review in *Marbury* "should at first view be considered by some, as an attempt to intrude into the cabinet, and to intermeddle with the prerogatives of the executive," Marshall wrote:

> It is scarcely necessary for the court to disclaim all pretensions to such a jurisdiction. An extravagance, so absurd and excessive, could not have been entertained for a moment. *The province of the court is, solely, to decide on the rights of individuals*, not to inquire how the executive, or executive officers, perform duties in which they have a discretion.[26]

What Marshall appears to be saying in these passages is: (1) it is the duty of courts to resolve individual disputes; (2) as an essential element of that task, it is incumbent upon the court to resolve a conflict between two competing and assumedly contradictory laws relied upon by the litigants; and (3) therefore, where one litigant relies on a statute, and the other litigant relies on a constitutional provision claimed to conflict with that law, the court must decide whether a conflict actually does exist, and if so which is to prevail; otherwise, it cannot perform its central function of resolving individual disputes.

Although the best known early Supreme Court decision imposing the injury-in-fact prerequisite surprisingly failed even to mention *Marbury*,[27] the connection between this passage in Marshall's opinion and injury-in-fact should be obvious: unless the plaintiff has suffered an injury in fact, there can be no real, concrete dispute between the individual litigants for the court to resolve. Absent an injury in fact, then, the court's action would amount to a naked political intrusion on and usurpation of the political authority of the representative branches.

However one feels about either the "private rights" adjudicatory model or the injury-in-fact requirement, it is probably inappropriate to rely on Marshall's analysis in *Marbury* to provide modern-day support for either one. Initially, although there can be little dispute about the facial import of the above-quoted passages, it is quite conceivable that Marshall's words should not be taken at face value. As Professor Monaghan has correctly noted, "[t]he assertion of this power to annul congressional and state legislation was, of course, heady and frightening stuff for any tribunal, particularly where opposition to the exercise of that power was frequent, loud, and intense."[28] Certainly, Marshall could have reasonably believed that the political repercussions of his assertion of this power could be minimized if he managed to maintain for the judiciary the non-political appearance akin to that of a mundane small claims court. It is not difficult to believe, despite his characterization of the case in terms of private rights, that the broader political impact of the decision was in reality central to his decision.[29]

In any event, to quote only these passages from Marshall's opinion is to take them out of context. At other points, he rationalized the judicial review power in a manner strikingly similar to the Counter-Majoritarian principle described previously.[30] To deny the power of the judiciary to consider the relevance of the Constitution, he wrote,

> would subvert the very foundation of all written constitutions. It would declare that an act, which, according to the principles and theory of our government, is entirely void; is yet, in practice, completely obligatory. It would declare, that if the legislature shall do what is expressly forbidden, such act, notwithstanding the express prohibition, is in reality effectual. It would be giving to the legislature a practical and real omnipotence, with the same breath which professes to restrict their

> powers within narrow limits. It is prescribing limits, and declaring that these limits may be passed at pleasure.[31]

Such an argument, Marshall said, "reduces to nothing what we have deemed the greatest improvement on political institutions—a written constitution. . . ."[32]

One may of course choose either to agree or disagree with Marshall's logic,[33] but it is difficult to deny that these statements at least imply his recognition of the frankly political function the judiciary is to serve within our constitutional system. Although in *Marbury* itself—and, indeed, in most cases—injury in fact is easily established, the logic of this judicial role in no way turns on whether or not the judiciary's resolution of a constitutional challenge will directly affect the concrete interests of the litigants.

The Injury-in-Fact Requirement: The Separation-of-Powers Rationale

The argument has been made that "the judicial doctrine of standing is a crucial and inseparable element of [the] principle [of separation of powers], whose disregard will inevitably produce . . . an overjudicialization of the processes of self-governance."[34] This same logic was relied upon by the Supreme Court in *Frothingham v. Mellon*,[35] one of its classic standing decisions:

> The functions of government under our system are apportioned. To the legislative department has been committed the duty of making laws; to the executive the duty of executing them; and to the judiciary the duty of interpreting and applying them in cases properly brought before the courts. The general rule is that neither department may invade the province of the other and neither may control, direct or restrain the action of the other. . . . We have no power *per se* to review and annul acts of Congress on the ground that they are unconstitutional. That question may be considered only when the justification for some direct injury suffered or threatened, presenting a justiciable issue, is made to rest upon such an act. Then the power exercised is that of ascertaining and declaring the law applicable to the controversy. It amounts to little more than the negative power to disregard an unconstitutional enactment, which otherwise would stand in the way of the enforcement of a legal right.[36]

The logic behind the asserted connection between the injury-in-fact requirement and separation of powers appears to focus on two factors. Initially, as Marshall implied in *Marbury*,[37] the requirement allows the judiciary to maintain the appearance of non-politicization, brought about by the "private rights" model—that is, performing the judicial review function, the courts are simply acting in the manner traditionally associated with courts, as resolvers of disputes between individuals. It is almost as if the Supreme Court, in deciding delicate and important questions of constitutional law, were no different from Judge Wapner, of television's "People's Court," resolving a contract dispute over the care and feeding of the plaintiff's poodle. Secondly, use of injury-in-fact as a prerequisite for the exercise of judicial review simultaneously reduces the sum total of instances in which that review power is exercised, and provides a justification for a counter-majoritarian disruption of and departure from the inertia of the normal democratic processes in favor of rule by the majoritarian branches. In the words of Justice Scalia, it is only concrete injury "that can separate the plaintiff from all the rest of us who also claim benefit of the social contract, and can thus entitle him to some special protection from the democratic manner in which we ordinarily run our social-contractual affairs."[38]

The injury-in-fact requirement is also thought to flow from a particular conception of the substantive role of judicial review, as the protection of minority rights against majoritarian encroachment. As Justice Scalia has argued:

> [T]he law of standing roughly restricts courts to their traditional undemocratic role of protecting individuals and minorities against impositions of the majority, and excludes them from the even more undemocratic role of prescribing how the other two branches should function in order to serve the interest *of the majority itself*. . . .
> [T]he doctrine of standing, as applied to challenges to governmental action, is an essential means of restricting the courts to their assigned role of protecting minority rather than majority interests.[39]

Closer analysis reveals, however, that none of these separation-of-powers arguments successfully rationalizes the injury-in-fact requirement.

The Fallacy of the "Private Rights" Model

No one could doubt that a fundamental purpose of the exercise of judicial jurisdiction is to vindicate individual rights and claims. Thus, it makes perfect sense to employ injury-in-fact—at least in a meaningful sense of that term[40]—as a *sufficient* condition for the exercise of federal judicial power. But it would be equally absurd to doubt that the judicial role, at least in the exercise of the power of judicial review, extends well beyond the vindication of such interests. As explained earlier,[41] the Counter-Majoritarian principle recognizes the important systemic political role the judiciary serves as enforcer of the counter-majoritarian Constitution. Providing a particular individual with a remedy is at best incidental to performance of this function.

This insight has its greatest force at the level of the Supreme Court, which agrees to hear a case only if there is present an important and disputed or unresolved issue of federal law.[42] Could anyone reasonably suggest, for example, that the reason for the national controversy that arose out of the Court's decision in *Roe v. Wade*[43] was concern over whether Jane Roe would be forced to have her baby (especially in light of the fact that she had already given birth to the baby prior to decision)? Surely, the future micro-impact of the decision on Jane Roe was at most a secondary national concern. Of obviously greater import was the decision's *macro*-impact on the national political process as a whole. This is not to suggest, of course, that the judicial exercise of the judicial review power will have no concrete practical impact on the lives of individual litigants. It is, rather, that that impact will generally go well beyond the interests of the individual litigant bringing the suit.

Chief Justice Marshall's clever disguise of the judicial review power as merely the performance of the traditional and non-political judicial role of individual dispute resolver may or may not have convinced the Jeffersonian Republicans. But it would surely defy reality today to continue the charade of the "private rights" adjudicatory model in constitutional litigation.

Injury-in-Fact as an Instrument of Judicial Restraint

A more arguable justification for the injury-in-fact requirement is that it both reduces the number of instances in which the judiciary will even be given the opportunity to strike down the actions of the majoritarian branches, and therefore limits the situations in which basic democratic principles will be undermined to the out-of-the-ordinary case. Both these rationales suggest that the injury-in-fact requirement preserves separation of powers by imposing a substantial degree of judicial restraint on the federal judiciary. However, both arguments misperceive the proper judicial role in our political system. Injury-in-fact is neither a necessary nor sufficient feature of judicial restraint, as that concept is properly understood.

That injury-in-fact fails as an effective guarantor of judicial restraint is illustrated by the so-called economic due process cases, decided in the early part of the century.[44] No one could question the presence of injury-in-fact in those cases because the plaintiffs clearly suffered economic loss as a result of the challenged regulations. Yet many commentators consider those decisions to be the height of judicial usurpation, and they have long since been largely repudiated by the Court.[45] These decisions demonstrate that the appropriate battleground for judicial restraint is in the fashioning of the substantive decision. Imposition of injury-in-fact as a jurisdictional prerequisite does little to assure that the judiciary does not exceed the bounds of its authority.[46]

It is true, of course, that use of an injury-in-fact requirement reduces the sum total of constitutional challenges to majoritarian action, and in that sense the requirement could be thought to foster judicial restraint. But that fact alone should not serve as a sufficient justification for adoption of a jurisdictional rule. For example, a rule randomly excluding from federal court jurisdiction every fourth constitutional case that has been filed would reduce the number of constitutional challenges by 25 percent, yet surely no one would suggest that therefore such a practice represents a wise instrument of judicial restraint. So long as the non-political disguise of the "private rights" model is discarded,[47] and so long as the federal judiciary adheres to the basic contours of a "case,"[48] there is no reason to believe that the injury-in-fact requirement is any more rational a means of ensuring judicial restraint than a process of random selection.

Indeed, one could persuasively argue that rigid adherence to injury-in-fact has substantially interfered with the judiciary's performance of its checking role. Violations of several constitutional provisions, both regulating governmental operations[49] and protecting civil liberties,[50] generally do not give rise to specialized or individualized injury. The presence of the injury-in-fact requirement has therefore occasionally precluded the courts from resolving legitimate constitutional questions concerning these provisions.[51]

An illustration of this category of cases is the decision in *City of Los Angeles v. Lyons*.[52] In *Lyons*, the Court denied standing, for the purposes of seeking injunctive relief,[53] to an individual who had been the victim of an allegedly unconstitutional "chokehold" by the city's police during a routine traffic stop.[54] In an opinion by Justice White, the Court reasoned:

> In order to establish an actual controversy in this case, Lyons would have had not only to allege that he would have another encounter with the police but to make the incredible assertion either, (1) that *all* police officers in Los Angeles *always* choke any citizen with whom they happen to have an encounter, . . . or, (2) that the City ordered or authorized police officers to act in such a manner. . . .
>
> [I]t is surely no more than speculation to assert either that Lyons himself will again be involved in one of those unfortunate instances, or that he will be arrested in the future and provoke the use of a chokehold. . . .
>
> Absent a sufficient likelihood that he will again be wronged in a similar way, Lyons is no more entitled to an injunction than any other

citizen of Los Angeles; and a federal court may not entertain a claim by any or all citizens who no more assert that certain practices of law enforcement officers are unconstitutional.[55]

Although it is true that Lyons or anyone else in his position had standing to seek damages, as dissenting Justice Marshall correctly pointed out, "[s]ince no one can show that he will be choked in the future, no one—not even a person who, like Lyons, has almost been choked to death—has standing to challenge the continuation of the policy. The City is free to continue the policy indefinitely as long as it is willing to pay damages for the injuries and death that result."[56]

Of course, it is conceivable that the constitutional challenges in *Lyons* should have been rejected on the merits. But, if so, the violation of the precept of judicial restraint would come in the ultimate judicial invalidation of the challenged governmental action, not in the mere fact of the court's willingness to adjudicate the constitutional challenge. Moreover, unless and until the merits of the constitutional challenge are examined, it is impossible to know whether the exercise of the judicial review power would in fact constitute a violation of separation of powers. Surely, separation-of-powers precepts are not violated by a judicial invalidation of governmental action that all agree actually does violate the Constitution, and the presence or absence of injury-in-fact says absolutely nothing about the substantive merits of the constitutional challenge being raised. It is for these reasons, then, that the argument linking injury-in-fact and separation of powers ultimately fails.

Injury-in-Fact and the Theory of Judicial Review

Justice Scalia has argued that the rationale for the exercise of judicial review power logically dictates the injury-in-fact prerequisite. Because, according to Scalia, the only justification for departure from the norm of democratic rule is the need to protect minority rights against majoritarian encroachment, it follows that there is no justification for such a departure when all members of society are equally affected by unconstitutional governmental action.[57] Justice Scalia's theory of judicial review appears similar to the position taken by Dean Choper,[58] the serious analytical flaws of which are many.[59] By its terms, the Constitution is counter-majoritarian in *all* its provisions. The fact that majoritarian action does not threaten individual liberty does not necessarily mean that all constitutional dictates have been observed. Thus, the logic of judicial review dictates a need for protection of society as a whole from the unconstitutional actions of the majoritarian branches.

Even if one were to accept the Scalia-Choper "minority rights" rationale, however, the injury-in-fact requirement would not logically follow. There are numerous situations in which individual plaintiffs easily meet the injury-in-fact prerequisite to assert violations of constitutional provisions having nothing to do with the protection of minority rights. For example, the plaintiff in *Northern Pipeline Co. v. Marathon Pipe Line Co.*[60] was forced by federal statute to adjudicate its common law claim against a bankrupt in a federal court whose judges lacked Article III protections, and was therefore able to challenge the jurisdiction of the Article I bankruptcy courts on separation-of-powers grounds.[61] A private individual subject to regulation by a federal statute has standing to challenge the law as beyond the scope of the congressional power to regulate interstate commerce,[62] thus raising issues of constitutional federalism. Although in both these instances the individual plaintiff suffers more than sufficient harm to satisfy the injury-in-fact requirement, in neither case is the court called upon to vindicate a constitutional right of a minority in need of protection against the majority. Rather, in both the court is asked to interpret and enforce the Constitution's structural provisions. In contrast, in numerous cases brought to enforce the First Amendment's establishment clause,[63] it is all but impossible for a plaintiff to establish an injury beyond that suffered by society as a whole.[64] Yet one could reasonably conclude that such cases do involve the protection of individual liberty. Under Justice Scalia's logic, then, in none of these situations do the standing results comport with those dictated by the use of the injury-in-fact requirement.

Injury-in-Fact: The "Passive Virtues" Rationale

For the very reason that constitutional decisions must be grounded in principle, Professor Bickel argued that the Supreme Court may appropriately resort to the so-called "passive virtues"—including the standing doctrine—in a starkly political effort to avoid having to reach a decision on the constitutional merits.[65] These "techniques and allied devices for staying the Court's hand," Bickel said, "cannot themselves be principled in the sense in which we have a right to expect adjudications on the merits to be principled. They mark the point at which the Court gives the electoral institutions their head and itself stays out of politics, and there is nothing paradoxical in finding that here the Court is a most political animal."[66]

Of course, if Bickel were so concerned that the Supreme Court invalidate majoritarian action only when it could do so on the basis of principle,[67] one might suggest that the Court could decide the case on its merits, and simply uphold the challenged governmental activity when no such principled grounds presented themselves. But, just as Bickel expressed concern about Supreme Court invalidation of majoritarian action without a proper grounding in principle, so, too, was he concerned about the political implications of a formal judicial validation of such action. "Not only is the Supreme Court capable of generating consent for hotly controverted legislative or executive measures," he argued, "it has the subtler power of adding a certain impetus to measures that the majority enacts rather tentatively."[68] Simply put, Bickel's argument was that "[t]o declare that a statute is not intolerable in the sense that it is not inconsistent with the principles whose integrity the Court is charged with maintaining . . . amounts to a significant intervention in the political process, different in degree only from the sort of intervention marked by a declaration of unconstitutionality."[69] Thus, "it is no small matter . . . to 'legitimate' a legislative measure. . . . Regardless of what it intends . . . the Court can generate consent and may impart permanence."[70]

The problems with this analysis as a rationale for the injury-in-fact element of the standing requirement are many. Initially, as Professor Gunther has noted, although Bickel's "legitimation" concern "has a kernel of truth, perhaps even a sliver of utility . . . it is too slight a foundation to support the elaborate analysis."[71] This is because, in Gunther's words,

> [t]he legitimation notion is open to question as a description of the political impact of a Supreme Court decision rejecting a constitutional challenge on the merits—especially when that impact is described as sharply different from the effect of a Court failure to invalidate a law on other grounds. And even if legitimation were an adequate descriptive concept, it would be an unacceptable source of normative standards: it would endorse conjecture about the complexities of political reactions as a primary ingredient of Court deliberations.[72]

Moreover, it should be noted that Bickel's exclusive concern was with the exercise of the *Supreme Court's* jurisdiction; he appears to place no emphasis on the reach of lower federal court power. This limitation seems to make sense, in light of his concern about the unique political impact that results from the Supreme Court's national prestige.[73] Yet standing doctrine, as well as all of the other so-called "passive virtues," of course act as limitations on lower court jurisdiction as much as on Supreme Court authority. Under its discretionary certiorari power—expanded, since Bickel wrote, to be all but total in its scope[74]—the Supreme Court can easily avoid the dangers he feared, simply by denying application for the writ.[75] The Court can do so, without undermining the lower federal courts' performance of the function of providing a counter-majoritarian interpretation of constitutional directives.

More importantly, unless legal doctrine is to be manipulated in a totally unprincipled manner—without regard to logic, language, or concept[76]—it will be totally fortuitous whether Bickel's political concerns and the requirements of injury-in-fact will in any way overlap. Presumably, there will be many cases, under his rigid demand for so-called principled constitutional decisionmaking on the merits, in which Bickel would prefer that the Court abstain, yet injury-in-fact will be easily and unambiguously established.[77] On the other hand, there is no reason to believe that the substantive constitutional issues raised by a plaintiff failing the injury-in-fact test will inherently fail to lend themselves to principled resolution on the merits.

Finally, one may question Bickel's fundamental premise: that it is dangerous for the public to learn that the Supreme Court constitutionally validates majoritarian action because of the possibility that the public would misinterpret that judicial act as a form of normative concurrence. The assumption that the public cannot be trusted to understand the implications of factual information is directly at odds with the premise of the First Amendment right of free expression. In the political realm, the answer to speech—even false or misleading speech—is more speech, not suppression.[78] If there exists a danger that the public will construe Court validation to be more than it actually is,[79] the answer is to encourage an increase in public awareness of the true political implications of a Supreme Court finding of constitutionality.

In any event, it is not unreasonable to believe that the Court's ruling on the constitutional validity of governmental action will and should have a legitimate impact on the public's political and normative perceptions about that action. For example, those concerned about the free speech implications of a total ban on a certain form of advertising might alter their positions as a result of a Supreme Court holding that such a restriction does not violate the First Amendment.[80] Conversely, one who supports legislation prohibiting flag desecration may reasonably be given pause by a Supreme Court decision concluding that such laws impermissibly interfere with freedom of expression.[81] The point is that the Court's constitutional pronouncements are inextricably intertwined with the normative political and social debate on governmental action. Acting on Bickel's concern would therefore preclude a potentially important and legitimate contribution to that debate.

Bickel contended, however, that the standing and "case-or-controversy" requirements serve a valuable function in ensuring that "the judgment of courts may be had in concrete cases that exemplify the actual consequences of legislative or executive action."[82] This is vital, he asserted, because "there are sound reasons . . . for believing that the hard, confining, and yet enlarging context of a real controversy leads to sounder and more enduring judgments."[83] But, although Bickel's point is no doubt valid in many situations, it is not always so, as the Court's willingness, in certain instances, to invalidate statutes on their face demonstrates.[84] Whether the Court will find a statute to be appropriate for facial invalidation or instead require case-by-case ruling on constitutionality as applied turns exclusively on examination of substantive constitutional principles and the nature of the challenged statutes, under the so-called overbreadth doctrine.[85] It in no way turns on the nature of the plaintiff's interest in the litigation.[86] Thus, as was shown to be true for the separation-of-powers rationale, the injury-in-fact requirement proves to be too clumsy a device to distinguish between cases lending themselves to broad-based constitutional decision and those requiring a narrower resolution. Rather, such a distinction can be drawn only on the basis of a careful analysis of substantive considerations.

Injury-in-Fact: The Instrumental Rationale

Inclusion of the injury-in-fact requirement as part of Article III's "case-or-controversy" requirement has on occasion been defended on instrumental grounds, as a necessary means of ensuring the fairness and accuracy of the litigation process. The leading advocate of this position has been Lea Brilmayer, who has argued that viewing injury-in-fact as part of the "case-or-controversy" requirement fosters "three interrelated policies of Article III: the smooth allocation of power among courts over time; the unfairness of holding later litigants to an adverse judgment in which they may not have been properly represented; and the importance of placing control over political processes in the hands of the people most closely involved."[87] She labeled these values "restraint," "representation," and "self-determination."[88] However, as the following discussion will demonstrate, none of these rationales justifies inclusion of injury-in-fact as an element of Article III's "case-or-controversy" requirement.

Restraint

Professor Brilmayer noted that, "[w]hen faced with problems of whether particular issues are properly presented for adjudication, courts frequently allude to judicial restraint as a reason for hesitation about passing on the merits."[89] She argued that the most appropriate rationale for such restraint is

> the relationships among courts over time. Stare decisis in effect subordinates the opinions and policy choices of later courts to those of the

> present court. . . . To allow a court to settle any matter it wished to address would give precedence to the preferences of earlier courts, who are able to tie the hands of the subsequent ones. There is a clear need for some mechanism to allocate decisonmaking responsibility among successive courts, by specifying the point at which an issue may be addressed.[90]

Even if one were to accept Professor Brilmayer's reasoning, however, acceptance of injury-in-fact does not follow, unless she can further establish a logical connection between that requirement and the appropriateness of an issue for judicial resolution. Although she contended that "procedural innovation to allow litigation of abstract issues undermines" the institution of stare decisis,[91] it is by no means clear why this is so. More importantly, as already noted,[92] whether a court wishes to decide a constitutional issue on a generalized or abstract basis will be determined by an analysis of substantive factors, going to the constitutional merits. In the event that such an analysis dictates the appropriateness of an abstract determination, whether or not the plaintiff raising the issue suffered injury-in-fact would seem to be irrelevant.

Representation

Professor Brilmayer believes that "fairness problems . . . would arise if an ideological challenger—a challenger without the traditional stake—were permitted to litigate a constitutional claim."[93] In support, she points to "the similarities between justiciability doctrine and the requirement, in class action litigation, that the named plaintiff be a member of the class he seeks to represent."[94] Initially, one may question her analogy because the res judicata effect of a class action determination on absent class members is considerably more powerful than a simple stare decisis impact.[95] More importantly, for Professor Brilmayer's argument to support the injury-in-fact requirement, she must establish the existence of a direct correlation between that requirement and the likelihood of a more effectively conducted litigation. That is a connection that even advocates of the injury-in-fact requirement have doubted.[96]

The theory behind the asserted connection is, basically, a rationale premised on greed: the assumption that an individual who has something personally to gain or lose as the result of a litigation will take that litigation more seriously, and therefore prepare and conduct the litigation more effectively than one who is motivated either by concern for the interests of others or by purely ideological factors. However, no empirical, psychological, or anthropological evidence has been cited in support of this assumption, and it is by no means clear that it can be intuitively derived. In fact, a strong argument could be fashioned that the presence of injury-in-fact is, as an abstract matter, neither a necessary nor sufficient condition for the effective conduct of litigation. On the one hand, it is certainly conceivable that litigants motivated purely out of ideological concern, possessing both ample financial resources and experienced counsel, would mount an extremely elaborate and effective case, even when they themselves had suffered no direct financial or personal harm. One who doubts that pure ideology can prove to be an extremely powerful motivator need only consider the enormous intensity, on both sides, of the current abortion debate, or the powerful and negative reaction of many to the Supreme Court's decision holding flag desecration statutes unconstitutitonal,[97] even though in neither case are most of the participants in any way personally affected, in the "injury-in-fact" sense. On the other hand, one who has suffered a real but minimal injury-in-fact[98] is not likely to be willing to expend substantial resources in order to vindicate his legal right.[99] Thus, to the extent we choose to fashion standing requirements with a concern for those unrepresented future litigants who may be precedentially affected by a judicial decision, it is highly unlikely that injury-in-fact would be the standard of choice.

This does not mean that injury-in-fact should be rejected as a *sufficient* basis for meeting the standing requirement. Although the presence of injury-in-fact may not provide assurance that a legal issue will be fully explored in the course of a litigation, an individual's right of access to the courts to vindicate his personal rights is itself a legitimate basis for extending standing. Nor does it mean that the category of standing prerequisites should become a null set. The point, rather, is that standing requirements should be more appropriately tailored in order to assure more directly a full and effective exploration of the legal issues raised.

The most appropriate means of doing so would be to draw an analogy to one of the class action prerequisites not mentioned by Professor Brilmayer: the requirement that the named party "adequately represent" the interests of the absent class members.[100] Factors normally examined in making this assessment are the financial resources the named party is able and willing to commit to the litigation and the competence and experience of counsel.[101] Although in certain cases imposition of this standard would add to the judicial burden, in the majority of suits brought by non-injured plaintiffs the party will likely be an established institutional litigant, about whose competence and seriousness of purpose there will be little doubt. Moreover, unless a suit is collusive—a fact that courts have traditionally been relied upon to ascertain in other contexts[102]—it is unlikely that a non-injured or institutional plaintiff will go to the time and expense of bringing a litigation raising a constitutional issue, unless that issue is extremely important to that plaintiff.

Self-Determination

Professor Brilmayer argued that allowing litigants to raise the rights of others would endanger the self-determination value of allowing injured individuals to make their own choices about whether or not to sue to vindicate their personal rights.[103] Even if her analysis were accepted, however, it would have no relevance to the important situations—involving such areas as establishment of religion[104] and certain governmental operations[105]—where the standing problem results from the failure of *any* individual to have incurred an injury beyond that suffered by the populace as a whole.[106] Moreover, suits brought by purely ideological plaintiffs are likely to present facial challenges to governmental action, rather than to the application of such action to particular individuals. In any event, to take account of Professor Brilmayer's concern, it might be reasonable to preclude ideological standing in cases challenging particular applications of laws to specific individuals absent the individual's formal consent. However, this would not require injury-in-fact as a necessary condition for standing in all cases.

The "Judicial-Political" Model, "Case-or-Controversy," and the Remaining Passive Virtues: Mootness and Ripeness

Defining the Contours of the "Judicial-Political" Model

To this point, I have argued that recognition of the important political role played by the federal judiciary in its constitutional decisionmaking dictates rejection of the "private rights" adjudicatory model and its consequential imposition of the injury-in-fact requirement for standing. As the preceding discussion demonstrated,[107] however, it does not follow that there should be absolutely no requirements for standing in constitutional cases, but merely that those requirements should be more appropriately structured to fulfill the judiciary's political role. Nor am I urging that the courts ignore the dictates of Article III's "case-or-controversy" requirement, but rather that that requirement should be redefined to take account of the hybrid judicial and political functions performed in the adjudication of constitutional issues.[108] Although it would reject the logic and history of the federal judicial role to ignore the political impact of the courts' constitutional decisions, to abandon any semblance of a "case-or-controversy" requirement would similarly ignore the framers' obvious attempt to distinguish the judiciary's operation from that of the two representative branches of government.

The federal courts are not, as the Supreme Court has stated,[109] merely debating societies, designed solely for the airing and discussion of abstract issues of constitutional theory. The "case-or-controversy" requirement can, therefore, reasonably be read to demand that real life consequences turn on the court's resolution of a dispute brought before it, and that the court's resolution of that dispute be enforceable. It also should be construed to mean that the federal judiciary cannot itself initiate legal action, but rather must rely on others to do so. Such a requirement makes sense from the perspective of democratic theory, as an attempt to confine the authority of the unrepresentative branch to disrupt the operation of the other branches. Finally, the "case-or-controversy" requirement should be construed to prohibit the federal judiciary from acting in a directly legislative or executive fashion: the federal courts cannot issue free-standing and binding legislation, nor can they administer governmental programs that are not incidental to the performance of the judicial function.[110] Such limitations ensure both that the federal judiciary will function as courts and not as legislatures or executives, while not interfering significantly with performance of their political role as enforcer of the counter-majoritarian constitutional checks.

It is true that similar arguments could be relied upon to justify an injury-in-fact requirement for standing. There is, however, a key difference: the prohibition on adjudicating purely hypothetical disputes does not significantly undermine the federal judiciary's performance of its political function because there should be a sufficient opportunity to provide a constitutional check if and when the proposed legislation or executive action actually takes place. If, on the other hand, that action never does take place, then presumably a need never existed for the judicial check in any event. In contrast, in a number of situations imposition of an injury-in-fact requirement may completely preclude an opportunity for judicial action, despite the clear need for the provision of a constitutional check. Put another way, the presence or absence of a plaintiff's injury-in-fact is logically irrelevant to the need for or quality of the performance of the federal judiciary's political function; the presence or absence of a real-life basis for dispute may well be relevant to both.

Recognition of the need to define the federal judicial role in constitutional cases in terms of the "judicial-political" adjudicatory model would have important implications for two other traditionally accepted limitations on the exercise of federal court jurisdiction: the doctrines of mootness and ripeness. These doctrines are currently structured largely to reflect the logic of the "private rights" model.[111] In certain instances, however, the Supreme Court has twisted and contorted the doctrines in an attempt to accommodate performance of the Court's political function. In so doing, the Justices ultimately satisfy the requirements of neither model.

Mootness Under the "Judicial-Political" Model

Refusing to adjudicate cases that have become moot makes perfect sense under the "private rights" model. If the concrete rights and interests of individual litigants will not be affected by judicial resolution of a legal issue, under the logic of the "private rights" model the rationale for requiring such resolution vanishes. Of course, questions may arise in individual cases as to whether, because of a change in circumstances, the parties will actually be affected by an adjudication,[112] but, once such a determination has been made, the logical implications of the "private rights" model are clear.

If the "private rights" model were replaced in constitutional adjudication by the "judicial-political" model, the mootness doctrine would not be abandoned. However, its rationale—and, in some instances, its application—would be altered significantly. Under this model, the conceivable rationales for refusing to adjudicate a case that has become moot would be that (1) there no longer exists a real controversy implicating the constitutional issue sought to be adjudicated, rendering a judicial decision both unenforceable and hypothetical; and (2) the absence of the possibility of any direct concrete benefit renders the plaintiff an inadequate representative to assure thorough exploration of the constitutional issues raised in the case.

To understand how the mootness doctrine might differ under the two models, it is helpful to apply both to the facts of two well-known Supreme Court decisions, *DeFunis v. Odegaard*[113] and *Honig v. Doe*.[114] *DeFunis* concerned an equal protection challenge by a white applicant, denied admission to the University of Washington Law School, to the school's preferential admissions program for minority applicants. The state trial court granted his request for an injunction commanding the school to admit him. While the litigation proceeded, DeFunis continued his legal studies. When the United States Supreme Court first considered his petition for certiorari, he was in the first term of his third and final year of law school. The Court granted certiorari, but ultimately held the case to be moot. "Since he has now registered for his final term," the Court reasoned, "it is evident that he will be given an opportunity to complete all academic and other requirements for graduation, and if he does so, will receive his diploma regardless of any decision this Court might reach on the merits of this case."[115] Therefore, the Court concluded, "[a] determination by this Court of the legal issues tendered by the parties is no longer necessary to compel that result and could not serve to prevent it."[116]

Application of the mootness doctrine in *DeFunis* appears to comport with the logic of the "private rights" model because judicial resolution was not likely to affect the plaintiff's interests in one way or the other.[117] Under the "judicial-political" model, however, this fact would be far from dispositive. Although the rights of DeFunis himself might not be affected by Supreme Court resolution, it is clear that the viability of the University of Washington Law School's affirmative action program, as well as that of many other law schools, could easily turn on the Court's decision. Thus, the requirement that judicial decision have more than a hypothetical impact would have been satisfied. The remaining question would be whether the fact that DeFunis himself would no longer be affected rendered him an inadequate representative. But, as Justice Brennan commented in dissent, "there is no want of an adversary contest in this case."[118] He noted that the event that supposedly rendered the case moot, DeFunis's registration for the spring term, occurred "only after the case had been fully litigated in the state courts, briefs had been filed in [the Supreme] Court, and oral argument had been heard."[119] Hence, there was no basis for finding DeFunis to inadequately represent one side of a constitutional issue. Under the "judicial-political" model, then, there would have been no basis for avoiding adjudication on mootness grounds in *DeFunis*, even though mootness plays a role as a general matter in the implementation of this model.

The relevance of the "judicial-political" model to the facts of *Honig* is somewhat problematic because the case concerned an issue of statutory interpretation, rather than constitutional analysis. Inasmuch as the logic of the "judicial-political" model derives from the premises of the Counter-Majoritarian principle, focusing on the judiciary's role as a constitutional check on the representative branches,[120] that model is not directly applicable to cases of statutory interpretation.[121] The case may nevertheless serve as a factual analogy for cases presenting constitutional issues.

In *Honig*, a local school district in California had sought to expel two emotionally disturbed students for disruptive conduct related to their disabilities. The students brought an action against the school district for violation of the Education of the Handicapped Act.[122] When the case reached the Supreme Court, that Court found the case moot as to one of the students because he was 24 years old at the time while the Act limits eligibility to disabled children between the ages of three and 21.

The Court found the case not to be moot as to the second student, however, because he

> is currently 20 and has not yet completed high school. Although at present he is not faced with any proposed expulsion or suspension proceedings, and indeed no longer even resides within [the school district], he remains a resident of California and is entitled to a free appropriate public education within that State. . . . Given [the student's] continued eligibility for educational services under the EHA, the nature of his disability, and [the school district's] insistence that all local school districts retain authority to exclude disabled children for dangerous conduct, we have little difficulty concluding that there is a reasonable expectation that [the student] would once again be subjected to unilateral "change in placement" for conduct growing out of his disabilities. . . .[123]

Although the Court was correct in suggesting the possibility that the student in question would once again face the same problem that led to the suit before he turned 21, the likelihood was at best problematic.[124]

If one were to view the issue from the perspective of the "private rights" model, the question would be whether the plaintiff's personal interest would still be affected by judicial resolution of the legal issue. From this perspective, the matter could reasonably be resolved either way. If one were to employ the standards of the "judicial-political" model, however, the test would be whether the student would be sufficiently motivated to litigate the legal issues to the fullest. From that perspective, one might seriously doubt whether such motivation would be present, given the questionable likelihood that his interests would be directly affected by the outcome. Of course, it is conceivable that in reality the litigation was in the hands of groups or individuals with a more long-term interest in the resolution of the particular legal issue involved in the case. But, if so, it would make sense for the Court to engage in the type of inquiry previously suggested for the determination of standing under the "judicial-political" model: whether those effectively responsible for the litigation constitute adequate representatives of one side of the legal issue.[125] Reliance on the fiction of the "private rights" model effectively precludes a careful examination of these truly important factors.

Application of the "judicial-political" model to the facts of *Honig*, then, demonstrates that the mootness doctrine will not necessarily play a more limited role as a restraint on the exercise of judicial jurisdiction under that model than under the "private rights" model. Rather, in adjusting the mootness doctrine more directly to fulfill the federal judiciary's political role, that doctrine's prohibitions would expand in certain instances and contract in others.

Ripeness

"The power of courts, and ultimately of this Court, to pass upon the constitutionality of acts of Congress," the Supreme Court has declared, "arises only when the interests of litigants require the use of this judicial authority for their protection against actual interference. A hypothetical threat is not enough."[126] In part for this reason, the Court has imposed the requirement that a case be "ripe" before the federal judiciary will be allowed to exercise its jurisdiction.[127] Such a limitation on judicial jurisdiction does not appear unreasonable even under the framework of the "judicial-political" adjudicatory model, on several grounds. The "case-or-controversy" requirement can reasonably be construed to demand existence of a real dispute, in order to avoid adding to the judicial burden and unnecessary judicial encroachment into the operation of the representative branches.

The ripeness doctrine could arguably be justified on the basis of a need for a better developed factual basis on which to judge the constitutionality of government action.[128] Thus rationalized, the doctrine excludes from federal jurisdiction not only purely hypothetical disputes, but also live disputes deemed in need of greater development. The extent to which such an extension of the ripeness concept should be made is debatable. The extension cannot be justified on grounds related to the maintenance of a judicial appearance, even under the "private rights" adjudicatory model. Moreover, such an extension may threaten the effective performance of the judiciary's political role in situations where a ruling on the merits is called for because a refusal to adjudicate constitutional challenges leaves the inertia in favor of the challenged legislation, which of course would remain in effect. In any event, to the extent it is appropriate for a court to decline to rule on a constitutional challenge because of an undeveloped factual context, such a decision will be grounded in an analysis of substantive factors related to the particular constitutional challenge, including issues of substantive constitutional theory.[129] The point to be emphasized, then, is that the issue is not properly viewed as exclusively a matter of judicial jurisdiction.

Conclusion

Neither history, logic, nor political theory justifies the "private rights" model of constitutional adjudication and the justiciability doctrines that flow from it. Once one recognizes the validity of the Counter-Majoritarian principle as the rationale for judicial review, it is not difficult to see that the courts' proper role in our political system extends far beyond the resolution of individual disputes.

Rejection of the "private rights" model need not lead to the abandonment of all distinctions between the federal judiciary and the purely political branches. Article III's case-or-controversy requirement, designed to preserve this distinction, should be interpreted to require that the federal courts perform their important political role in a judicial manner. Under this "judicial-political" model of constitutional adjudication, the federal courts would adhere to the doctrines of justiciability, but only to the extent those doctrines are designed to ensure effective performance of the judiciary's task, and to the extent they do not significantly undermine performance of the judiciary's political role of serving as an effective counter-majoritarian constitutional check on the majoritarian branches.

SEVEN

APPLYING THE COUNTER-MAJORITARIAN PRINCIPLE, II: Judicial Review and the "Political Question"

The so-called "political question" doctrine postulates that there exist certain issues of constitutional law that are more effectively resolved by the political branches of government[1] and are therefore inappropriate for judicial resolution. As a result, the courts hold such questions to be "non-justiciable," which means that the courts will neither approve nor reject the judgments of the political branches, and will instead let the political process take its course. A modern example of the doctrine's application is the federal courts' refusal to consider the legality of the President's activities in Nicaragua.[2]

The doctrine has always proven to be an enigma to commentators. Not only have they disagreed about its wisdom and validity (which is to be expected), but they have also differed significantly over its scope and rationale.[3] In fact, they have even disagreed over whether the doctrine exists at all.[4] At least part of the explanation for this confusion is the largely unpredictable method in which the Supreme Court has chosen to invoke the doctrine over the years.[5]

The academic debate has centered primarily over how "principled" use of the doctrine must be. One view, associated with Professor Bickel, asserts that the best means to assure that the Supreme Court's substantive constitutional decisions will be the outgrowth of logic and reason, rather than of a purely pragmatic result orientation, is to allow the Court to choose to avoid making such decisions on purely pragmatic or functional grounds.[6] In part, this "prudential" version of the political question doctrine[7] is characterized by an attitude that could legitimately be called "realpolitik": the Court must survive in an often hostile political world, and the best way to accomplish that feat and simultaneously maintain its legitimacy is to pick its fights. In addition, this version is justified by the belief that certain issues simply do not lend themselves to principled judicial resolution.

The contrary view, associated primarily with Professor Wechsler's famed article on neutral principles,[8] rejects any notion of a "prudential" political question doctrine. The only cases in which the Court may decline to exercise its jurisdiction, he argues, are those in which the Constitution itself has explicitly or implicitly committed the decision to another branch of government.

Adding to this debate are the more recent views of Professor Henkin, who draws a distinction between legitimate exercises of judicial review and recognition of limitations on the use of equity power with some discretionary judicial doctrine to abstain.[9] This analysis leads him to question whether a distinct "political question" doctrine, apart from traditional applications of judicial review, actually exists.[10]

Despite Professor Henkin's valuable insights,[11] however, a political question doctrine does in fact exist. Although perhaps some of the decisions in which it has been invoked theoretically could have been decided the same way on traditional legal grounds, the fact remains that they were in actuality premised on recognition of a certain discretionary judicial authority to defer to the other branches that potentially extends well beyond the traditional rationales.[12] Moreover, it is impossible to explain the results in some of these cases other than by the existence of such a discretionary doctrine.[13] In fact, it is my contention that, in a number of cases in which the Court purported not to invoke the political question doctrine, it was in fact applying many of the doctrine's precepts in rendering its decision.[14]

Although respected scholars have for years debated the scope and wisdom of the political question doctrine, none to date has fully explained why it should be given the total and complete repudiation it so richly deserves.[15] Ultimately, neither Wechsler's "classical" form of the doctrine nor Bickel's "prudential" version is valid—the "classical" form because, at least as applied by the Court and commentators, it represents a fundamentally flawed view of the concept of judicial review, and the "prudential" form because, quite simply, its moral, social, and political costs outweigh its speculative benefits. This chapter is designed to explain why the political question doctrine should play no role whatsoever in the exercise of the judicial review power.[16]

The History, Scope, and Rationale of the Political Question Doctrine: Does the Doctrine Exist?

Even if a political question doctrine—at least in the "prudential" sense envisioned by Bickel—did not exist in the courts, the articulate and persuasive argument, made by a renowned scholar, to justify the use of such a doctrine would be deserving of detailed response. Nevertheless, an examination of the relevant case law reveals that, despite Professor Henkin's contrary assertions, such a doctrine is very much alive in Supreme Court decisions.

The strongest evidence to support this contention are the numerous and extended references to the political question doctrine that the Court itself has made in modern times. It is true that the Court's most detailed analysis of the doctrine came in a case in which it ultimately rejected the doctrine's application, but that fact does not detract from use of the decision as an illustration of the doctrine's existence. After all, if no political question doctrine existed, there would have been no need for the Court to expend so much effort to explain why the doctrine was inapplicable.

The case was *Baker v. Carr*,[17] where the Court, in a detailed opinion by Justice Brennan, held that the political question doctrine did not bar the federal courts from considering an equal protection challenge to a state's voting apportionment structure.[18] In his opinion, Brennan provided lists of both the general criteria to determine the doctrine's applicability and the categories of cases to which the doctrine has been applied. As to the former, he wrote:

> Prominent on the surface of any case held to involve a political question is found a textually demonstrable constitutional commitment of the issue to a coordinate political department; or a lack of judicially discoverable and manageable standards for resolving it; or the impossibility of deciding without an initial policy determination of a kind clearly for nonjudicial discretion; or the impossibility of a court's undertaking independent resolution without expressing lack of the respect due coordinate branches of government; or an unusual need for unquestioning adherence to a political decision already made; or the potentiality of embarrassment from multifarious pronouncements by various departments on one question.[19]

Since the decision in *Baker*, though the Court declined to invoke the political question doctrine on one controversial occasion,[20] a majority expressly invoked the doctrine in one case, *Gilligan v. Morgan*,[21] which presented a constitutional challenge to the training and weaponry of the Ohio National Guard. In addition, a plurality of four Justices in *Goldwater v. Carter*[22] (decided after publication of Professor Henkin's article) expressly invoked the doctrine to avoid adjudicating a constitutional challenge by several members of Congress to the President's unilateral notice of termination of a mutual defense treaty with the Republic of China, pursuant to the treaty's termination clause, because of the absence of congressional approval. Moreover, the Supreme Court has avoided review of lower court determinations that the constitutionality of the Vietnam War[23] and covert activities in Nicaragua[24] were beyond the competence of the judiciary to adjudicate. Finally, the Supreme Court has in recent years at least intimated the possibility that the political question doctrine renders non-justiciable certain constitutional issues surrounding the operations of political parties.[25] Certainly most of these more recent applications could not be justified by some principled analysis that finds simply a textual commitment to another branch, as even Professor Henkin appears to concede as to the constitutionality of the undeclared war in Vietnam. Even if, as he argues,[26] *Gilligan* could have been resolved in the same manner by narrower means, it must be noted that the Court itself clearly did not view its rationale as so narrowly confined. Thus, whether or not a political question doctrine *should* be recognized as purely a normative matter, or whether the Court's modern decisions reflect a misreading or overextension of earlier cases, as has been suggested,[27] the fact remains that the modern Court has adopted such a doctrine, both in theory and practice.

It is largely irrelevant to the question of the doctrine's current viability, then, whether or not the modern Court has misconstrued antiquated precedent. At least in this area, if only implicitly, the Court is likely motivated more by the prudential policy considerations to which Professor Bickel has pointed than it is by the desire to maintain rigid adherence to precedent. It is not uncommon, however, for a Supreme Court intent on developing a doctrine for policy reasons to attempt to mold precedent in an effort to characterize its new doctrine as merely an outgrowth of past decisions. To be truly helpful, therefore, criticism of modern Court doctrine must go well beyond a critique of its use of precedent.

In any event, a more than plausible argument can be made to support the existence (at least as a descriptive matter)[28] of a prudential version of the political question doctrine long before *Baker*. Although the doctrine's origins are claimed to go back to the 1800s,[29] at least by 1924 one commentator could note:

> There are certain cases which are completely without the sphere of judicial interference. They are called, for historical reasons, "political questions." [The term] applies to all those matters of which the court, at a given time, will be of the opinion that it is impolitic or inexpedient to take jurisdiction. Sometimes this idea of inexpediency will result from the fear of the vastness of the consequences that a decision on the merits might entail. Sometimes it will result from the feeling that the court is incompetent to deal with the particular type of question involved. Sometimes it will be induced by the feeling that the matter is "too high" for the courts. But always there will be a weighing of considerations in the scale of political wisdom.[30]

Although perhaps employing different rationales, other commentators of the period also recognized the existence of such a doctrine.[31]

The case sometimes deemed the classic representation of the early political question doctrine is *Luther v. Borden*,[32] which arose out of the Dorr rebellion of 1842 against the charter government of Rhode Island. The traditional view of the case is that, when asked to consider whether the charter government violated the Article IV, section 4, guarantee of a republican form of government, the Court invoked the political question doctrine because of

> the commitment to the other branches of the decision as to which is the lawful state government; the unambiguous action by the President, in recognizing the charter government as the lawful authority; the need for finality in the executive's decision; and the lack of criteria by which a court could determine which form of government was republican.[33]

Professor Henkin, however, suggests that "the *Luther* decision gave [the political branches] no extra-ordinary deference" and that

> [t]he Court was not refusing to scrutinize the constitutionality of what the political branches had done. To the contrary, it found that the actions of Congress and the President in this case were within their constitutional authority and did not violate any prescribed limits or prohibitions. They were therefore law for the courts and there could be no basis for any court to disregard them.[34]

Henkin therefore concludes that "Luther . . . established no pure 'political question doctrine.' "[35]

Professor Henkin's analysis amounts to little more than a play on words. True, the *Luther* Court ultimately concluded that the guarantee clause vested in the political branches of the federal government exclusive authority to interpret the meaning of and to enforce that provision. But there is certainly no more obvious textual basis to support such a conclusion[36] than there is for any other provision of the Constitution: no constitutional provision describing legislative or executive power expressly dictates judicial power to review the constitutionality of the exercise of those powers.[37] Nor did the Court cite any historical evidence concerning the intent of the framers to support such a unique construction. Instead, the opinion construed the provision in this manner because the Court believed that a construction authorizing judicial intervention could well lead to chaotic, or even disastrous, results.[38] Thus, it is not a satisfactory answer to suggest that in a case like *Luther* "the court does not refuse judicial review; it exercises it."[39] It "exercises it" only to the extent of twisting a constitutional provision's meaning in order effectively to *exclude* judicial review, or at least meaningful judicial review, precisely because of the type of prudential reasons cited by Professor Bickel.

Luther, then, actually is the epitome of the political question doctrine that it has traditionally been construed to be.

This discussion of *Luther* has been included to demonstrate that the historical origins of the modern political question doctrine are more sound than certain critics believe. But an extended and detailed analysis of precedent is, candidly, of only limited value in a modern normative debate over Supreme Court doctrine. Whatever the historical record, the modern Court has recognized the possibility that it should avoid involvement in certain so-called "political" disputes, largely because of an unstated fear that resolution is for some reason beyond its province—either because the dispute does not lend itself to the development of judicial standards, or because the Court deems itself incapable of assessing the potentially momentous impact of its decision, or because the Court is concerned about the adherence to its decision by the political branches.[40]

The Logic and Structure of the Political Question Doctrine

The "Classical" Version of the Political Question Doctrine

Professor Wechsler has argued that the only appropriate use of a political question doctrine is to guide the Court in deciding under what circumstances "the Constitution has committed to another agency of government [than the courts] the . . . determination of the issue."[41] This substantially narrowed version of the doctrine is thought to have the benefit of confining the Court's determinations to truly principled exercises. However, even in this supposedly principled form, the political question doctrine, at least as it has been applied, is unacceptable because it disregards long-accepted principles of judicial review.

In understanding this point, it is important to draw certain distinctions. Professor Henkin is surely correct when he argues that in a number of so-called political question cases the Court "is not refusing to pass on the power of the political branches; it passes upon it, only to affirm that they had the power which had been challenged and that nothing in the Constitution prohibited the particular exercise of it."[42] For example, Henkin points to the Court's conclusions that it is "bound by the Executive's determination that a particular regime was the government of a foreign state; that given territory belonged to a foreign state [and] that an island belonged to the United States. . . . "[43] In such cases, the Court is not abdicating its power to interpret and enforce a constitutional provision; rather, it is simply holding that nothing in the Constitution directs the executive as to *how* to make such determinations.[44] Thus, purely as a matter of constitutional analysis, there is no issue about how the decisions are made, but only about who is authorized to make them. The Court easily answers this latter question by finding that the day-to-day conduct of foreign relations lies in the hands of the executive branch.[45]

To the extent Professor Wechsler intended to refer exclusively to such issues, he would no doubt be correct. But both Wechsler and Henkin fail to see the distinction between a judicial conclusion that the Constitution is silent on the exercise of executive or legislative authority and a judicial decision to allow the political branches to act as the final arbiter of a specific constitutional directive concerning the exercise of their power. There is, in fact, all the difference in the world, in terms of valid judicial review theory, between the two types of decisions.

The contrast can be seen by examining the constitutional provision involved in *Luther*, the so-called guarantee clause.[46] Henkin believes that *Luther* can properly be grounded on the view that the phrase "the United States shall guarantee," in Article IV, "plausibly refers to the political branches, and it is not implausible to read it as excluding monitoring and enforcement by the courts. If so, we may have a unique constitutional clause excluding the courts; but that hardly adds up to a 'political question doctrine.' "[47] The problem with this analysis is that it may well prove considerably more than Professor Henkin intended to prove. It is difficult to construe a constitutional provision as excluding judicial review on the basis of the facts that (1) the courts are not mentioned; and (2) other branches are mentioned (even if the words "United States" were construed to include only the political branches), because the power of the judiciary to engage in judicial review is not explicitly mentioned in *any* constitutional provision. For example, Article I, section 8, refers to the powers that Congress may exercise. Indeed, it makes more explicit reference to the power of the political branches than does the guarantee clause, which refers only to "the United States." At no point does the provision indicate that the courts may review legislation to determine whether Congress has exceeded its enumerated powers. If the words "the United States shall guarantee" in Article IV are construed to vest in the political branches exclusive power to interpret the phrase "republican form of government," why do the words of Article I not have the same effect? There is, then, absolutely nothing in the text of the guarantee clause to distinguish the relevance of judicial review from any other provision.[48] Indeed, I fail to see why the presence of a "republican form of government" in a state does not amount to a question of "constitutional fact" under the logic of *Crowell v. Benson*,[49] one which the concept of separation of powers dictates must be finally decided by the judicial branch.

Even in cases falling within the former category—those in which the constitutional provision fails to direct the political branches how they are to exercise the authority vested in them—exponents of the classical version of the political question doctrine have failed to recognize that, even if a constitutional provision is silent on the question of how the power is to be exercised, one of the constitutional protections contained in the amendments may well impose limitations on the exercise of that power.

For example, Professor Wechsler noted that arguably

> the power of Congress to 'make or alter' state regulations of the 'Manner of holding Elections for Senators and Representatives,' implying as it does a power to draw distinct lines or to prescribe the standards to be followed in defining them, excludes the courts from passing on a constitutional objection to state gerrymanders, even if the Constitution can be thought to speak to this kind of inequality and the law of remedies gives disadvantaged voters legal standing to complain.... [50]

With the benefit of hindsight, of course, we can today say with certainty that this argument has been rejected by the Supreme Court, which has held that the Fourteenth Amendment's equal protection clause[51] severely restricts state gerrymandering.[52] The important point, however, is that under traditional judicial review theory, the absence of a limitation on the exercise of legislative or executive authority within the body of the constitutional provision granting that authority should not preclude judicial application of the standards embodied in relevant constitutional amendments. The entire premise of the amendment concept is that an amendment supersedes anything contained in the body of the Constitution that is inconsistent with the amendment's directives. Thus, even if a constitutional provision vesting power in the political branches appears to be facially neutral as to how that power is to be exercised, it does not necessarily follow that all applications of that power are insulated from constitutional scrutiny. Therefore, the "textually demonstrable commitment" concept, even in its most narrowed form, must be further confined by recognition of the potential applicability of constitutional enclaves contained within the amendments.

This point illustrates the highly tenuous reasoning underlying the Court's conclusion that the political question doctrine—at least in its classical form[53]—precluded review in *Gilligan v. Morgan*.[54] Respondents there contended that the Fourteenth Amendment's due process clause[55] required the federal judiciary to evaluate the "training, weaponry and orders" of the Ohio National Guard. In reply, the Chief Justice stated: "In relying on the Due Process Clause of the Fourteenth Amendment, respondents seem to overlook the explicit command of Art. I, § 8, cl. 16," [56] the provision vesting in Congress the power to prescribe the training of the militia.[57] There may well have been numerous grounds on which to reject the respondents' requested relief in *Gilligan*.[58] Indeed, if one were to accept some form of "prudential" political question doctrine one might arguably find justification for the Court's conclusion. But I fail to understand a logic that suggests that an appeal to the due process clause of either the Fifth or Fourteenth Amendments can be precluded by a constitutional provision's vesting of power in one of the political branches of government. If the particular exercise of power violates the due process clause, then the fact that a provision in the body of the Constitution authorizes the practice is wholly irrelevant.

In sum, Professor Henkin is correct when he argues that the so-called classical version of the political question doctrine requires no special judicial deference. Rather, it is simply the product of the application of neutral principles of judicial review. Recognition of this fact, however, logically leads to significant refinements of this version of the doctrine. First, the mere fact that a constitutional provision expressly refers to the exercise of power by the political branches but not to the review function is irrelevant because judicial review is *nowhere* mentioned in the Constitution.[59] Such reasoning, then, may ultimately prove too much. Thus, clauses like the guarantee clause should not, for textual reasons at least, be immune from judicial review. Second, even if a constitutional provision provides no standards by which to judge the exercise of political power, such exercises may well be subject to control through protections contained in the constitutional amendments.

The "Prudential" Version of the Political Question Doctrine

There exists some degree of doubt concerning the contours of the so-called "prudential" version of the doctrine, largely because modern commentators have imposed distinctions that may not actually exist. For example, Professor Scharpf has distinguished the "prudential" version from a "functional" approach.[60] Yet, at least in a broad conceptual sense, the "functional" approach, as Scharpf describes it,[61] appears to be merely a subset of a "prudential" doctrine. In my discussion, then, it is necessary to make clear that by "prudential" I refer to all rationales for effective judicial abdication of review power, other than a basis in the text of the Constitution. In this sense, this branch of the doctrine is distinguished from Wechsler's "classical" version, which, as we have seen, when properly applied is no "doctrine" at all but merely the exercise of traditional judicial review.

The rough contours of the prudential doctrine are embodied in the often-quoted statement of Professor Bickel:

> Such is the foundation . . . of the political-question doctrine: the Court's sense of lack of capacity, compounded in unequal parts of (a) the strangeness of the issue and its intractability to principled resolution; (b) the sheer momentousness of it, which tends to unbalance judicial judgment; (c) the anxiety, not so much that the judicial judgment will be ignored, as that perhaps it should but will not be; (d) finally ("in a mature democracy"), the inner vulnerability, the self-doubt of an institution which is electorally irresponsible and has no earth to draw strength from.[62]

This statement simultaneously provides both the criteria of application and the various rationales for use of the prudential political question doctrine.

A parsing of Bickel's quotation reveals the following justifications for use of such a doctrine: (1) the inability of the judiciary to develop general principles and rules of construction of a particular constitutional provision; (2) the judiciary's lack of institutional capacity to review particular judgments of one or both of the political branches; and (3) the judicial humility that flows from the judiciary's inherently undemocratic nature. To these three rationales can reasonably be added a fourth, one that is mentioned in the Bickel quotation primarily for purposes of rejecting it: the fear that the judiciary's authority and legitimacy will be undermined by a blatant disregard of its decision by the political branches. Any attempt normatively to reject the prudential political question doctrine must deal with the wisdom of each of these four rationales.

First, however, it is necessary to consider the argument, attributable primarily to Wechsler, that the judiciary *cannot* establish a prudential doctrine, whether or not it *should* do so. Wechsler's attack on this branch of the political question doctrine is remarkable mainly for its absence of a policy critique of the doctrine's wisdom. His point, rather, appears to be that the accepted role of the judiciary and of its authority of judicial review render it powerless to establish such a doctrine. His critique, then, is a structural attack, rather than one based in policy.

Professor Wechsler, relying on both the supremacy clause[63] and the deceptively simple reasoning of Chief Justice Marshall in *Marbury v. Madison*,[64] rejects the postulate "that a court, in a case properly before it, is free . . . either to adjudicate a constitutional objection to an otherwise determinative action of the legislature or executive, national or state, or to decline to do so, depending on 'how importunately' it considers the occasion to demand an answer. . . ."[65] He concludes that "[f]or me, as for anyone who finds the judicial power anchored in the Constitution, there is no such escape from the judicial obligation; the duty cannot be attenuated in this way."[66] Largely on the basis of a constitutional provision that by its terms concerns itself exclusively with matters of federalism and state court obligations (the supremacy clause), Wechsler has recognized an unwaveringly rigid judicial obligation to interpret and enforce the Constitution, regardless of what many would consider the socially and politically disastrous consequences that would follow. His conclusion may be a valid one—indeed, it is similar to the conclusion that I ultimately reach. But I fail to see how the position in support of such a view can avoid dealing with the arguably strong policy considerations generally relied upon to justify a prudential political question doctrine.

In the final analysis, the most persuasive arguments in support of the power of judicial review are premised not on the rigid structural commands of the Constitution itself, but on theories of normative policy.[67] It is difficult, then, to refute policy arguments urging an abdication of this authority in narrow circumstances without considering the validity of those policy arguments.[68] It is to such a discussion that I now turn.

The Policy Critique of the Prudential Doctrine

Although I ultimately reject all four of the proffered rationales for the prudential political question doctrine, even a cursory analysis reveals a marked gradation in their persuasiveness. Two of the rationales—the inherently undemocratic nature of judicial review[69] and Bickel's "intractability to principled resolution"[70]—are clearly without significant merit. The remaining two rationales—the simultaneous anxieties that the judicial judgment will be ignored and that it will not be ignored but should be—present somewhat thornier problems.

The Undemocratic Character of Review. Although the unrepresentative nature of the judiciary is an important factor in the modern debate over the proper scope of judicial review,[71] it has no place in the political question debate. Arguably, one might deem it relevant in deciding how invasive of majoritarian prerogatives the judiciary's review will be pursuant to a potentially open-ended constitutional provision, such as the equal protection clause. But so long as one accepts the concept of judicial review in the first place, this factor cannot logically preclude review (which is, after all, the effect of the invocation of the political question doctrine).

Under the Counter-Majoritarian principle,[72] the basic function of unrepresentative judicial review is to assure that the constitutional restraints on majoritarian will are enforced. If the majoritarian branches could act as final arbiters of the limits of their own power, there would have been little purpose in imposing super-majoritarian constitutional limitations in the first place. Thus, if a constitutional provision, reasonably interpreted, prohibits an action by one of the political branches, it is unresponsive to argue that the courts should abstain from exercising their review power because of their undemocratic nature.

To be sure, the political question doctrine is often invoked when—indeed, because—the limits imposed on the political branches by a constitutional provision are unclear.[73] However, the goal of the discussion at this point is not to attack the entire political question doctrine, but to demonstrate that, if there is to be such a doctrine, it must be for some reason or reasons other than the inherently undemocratic character of judicial review.

"Intractability to Principled Resolution". Perhaps the most widely cited ground in support of the prudential doctrine is the view that certain constitutional provisions do not lend themselves to the development of workable, generalizable standards of construction—what Scharpf has referred to as the "cognitive" theory.[74] As one jurist described the theory many years ago,

> [w]hat-ever may be the difficulties in definitively describing the differences between the judicial and the legislative department it seems settled and clear that the court must have some rule to follow before it can operate. Where no rule exists the court is powerless to act. From this it follows that the courts cannot enter into questions of statecraft or policy.[75]

If one examines the litany of case law either interpreting the broad language of the due process or equal protection clauses or establishing standards on which to invoke the First Amendment right of free speech, one must suspect the disingenuousness of the "absence-of-standards" rationale.[76] Over a period of many years, the Supreme Court has developed numerous specific principles of personal jurisdiction[77] and concepts of fair procedure[78] without the slightest hint of guidance from either the language or history of the due process clause. Similarly, the Court has adopted shifting standards of scrutiny under the equal protection clause that find little or no basis in the vague terms of that provision.[79] The First Amendment guarantee is only one more illustration of many to indicate that whenever the Court truly desires, it can find workable—if not perfect—standards of application in interpreting exceedingly vague constitutional language.

The dubious nature of the "absence-of-standards" view is illustrated by Justice Brennan's opinion in *Baker v. Carr*,[80] where he suggested that a constitutional challenge to state gerrymandering pursuant to Article IV's guarantee clause would be dismissed for lack of susceptibility to workable judicial standards, though a similar challenge brought under the equal protection clause somehow failed to present the same difficulty. Of course, the same standards could have been developed, regardless of the asserted constitutional rationale. It is difficult for me to understand why the words "republican form of government" in Article IV are thought not to be susceptible to judicial interpretation,[81] but the words "due process" or "equal protection" are deemed not to suffer from this difficulty. Ultimately, *any* constitutional provision can be supplied with working standards of interpretation. To be sure, those standards often will not clearly flow from either the language or history of the provision, but that fact does not distinguish them from many judicial standards invoked every day. If we were really to take seriously the "absence-of-standards" rationale, then we would once again be proving considerably more than most of us had intended, for a substantial portion of all constitutional review is susceptible to the same critique.

Professor Jaffe, however, has argued that in certain instances the point is not that the courts *cannot* develop workable standards, but that they *should* not:

> Many of the questions that arise are of the sort of which we do not choose, or have not been able as yet to establish, strongly guiding rules. We may believe that the job is better done without rules, or that even though there are applicable rules, these rules should be only among the numerous relevant considerations.[82]

Bickel argues "that some questions are held to be political pursuant to a decision on principle that there ought to be discretion free of principled rules."[83]

In considering this justification, we must once again draw subtle but important distinctions. As already seen, in certain cases it is nothing more than the application of traditional judicial review principles for the Court to hold that a particular judgment is committed to the discretion of one of the political branches. This is simply because the constitutional provision delegating that authority is neutral as to how the authority is to be exercised.

At least to a certain extent, Professor Jaffe's comment was directed toward this conclusion. He cites as an example the President's decision whether to recognize a foreign government: "It is the President alone who is competent—that is, has jurisdiction—to make this decision. The Constitution itself is construed to assign this jurisdiction."[84] One can have no quarrel with this view. Even if the issue of whether the present government of a nation is to be recognized arises during the course of private litigation, it would not seem to violate separation of powers for a court to defer to the executive branch's determination of the question because such deference does not undermine the judiciary's function as interpreter of the Constitution; the Constitution simply does not speak to the issue.[85] It is more difficult to justify this "normative" rationale in cases in which it is claimed that a constitutional provision has been violated by executive or legislative action.

The natural question to raise about the Jaffe-Bickel position in this context concerns the most appropriate source of the decision that in a particular case, in Bickel's words, "there ought to be discretion free of principled rules." When the Constitution's framers intended that one of the political branches retain discretion to act not in accordance with principle, the document effectively says so, by vesting decisionmaking power in those branches without simultaneously indicating how that power must be exercised. But if the document provides, for example, that it is Congress' province to declare war,[86] one may ask why it is appropriate for the courts, interpreting and enforcing the document, to overrule the Constitution's allocation of power by concluding that the conduct of military affairs, even to the point of waging war, must lie in the executive's uncontrolled discretion. Surely, the exercise of such judicial power does not represent the principled constitutional interpretation for which Professor Bickel strove. Similarly, if the First Amendment right of free expression was intended to serve as a limitation on congressional power, I fail to see from where the judiciary derives the authority to conclude that the decision whether to imprison subversives who speak out against the government must be totally within congressional and executive discretion. This does not mean that I believe that in rendering such decisions the judiciary must give no deference whatsoever to the expertise of the political branches or to the possible need for some form of reasonable immediate action on the part of the executive, particularly in the conduct of foreign affairs. But it is vital to distinguish between appropriate "substantive" deference—in which the judiciary, while retaining power to render final decisions on the meaning of the constitutional limits, nevertheless takes into account the need for expertise or quick action—and unacceptable total "procedural" deference, where the court concludes simply that resort to the judiciary constitutes the wrong "procedure," because the decision is exclusively that of the political branches.[87]

Bickel's primary concern appears to be the impossibility of the judiciary's supervising the finding of "necessity" in a principled manner.[88] But this demonstrates that the preoccupation with the need for rigid, general, and categorical rules of judicial decision can lead to an effective abdication of judicial authority to ensure adherence of the majoritarian branches to the super-majoritarian limits of the Constitution in the many cases that do not lend themselves to this type of resolution. As a result, although perhaps the judiciary is saved the difficult task of resolving constitutional issues pragmatically, the majoritarian branches are left totally unchecked. In balancing the comparative evils, it is not difficult to find far less danger when the judiciary examines necessity in cases in which constitutional rights are at stake than when it abdicates in favor of the unbridled power of the political branches.

The concern for principled decisionmaking as a rationale for the political question doctrine represents an unduly narrow, short-sighted, and even solipsistic view of the judiciary's function in a constitutional system. The approach examines only the impact of decision on the judiciary itself; so long as the judiciary's adherence to principle is maintained, no problems are thought to exist.[89] The fact that as a result constitutional rights and precepts may be violated by a political branch that has consciously or unconsciously overestimated the necessity for such action appears to be of little concern. If the judiciary declines to resolve sensitive constitutional disputes, the nation is effectively left in a constitutional state of nature, in which the constitutional position that prevails is the one that is the politically or physically most powerful.

In light of our initial assumption that in general the judiciary must have the final say as to the constitutionality of the activities of the political branches, primarily for the reason that the political branches should not be permitted to sit in final judgment on the constitutionality of their own actions, the moral and social posture of the judiciary is not aided by abdication of its ultimate function. Although common sense may dictate an appropriate degree of substantive deference,[90] the broad policies behind the concept of judicial review require that the judiciary exercise its function, even if this results in an abandonment of rigid adherence to generalized principle in favor of partially intuitive judgments on the issue of necessity.

In any event, it is by no means clear that a judicial ruling on the issue of legislative or executive necessity represents a departure from the performance of the traditional judicial function. Courts are often called upon to apply generalized and ambiguous abstract principles to specific factual situations, even when the application of those principles is unclear. If the substantive interpretation of a particular constitutional provision is that the legislature or executive is prohibited from taking certain action absent the presence of some true or compelling necessity (as it generally is for such venerable constitutional protections as free speech and procedural due process), then a judicial judgment of necessity amounts to nothing more than the traditional application of abstract substantive principle to specific fact situations.

Although the extreme deference of the political question doctrine may not be justified by some notion of the need for principled decisions, a stronger pragmatic argument may be fashioned on another basis. For, even if one believes that there is nothing inherent in the performance of the judicial function that precludes it from judging "necessity," there arguably exist serious pragmatic barriers to the judicial determination of such questions. Any critique of the political question doctrine must deal with the argument that the judiciary is, at least in certain cases, institutionally incapable of judging the actions of the political branches.

The Judiciary's Capacity to Review. One of Bickel's rationales, it should be recalled, was "the anxiety, not so much that the judicial judgment will be ignored, as that perhaps it should be but will not be. . . ."[91] The concern, in other words, is that in certain instances, for one reason or another, judging the practical impact of its decision will lie beyond the judiciary's capacity. This is what Professor Scharpf refers to as the "functional" theory, the only one that he believes explains the various invocations of the doctrine.[92] In brief, the doctrine has been applied "where the Court has generally been hesitant to trust its own understanding of the broader situation."[93]

An initial point to note is that, even if one accepts such a rationale, it justifies invocation of the political question doctrine only in a relatively rare set of cases—primarily those dealing with certain aspects of foreign relations and perhaps emergency threats to internal security. But serious questions may be raised about the validity of the rationale in any of its applications.

A major problem with the lack-of-capacity rationale is that, once again, it proves too much, at least if one accepts the broad principle of judicial review in the first place. Is the Court to be bound by the government's assertion that the publication of the content of the Pentagon Papers will seriously threaten both our world image and our military posture in Southeast Asia?[94] If so, must the judiciary take the next logical step, and unquestioningly accept the government's assertion that public criticism of our military activities in Southeast Asia unduly threatens our military success and endangers our soldiers by encouraging the enemy to continue fighting? The point, simply, is that if the constitutional limitations on majoritarian power are to mean anything, at some point the judiciary must be able to question the political branches' assertion of factual necessity.

The pragmatic arguments made against judicial review of a finding of necessity at most establish a varying need for *substantive* deference, not for the total abdication of judicial authority. The level of the deference will presumably vary, depending on the severity of both the asserted emergency and of the loss of liberty involved. The claim that the judiciary may often lack access to information available to the executive[95] cannot justify abandonment of the review function because the judiciary may simply require the executive to justify its actions by supplying the information that led it to act. Although the Court faces obvious problems in scrutinizing the accuracy and completeness of the government's factual assertions, at least such an approach provides greater protection against encroachment on liberty by the majoritarian branches than does total judicial abdication. This is effectively what happened in the courts of appeals in the two Pentagon Papers cases: the government was required to prepare special briefs, for *in camera* judicial inspection, attempting to explain what specific harms would flow from publication.[96]

Moreover, in certain instances the Constitution itself renders necessity largely irrelevant. For example, Article I, section 8 vests in Congress the exclusive power to declare war. It does not provide that, if necessary, the President may conduct a war that Congress has not declared. Of course, the question of what military activity constitutes the conduct of a "war" is not free from ambiguity, and it would probably be appropriate for the judiciary, in defining the term, to take into account the need in modern foreign relations for limited military activities in emergency situations short of a declared war. But if the Court concludes, on the basis of an evidentiary record, that the military activities amount to a "war" in everything but name, the Constitution does not authorize a "necessity" exception. Indeed, it is difficult to imagine how a "necessity" argument could be fashioned in any event. So long as it is no longer a matter of immediate emergency, on what pragmatic basis could the President justify the conduct of an undeclared war? That Congress is too dumb or stubborn to recognize the need seen by the executive? Such an argument must of course be rejected because it undermines the checks-and-balances concept underlying the vesting of the power to declare war in Congress.

No more compelling than the informational problem is the so-called "embarrassment" danger—i.e., by overruling the executive in foreign affairs the judiciary risks embarrassing the government by having the nation appear to the rest of the world to be speaking with conflicting voices.[97] Although perhaps this argument may have some force when foreign relations issues arise in non-constitutional disputes between private parties,[98] it cannot outweigh the need for the judiciary to perform its function of judicial review. Presumably the same argument could be made when the Senate fails to ratify a treaty negotiated by the executive branch. In that instance, other countries are asked to understand our complex constitutional system of checks and balances, and we somehow manage to survive as a nation. There is no reason why the same practice could not apply when the judiciary exercises its function of constitutional review.

Judicial Fear of Disregard by the Political Branches. The final rationale for the prudential version of the political question doctrine is one that modern commentators have generally rejected, yet it may be the primary—if unstated—explanation for some of the classic judicial refusals to review. That rationale is the fear that the judiciary's authority and legitimacy will be significantly undermined if the political branches ignore the judicial decision in an area of sensitive political concern.

One early commentator expressly relied on this factor in explaining use of the political question doctrine.[99] However, Professor Bickel expressly rejected this ground.[100] Professor Scharpf indicates doubt that the rationale could explain many of the political question decisions, some of which arose between two private parties and where there would be little question that they would obey the decision.[101] Scharpf suggests that the Court may avoid delicate decisions without employing "the heavy artillery of the political question doctrine to cover its retreat from trouble in an individual case."[102] Instead, he reasons, the Court may simply rely on its inherent discretionary power to avoid decision. But the lower courts do not benefit from all of the same discretionary authority, so on occasion they may—and in fact have[103]—been forced to rely on the political question doctrine in cases in which the Supreme Court has the luxury of simply denying review.

Scharpf is correct in noting that the fear of disregard is relevant to only a small fraction of the traditional political question cases. Even in many cases to which the federal government is a party, particularly in the domestic area, it is highly unlikely that the dangers of adherence to a decision would be so great as to justify the risk of political backlash that the government's disregard of a Supreme Court decision would entail. Thus, once again it is worthy of note that even if we were to accept this rationale, it would justify only a handful of the political question decisions, primarily in the sensitive area of foreign relations. On balance, however, this rationale, like the others, fails.

The argument is premised on the assumption that the judiciary will better preserve its legitimacy and authority if, on its own motion, it declines to adjudicate a highly sensitive constitutional issue than if it does decide the question. This is at best a dubious premise. If the judiciary is deemed by society as the final arbiter of the Constitution's meaning, the fact that the judiciary has allowed what many consider an unconstitutional government action to continue without even considering the validity of the constitutional challenge will likely magnify the judiciary's impotence in the eyes of many.

No doubt, some members of the public believe that in a democracy the judiciary should never overrule judgments of the majoritarian branches, and these individuals would quite probably express agreement with the Court's decision to abstain. That decision, however, would not increase the respect these individuals have for the judiciary's authority, but merely reaffirm their lack thereof. Indeed, it is arguable that the judiciary's abdication of its review function would create a problem of rising expectations in those who question the general legitimacy of judicial review, rendering potentially more politically troublesome the Court's subsequent decision to exercise its power of review. For if the Court declines to exercise review in one instance on the basis of wholly pragmatic fears and discretionary judgment, it will have a more difficult time justifying its decision not to abstain in another politically sensitive matter. And those who do look to the judiciary in general, and the Supreme Court in particular, as the protector against a lawless government and guardian of individual liberty against the majoritarian branches would quite probably question the courts' commitment if they allowed unconstitutional governmental action to go unchecked. Thus, Justice Jackson was incorrect when, in *Korematsu v. United States,*[104] he urged the Court to avoid dealing with the constitutional issues surrounding the Japanese relocations. If such governmental conduct were thought by many to be unconstitutional, the Court would expend significantly greater moral capital by allowing such gross deprivations of liberty to continue unreviewed. Whatever the risks to the Court's stature that might result from a disregard of its decision by the political branches, then, the risks to its legitimacy are at least as great from the Court's refusal to review allegedly unconstitutional governmental action.

In any event, it is by no means clear that the political branches would ever openly disregard a decision of the Supreme Court finding their actions illegal. The political risks of such disregard may be so great as to surpass the problems created by adherence. Thus, President Nixon could not have seriously considered ignoring the Court's conclusion that he must supply his tapes to the special prosecutor[105] because the political costs would have been too high. Similarly, it is likely that President Johnson would have met political disaster sooner than he did if he had continued military actions in Vietnam after the Supreme Court had held those actions to be an unconstitutional undeclared war. The history of President Roosevelt's unsuccessful Court-packing plan teaches that there is a mystique about the Supreme Court in the minds of many members of the public that gives rise to grave danger to any political official who openly ignores the Court's directives.

It is true that an unpopular Supreme Court decision may lead not to direct disregard of its command but to an attempt by the political branches to curb the jurisdiction of the federal judiciary. The extent to which the political branches may employ jurisdiction-curbing techniques to curb the reach of a substantive constitutional holding is subject to doubt.[106] But to the extent such jurisdiction curbing is accepted as a legitimate constitutional check on the judiciary's power, then so be it;

the impact of such action cannot rise to the level of the humiliation many believe the open disregard of a Supreme Court decision would engender. In any event, the substantial political barriers that recent attempts to enact such jurisdiction-curbing legislation have encountered[107] are still further evidence that the Court possesses considerably greater political protection than many believe.

The New Defense of the Political Question Doctrine

In recent years, academic support for the political question doctrine has, in some circles, been revived. Professor Peter Mulhern argues "that critics of the political question doctrine rest their criticisms on a interpretation of our constitutional practice that fails the threshold test for fit" with our constitutional tradition.[108] He makes the following arguments in support of his contention that the judiciary does not possess a monopoly on enforcement of counter-majoritarian constitutional protections:

1. Article III limits the judiciary's authority to the adjudication of live cases or controversies, and in any event "the Constitution gives Congress extensive control over the federal courts' jurisdiction," permitting "Congress to block judicial consideration of many constitutional questions."[109]

2. "Congress and the President have a duty to ensure that their actions conform to the law."[110] Thus, "[w]hen courts abstain from striking down some act of a political branch of government out of deference, they impose a duty of constitutional interpretation on the branch of government to which they defer."[111]

3. "The [legal realists'] collapse of [the] distinction [between legal and nonlegal issues] calls into question the basis of judicial authority,"[112] because "[l]egislatures, not courts, were supposed to balance 'conflicting human values.' Courts had no special claim of competence to strike that balance."[113]

Upon close examination, it becomes clear that none of these rationales justifies the political question doctrine as it is traditionally understood. Before we undertake that examination, however, it is worthy of note that Professor Mulhern's own normative conception of the political question doctrine is very different from the traditional understanding, and the rationales which he adopts in no way logically support his suggested revision of the doctrine, even if one were to assume their validity in the abstract. Mulhern urges a "shared responsibility" model of constitutional interpretation,[114] which, in turn, provides the basis for determining applicability of the political question doctrine. He asserts that "[p]rotecting oppressed individuals from abuses of government power is the core of [the] sphere" in "which the courts [should] consider themselves responsible for constitutional interpretation."[115] However, under his version of the doctrine, courts "make no attempt to affect the constitutional balance between the state and federal governments,"[116] and "they avoid most issues concerning the proper balance of power between Congress and the President."[117] Surely, when one thinks of the traditional political question doctrine, this is not the division of authority that comes to mind.[118] More importantly, it could hardly be reasonably argued that the rationales Mulhern suggests justify such a distinction. For example, Congress's power to control federal jurisdiction under Article III applies with equal force in individual rights case as in separation-of-powers or federalism cases. The same is true of Article III's case-or-controversy requirement, as well as of the majoritarian branch's duty to enforce the Constitution and of the supposed collapse of legal formalism. Thus, to the extent one accepts Professor Mulhern's arguments at all, he appears to have proven considerably more than he intended to. Moreover, the same is true, even if Mulhern had purported to defend the political question doctrine in its traditional form. For all the factors upon which he relies are in no way limited in their logic to the narrow situations in which the political question doctrine has been applied.[119]

The most significant defect in Professor Mulhern's analysis, however, is that he has either misstated legal practice or grossly overstated the implications of the points on which he relies. For example, he relies on Congress's Article III power to control federal jurisdiction in order to establish that our tradition does not recognize a "judicial monopoly" on constitutional interpretation.[120] However, he completely ignores the widely recognized[121] due process limitation on Congress's power, preventing *total* preclusion of judicial review in constitutional rights cases. Thus, although Congress might retain power to control federal jurisdiction *or* state jurisdiction in such cases, it is clear that a congressional preclusion of *both* would deny the litigants the fair adjudicator required by due process.[122] Far from undermining the "judicial monopoly" logic, then, the relevant case law actually implements it.

Even more dubious is Professor Mulhern's reliance on the obligation of the majoritarian branches to conform their actions to the law. This obligation applies, of course, in *all* cases, yet the political question doctrine has clearly not been so broadly applied. Thus, the Supreme Court has recognized that, in most cases, reliance on the existence of this obligation is an insufficient basis on which to dispense with judicial review. In any event, reliance on this factor as a basis for precluding judicial review ignores the logic of the Counter-Majoritarian principle.[123] Unless and until Professor Mulhern provides a persuasive basis on which to reject the notion that reliance on a majoritarian branch to police itself effectively undermines the counter-majoritarian nature of the Constitution,[124] his conclusory reference to the political branches' obligation to conform their behavior to the law remains inadequate to justify the doctrine.

Finally, Mulhern's reliance on the implications of the legal realist movement fails to rationalize the political question doctrine. Initially, if he is correct in his description of those implications, there is no basis on which to limit the doctrine's reach. Once again, an advocate of the political question doctrine has proven considerably more than he intended to prove.[125] More importantly, Mulhern has so grossly overstated the demise of principled legal analysis as to border on caricature. Recognition of the overlap between political values and constitutional analysis has long presented scholars with a difficult task of reconciliation.[126] None but the most extreme, however, would suggest that we today operate in the system of intellectual chaos that Mulhern envisions. But, if Mulhern actually were correct, it most certainly would not justify judicial abdication in constitutional cases. To the contrary, it is only if constitutional issues were easily resolved on the basis of a mechanical application of automatic factors that we could trust the political branches to police themselves. In such an event, everyone would know whether the branches had correctly applied constitutional dictates. It is for the very reason that the process of constitutional analysis is so imbued with unverifiable political value judgments that we must rely on the one branch not directly subject to majoritarian political pressures to make those judgments. Thus, Professor Mulhern is incorrect when he suggests that courts possess "no special claim of competence"[127] to strike the constitutional balance. Under the logic of the Counter-Majoritarian principle, it is the judiciary's consciously designed insulation from majoritarian political influence that provides the courts this special claim of competence.

The Political Question Doctrine And The Exercise Of Equitable Power

Professor Henkin argues that what has traditionally passed for the political question doctrine is in reality often nothing more than the traditional exercise of the discretionary power of a court "to withhold relief for 'want of equity.' "[128] "The equity practice of the federal courts has largely retained its historic scope, its historic exceptions, and its tradition of broad discretion and flexibility, leaving large room for 'wisdom' and 'prudence,' " he contends.[129] "There is no reason why these should not include considerations of federalism or the separation of powers, or institutional integrity and the inter-institutional harmony implied in the nature of judicial power and the character of judicial institutions in their relation to political power and political institutions."[130]

To a certain extent, Professor Henkin's point is well taken. The fashioning of the specific contours of relief may well involve elements of judicial discretion and flexibility not present in the reaching of the constitutional decision on the merits. Thus, if the Supreme Court had ruled that the Vietnam War was unconstitutional, there would be little doubt that it would have been appropriate for the judiciary to fashion an order of withdrawal that lodged substantial discretion in the hands of the military to conduct a withdrawal that was as safe as possible. It is considerably more difficult, however, to distinguish the inherent judicial discretion of equity practice from the more sweeping abstention of the political question doctrine when a court invokes the limits of equity as a justification for fashioning no relief whatsoever.

The problem can be seen in Henkin's characterization of *Gilligan* as simply a matter of equitable limitations on judicial power.[131] In support of his characterization of the Court's refusal to review the constitutionality of the training and weaponry of the Ohio National Guard, he cites the following passage from the Court's opinion:

> Moreover, it is difficult to conceive of an area of governmental activity in which the courts have less competence. The complex, subtle, and professional decisions as to the composition, training, equipping, and control of a military force are essentially professional military judgment, subject always to civilian control of the Legislative and Executive Branches.[132]

It is difficult to understand how the above-quoted analysis represents anything other than Professor Bickel's "prudential" version of the political question doctrine. The Court in this passage does not seem to be commenting upon the institutional and physical difficulties of having the courts enforce a finding of unconstitutionality (though this factor was apparently relevant to the Court's decision).[133] Rather, the Court is saying that no judgment can be made on the merits of the constitutional claim because the judiciary is effectively incapable of questioning the expertise of the professionals involved in the making of the original decisions.

An analysis more consistent with the position taken here would have recognized the need for both expertise and flexibility in the making of decisions about training, weaponry, and equipment, but would have simultaneously allowed the courts to provide a substantive constitutional floor in the event that any of those decisions clearly transcended constitutional bounds. To use extreme examples, let us assume that the National Guard training manual stated that blacks were to be treated more roughly than whites, or that any demonstrator professing a belief in Communism should be beaten. Surely, issues of executive and military expertise and flexibility are irrelevant to the constitutionality of such training. Yet use of an all-encompassing political question doctrine would presumably prevent even such obvious constitutional decisions. More realistic issues might have been somewhat more ambiguous as a substantive constitutional matter, but whatever deference that was appropriate could easily have been incorporated into the Court's traditional substantive constitutional analysis. Characterizing the Court's rationale as a matter of equity, rather than of the political question doctrine, does not render the decision any more defensible as a constitutional matter, and can only have the counter-productive effect of obscuring the real issues.

Although much of *Gilligan*'s rationale may be improperly characterized as merely an equity analysis, surely it is possible to conceive of cases in which the Court could reach a constitutional decision on the merits, invalidating governmental practice, yet nevertheless conclude that there exist insurmountable practical barriers to the fashioning of effective equitable relief. But, although Professor Henkin may be correct that equity has traditionally allowed substantial judicial discretion, it is important to avoid transforming this authority into the equivalent of the prudential political question doctrine. Once a court finds a statute or executive practice to be unconstitutional, it must recognize its obligation to fashion relief that will adequately protect the rights of the complaining individuals. To be sure, in so doing the court may appropriately take into account its institutional limitations as well as the need for executive flexibility and expertise. But it is difficult to imagine a case in which this calculus will or should lead to a total denial of effective relief.

Conclusion

Once we make the initial assumption that judicial review plays a legitimate role in a constitutional democracy, we must abandon the political question doctrine, in all its manifestations. The doctrine inherently implies that one or both of the political branches may continue conduct that could conceivably be found unconstitutional, without any examination or supervision by the judicial branch. The moral cost of such a result, both to society in general and to the Supreme Court in particular, far outweighs whatever benefits are thought to be derived from the judicial abdication of the review function.

This does not mean that the Court, in reaching its constitutional decisions, should not, in certain cases, take into account the comparative expertise that the political branches may have in deciding whether certain actions are essential, or the institutional limitations on the judiciary's power to supervise day-to-day operations of the government, particularly when emergency actions may be required. But, in each case, if the Court is to perform the essential function of protector against a lawless government, it must draw the final constitutional calculus. If in certain instances the Court abdicates this responsibility, it becomes logically difficult to distinguish the majority of cases in which the Court deems legitimate the exercise of its review power; a large number of prima facie incursions of liberty by the political branches could conceivably be justified on some notion of expertise.

None of the traditionally proffered rationales employed to justify the political question doctrine has merit. The classical version of the doctrine, to the extent it means anything more than requiring a judicial determination whether both the constitutional provision vesting a power in the political branches and the various constitutional enclaves against the exercise of governmental power are neutral about a specific exercise of that power, must be rejected as a contradiction of traditional principles of judicial review. The fact that a provision vesting power refers to the political branches and not to the judiciary cannot justify a finding of a textual commitment of discretion to the political branches because the same could be said of virtually every provision vesting authority in a political branch. Thus, the "textual commitment" concept cannot justify the Court's invocation of the political question doctrine in such areas as the guarantee clause.

Nor can the prudential version of the doctrine be justified on the basis of any of its asserted rationales:

1. Although the so-called "undemocratic" nature of judicial review could conceivably justify an appropriate degree of judicial deference to the political branches in certain cases, it cannot justify total judicial abdication, at least without undermining the use of judicial review in all of its applications.

2. The so-called "absence-of-standards" rationale borders on the disingenuous, because the Supreme Court has never been at a loss to decipher roughly workable standards for the vaguest of constitutional provisions when it so desires.

3. The fact that the exercise of judicial review may require the Court to supervise a determination of "necessity" by the political branches does not significantly undermine performance of the judiciary's hallowed function of deciding on the basis of general rules or principles because this function has traditionally involved the delicate job of applying broad

legal values or concepts (for example, "government may infringe individual liberty only when truly necessary to avoid serious societal harm") to complex specific factual situations. Although a finding of "necessity" may ultimately require some intuitive leaps, the obvious costs to a constitutional democracy, premised in part on the preservation of individual liberty against majoritarian encroachment, of leaving the majoritarian branches as the final arbiter of the constitutionality of their own actions are so great as to justify the decisional difficulties that the judiciary will be forced to incur. In short, it would more significantly undermine the performance of the judiciary's accepted role for the courts not to decide such questions than it would for the courts to decide them.

4. The judiciary's lack of expertise and limited access to information also cannot justify total judicial abdication of its review function. There is no reason that the judiciary cannot demand that the governmental body that has taken a constitutionally questionable action supply whatever information it employed to decide to take such action in the first place. Moreover, although the judiciary's lack of expertise may justify a certain degree of deference in rendering a substantive constitutional ruling, the grave potential dangers to individual liberty that would result from a total judicial abdication make clear that the courts must exercise some meaningful review, if only to provide a floor of constitutionally acceptable governmental behavior.

5. The fear that the Court's constitutional rulings will be ignored by the political branches, thereby reducing its public legitimacy and stature, cannot be accepted as a rationale for the political question doctrine. First, such dangers are at most remote because of the severe political consequences that are likely to affect the political branches as a result of such an openly lawless act. Furthermore, the Court perhaps risks a greater expenditure of its moral capital if it washes its hands of a sensitive constitutional issue, thereby allowing the political branches to continue without review the activity thought by many to be unconstitutional.

EIGHT

CONCLUSION: Final Thoughts on the Intertwining of Political Theory and Jurisdictional Doctrine

The goal of the preceding seven chapters has been twofold. First, they have attempted to demonstrate the need for a dramatic alteration in the Supreme Court's approach to the development of the law of federal jurisdiction in light of appropriate notions of American political theory. Second, they have examined how those changes should be reflected in the revision of several specific jurisdictional doctrines.

In a certain sense, the formal separation in the application of the Representational and Counter-Majoritarian principles to concrete jurisdictional doctrines may be misleadingly artificial. Although it is, I believe, accurate to critique judge-made abstention as inconsistent with the Representational principle and the existing doctrines of justiciability as inconsistent with the Counter-Majoritarian principle, either doctrine might arguably be subjected to attack on grounds of inconsistency with the alternative theoretical precept. On the one hand, because judge-made abstention in cases brought to enforce constitutional rights leads to the abdication of the federal judiciary's intended political role as constitutional check on the majoritarian branches, the doctrine could be deemed inconsistent with the Counter-Majoritarian principle. On the other hand, to the extent that doctrines of justiciability are admitted to be judge-made, rather than the product of an interpretation of the limits imposed by Article III's "case-or-controversy" requirement, they could be attacked as contradictions of the relevant jurisdictional statutes and therefore as inconsistent with the Representational principle.

This cross-application of the two theoretical precepts may be problematic, however. To the extent abstention implies merely deference to the state judiciaries, traditionally deemed adequate forums to protect federal constitutional rights against state encroachment,[1] the doctrine would not contravene the Counter-Majoritarian principle. Although the constitutional adequacy of state forums for this purpose might be seriously questioned,[2] application of the Counter-Majoritarian principle to the abstention doctrines would necessarily implicate the often frustrating debate over state-federal court "parity,"[3] an intellectual and practical quagmire that should be avoided if at all possible. Because abstention fails under the standards of the Representational principle, regardless of the outcome of the "parity" debate, it is probably wise to end the theoretical analysis at that point. Moreover, because the Court has traditionally purported—albeit incorrectly, in my opinion—to ground most of the justiciability doctrines in the Constitution itself, most of the critique of these doctrines from the perspective of the Representational principle is rendered moot. Nevertheless, it is at least worth noting that the two key theoretical precepts are not mutually exclusive in their application.

It should also be noted that the particular jurisdictional doctrines examined in the preceding chapters are merely illustrative of how the intertwining of political theory and jurisdictional doctrine would function. Conceivably, all jurisdictional doctrine could be tested under the two precepts I have gleaned from American political theory, with varying results.

Ironically, if such an analysis were applied to several Supreme Court doctrines in the area of diversity jurisdiction, one might well conclude that the Court has deemed itself more constrained by the text of jurisdictional statutes than it should. For example, it has held that its antiquated doctrines for the aggregation of claims for the purpose of meeting the diversity statute's jurisdictional amount requirement[4] can be altered only by congressional action,[5] despite the clear inconsistency of such forms of measurement with the attitudes of prevailing modern jurisprudence.[6] Yet the relevant statutory language implies neither the Court's initial narrow interpretation nor rigid adherence to whatever interpretation was first adopted. Thus, the Court has attempted to insulate its socially dubious construction of the jurisdictional amount requirement from attack on policy grounds by protecting it with the mantle of democratic legitimacy derived from its characterization as statutory construction. The Court has engaged in a similar practice in its application of the diversity statute to the determination of the citizenship of unincorporated associations.[7] In both cases, the Court has abused the Representational principle, by circumventing the need to justify its statutory "interpretations" on social policy grounds through reliance on an imaginary legislative judgment. Such a practice is rendered even more questionable when contrasted with the Court's cavalier treatment of both statutory language and congressional intent in the area of judge-made abstention[8] and in the creation of substantive federal common law.[9]

The preceding discussion underscores the fact that application of the precepts of American political theory to jurisdictional doctrine is too subtle and complex a task to lend itself to easy or predictable conclusions. Nor does such application lend itself to easy ideological "pigeon-holing." Much of the point of the analysis has been to emphasize how limited judicial authority to fashion jurisdictional doctrine solely on grounds of the judge's preferred social policy or political ideology should actually be. On the other hand, the federal judiciary's unrepresentativeness also dictates the need for a judicial aggressiveness in the exercise of its jurisdiction to interpret and enforce the counter-majoritarian Constitution against the majoritarian branches. The logic of this Counter-Majoritarian principle leads to a substantial reduction in the self-imposed limits on federal judicial power to adjudicate constitutional challenges.

Acceptance of the analytical models of jurisdictional analysis developed in this book would, I believe, go far toward establishing a proper reordering of the judicial role in the shaping of jurisdictional doctrine. It would dictate recognition of the inherent intertwining of federal jurisdiction with the complex network of normative precepts that make up our nation's prevailing constitutional-democratic theory—a recognition that, to this point at least, appears for the most part to have evaded the Supreme Court.

Endnotes

ONE

1. See, e.g., J. Ely, Democracy and Distrust: A Theory of Judicial Review (1980); M. Perry, The Constitution, the Courts, and Human Rights (1982); Michelman, Law's Republic, 97 Yale L. J. 1493 (1988).

2. The leading illustration of this limited genre is A. Bickel, The Least Dangerous Branch: The Supreme Court at the Bar of Politics (1962). However, Professor Bickel's jurisdictional analysis focused only on several jurisdictional doctrines thought to be derived from the "case-or-controversy" requirement of Article III. See discussion infra at 97–100. See also Hart, The Power of Congress to Limit the Jurisdiction of Federal Courts: An Exercise in Dialectic, 66 Harv. L. Rev. 1362 (1953).

3. U.S. Const. Art. III, § 1: "The Judges, both of the supreme and inferior Courts, shall hold their Offices during good Behavior, and shall, at stated Times, receive for their Services, a Compensation, which shall not be diminished during their Continuance in Office."

4. Article V provides that, to become law, a proposed amendment must be approved by two-thirds of both houses of Congress and ratified by three-fourths of the state legislatures or state conventions. Alternatively, the Article provides that Congress shall call a constitutional convention for proposing amendments, on the application of two-thirds of the state legislatures. The ratification procedure is the same.

5. As will be seen in subsequent discussion [infra at 87–89], to a great extent the Supreme Court has purported to ground these doctrines in the so-called "case-or-controversy" requirement of Article III, section 2. As such, they might not, as a technical matter, be properly described as "judge-made." However, it is my contention that neither conceptually nor linguistically are most of these doctrines necessarily derived from the "case-or-controversy" requirement, and they therefore must be deemed judicially created principles. See discussion infra at 90–109.

6. This argument was made by Professor Herbert Wechsler, who contended that judicial review was dictated by the supremacy clause of Article VI. Wechsler, Toward Neutral Principles of Constitutional Law, 73 Harv. L. Rev. 1, 2–4 (1959).

7. Article III, § 2, cl.1, expressly extends the federal judicial power to "all Cases, in Law and Equity, arising under this Constitution. . . . "

8. See, e.g., J. Choper, Judicial Review and the National Political Process (1980); E. Rostow, The Sovereign Prerogative: The Supreme Court and the Quest for Law 149 (1962). See discussion infra at 75–85.

9. 5 U.S. (1 Cranch) 137 (1803). See discussion infra at 90–92.

10. See U.S. Const. Art. III, § 2.

11. Article III, § 1, provides that there shall exist such inferior federal courts "as the Congress may from time to time ordain and establish." This greater power not to create lower federal courts is deemed to give rise to the lesser power to control their jurisdiction. See, e.g., Sheldon v. Sill, 49 U.S.(8 How.) 441 (1850). Article III, section 2, provides to the Supreme Court only a very limited original jurisdiction, and states that the Court's appellate jurisdiction is subject to "such Exceptions, and under such Regulations as the Congress shall make."

12. See M. Redish, Federal Jurisdiction: Tensions in the Allocation of Judicial Power 7–52 (2d ed. 1990).

13. See A. Bickel, supra note 2 at 111–98; Bickel, The Supreme Court, 1960 Term—Foreword: The Passive Virtues, 75 Harv. L. Rev. 40 (1961). See discussion infra at 97–100.

14. See discussion infra at 102–09.

15. Although, as noted previously [discussion supra at 4–5], judicial review appears to be *allowed* by the text of the Constitution, as a general matter, at least, it does not appear to be *compelled* by that text. The one exception are those cases where, in Justice Brandeis's words, "the constitutional requirement of due process is a constitutional requirement of judicial process." Crowell v. Benson, 285 U.S. 22, 87 (1932) (Brandeis, J., dissenting.)

16. This result would occur where Congress has directed the exercise of federal jurisdiction in order to enforce a substantive statutory program, but, without any congressional authorization, the federal courts decline to exercise their jurisdiction in such cases. See chapter 4, infra at 39–74.

17. R. Posner, The Federal Courts: Crisis and Reform 210 (1985).

TWO

1. Although the point should hardly need documentation, ample support for this proposition may be found in the historical and political literature. Tocqueville, for example, wrote that, "[w]herever the political laws of the United States are to be discussed, it is with the doctrine of the sovereignty of the people that we must begin." A. De Tocqueville, Democracy in America 55 (R. Heffner ed. 1956). He continued:

> In America, the principle of the sovereignty of the people is not either barren or concealed, as it is with some other nations; it is recognized by the customs and proclaimed by the laws; it spreads freely, and arrives without impediment at its most remote consequences. . . .
>
> At the present day, the principle of the sovereignty of the people has acquired, in the United States, all the practical development which the imagination can conceive. . . . Sometimes, the laws are made by the people in a body, as at Athens; and sometimes its representatives, chosen by universal suffrage, transact business in its name, and under its immediate supervision.
>
> Id. at 56–57.

The origins of representational self-determination as an underlying political value extend back to the pre-Revolution period. According to Gordon Wood, "[t]he people were the undisputed, ubiquitous source that was appealed to by both the advocates and the opponents of independence." G. Wood, The Creation of the American Republic, 1776–1787 330 (1969). As Madison wrote in Federalist No. 47, "the people are the only legitimate foundation of power. . . ."

That this fundamental underlying normative principle remains in force today cannot be doubted. As Michael Perry has written, "[w]e in the United States are philosophically committed to the political principle that governmental policymaking—by which I mean simply decisions as to which values among competing values shall prevail, and as to how those values shall be implemented—ought to be subject to control by persons accountable to the electorate." M. Perry, The Constitution, the Courts, and Human Rights 9 (1982) (footnotes omitted).

2. See discussion supra at 4.

3. U.S. Const. Amend. XIV, § 1, cl. 4.

4. See generally J. Ely, Democracy and Distrust: A Theory of Judicial Review (1980).

5. See, e.g., M. Perry, supra note 1, at 85.

6. See J. Pennock, Democratic Political Theory 310 (1979): "Elections are thought to constitute the great sanction for assuring representative behavior, by showing what the voters consider to be their interests by giving them the incentive to pursue those objectives." See also H. Mayo, An Introduction to Democratic Theory 103 (1960): "[E]verything necessary to [democratic] theory may be put in terms of (a) legislators (or decision-makers) who are (b) legitimated or authorized to enact public policies, and who are (c) subject or responsible to popular control at free election."

7. A. Meiklejohn, Political Freedom 9 (1960).

8. Professor Pennock refers to totalitarian theory as "a vulgarized form of collectivist theory," under which "the worth and meaning of the individual [is derived] from the political whole of which he is a part. . . ." Pennock, supra note 6, at 108.

9. See Sunstein, Beyond the Republican Revival, 97 Yale L.J. 1539 (1988). Professor Sunstein, who urges "an approach [to statutory construction] that repudiates the idea that the only role of the courts is to ascertain legislative intent in the particular case" [id. at 1582], has argued that "[p]ublic choice theory has shown that cycling problems, strategic and manipulative behavior, sheer chance, and other factors prevent majoritarianism from providing an accurate aggregation of preferences." Id. at 1545 (footnote omitted).

10. See, e.g., Symposium on the Theory of Public Choice, 74 Va. L. Rev. 167 (1988).

11. Sunstein, Interest Groups in American Public Law, 38 Stan. L. Rev. 29, 29 (1985).

12. Id. (footnote omitted).

13. Id.

14. Mikva, Foreword, 74 Va. L. Rev. 167 (1988). See generally Kelman, "Public Choice" and Public Spirit, 87 Pub. Interest 80 (1987).

15. Eskridge, Politics without Romance: Implications of Public Choice Theory for Statutory Interpretation, 74 Va. L. Rev. 275, 277 (1988).

16. Kelman, On Democracy-Bashing: A Skeptical Look at the Theoretical and "Empirical" Practice of the Public Choice Movement, 74 Va. L. Rev. 199, 201–02 (1988).

17. Mikva, supra note 14, at 169; see also Farber & Frickey, The Jurisprudence of Public Choice, 65 Tex. L. Rev. 873, 883–906 (1987).

18. To my knowledge, the term "neo-republican" has never been used by other scholars. I have chosen the term, in order to underscore the significant differences between the version of civic republicanism advocated by modern scholars and that developed in classical republican thought. See discussion infra at 14–15.

19. There exists some legitimate question concerning the judiciary's ability to discern exactly how often statutes actually suffer from this problem. See Posner, Economics, Politics, and the Reading of Statutes and the Constitution, 49 U. Chi. L. Rev. 263, 272–73 (1982), suggesting that

> [c]ourts do not have the research tools that they would need to discover the motives behind legislation. Nor can they just presume the presence of an interest group somewhere behind the scenes. Many statutes really are enacted in the public interest; in those statutes, the actual and the ostensible purposes coincide. Moreover, even where it is obvious that a particular statute was procured by some particular interest group . . . it will not be clear, at least without an inquiry that is beyond the judicial competence to undertake, how completely the group prevailed upon Congress to do its will. The statute as ultimately enacted may represent a compromise with other groups; if so, the "real" legislative purpose may be unclear.

20. See, e.g., Macey, Promoting Public Regarding Legislation Through Statutory Interpretation: An Interest Group Model, 86 Colum. L. Rev. 223, 223 (1986): "Too often the [legislative] process seems to serve only the purely private interests of special interest groups at the expense of the broader public interest it was ostensibly designed to serve." See also Eskridge, supra note 15, at 277 ("Public choice theory indicates that the legislature will produce too few laws that serve truly public ends, and too many laws that serve private ends"); Farber & Frickey, supra note 17, at 424 ("[public choice] scholarship suggests that congressional enactments are not motivated by conceptions of the public interest; rather, federal statutes might reflect private interest deals, re-election posturing, or arbitrary outcomes").

21. See discussion supra at 11.

22. For example, Justice Black, speaking for the Court in Eastern Railroad Presidents Conference v. Noerr Motor Freight, Inc., 365 U.S. 127 (1961), in holding that the Sherman Act does not preclude collective action to obtain legislation designed to harm competitors, stated: "It is neither unusual nor illegal for people to seek action on laws in the hope that they may bring about an advantage to themselves and a disadvantage to their competitors." Id. at 139. Learned Hand suggested that statutes "should be construed, not as theorems of Euclid, but with some imagination of the purposes which lie behind them." Lehigh Valley Coal Co. v. Yensavage, 218 F. 547, 553 (2d. Cir. 1914). Finally, Justice Holmes wrote that "it is no sufficient condemnation of legislation that it favors one class at the expense of another; for much or all legislation does that. . . . " O. W. Holmes, Herbert Spencer: Legislation and Empiricism, in Justice Oliver Wendell Homes: His Book Notices and Uncol-

lected Letters and Papers 104, 107–09 (H. Shriver ed. 1936). These sources were cited in Posner, supra note 19, at 267–68.

23. See sources cited in note 25, infra.

24. See, e.g., J. Pocock, The Machiavellian Moment: Florentine Republican Thought and the Atlantic Republican Tradition (1975); G. Wood, supra note 1.

25. See, e.g., Fallon, What Is Republicanism, and Is It Worth Reviving?, 102 Harv. L. Rev. 1695 (1989); Sherry, Civic Virtue and the Feminine Voice in Constitutional Adjudication, 72 Va. L. Rev. 543 (1983); Sunstein, supra note 11; Symposium, The Republican Civic Tradition, 97 Yale L.J. 1493 (1988).

26. As will be seen, this "modification" has been so extensive as to make the classical theory all but unrecognizable. See discussion infra at 14–15.

27. Sunstein, supra note 9, at 1541. See also id. at 1550. In this sense, neo-republicanism resembles classical theory, which posited "that there exists an objective public good apart from individual goods...." Fallon, supra note 25, at 1698 (footnote omitted).

28. Sunstein, supra note 9, at 1541.

29. "The emphasis on deliberation in republican thought is closely allied with the republican beliefs that the motivating force of political behavior should not be self-interest, narrowly defined, and that civic virtue should play a role in political life." Id. at 1550.

30. Id. at 1541. See also Sunstein, supra note 11, at 31–32, suggesting that the theory of civic republicanism posits that

> through discussion people can, in their capacities as citizens, escape private interests and engage in pursuit of the public good.... [T]his conception reflects a belief that debate and discussion help to reveal that some values are superior to others. Denying that decisions about values are merely matters of taste, the republican view assumes that "practical reason" can be used to settle social issues.

31. See discussion supra at 11.

32. See U.S. Const. Art. III, section 1, guaranteeing federal judges life tenure during good behavior and prohibiting reduction in their salaries.

33. Sunstein, supra note 11, at 31–32.

34. J. Mansbridge, Beyond Adversary Democracy 16 (1983).

35. Id. at 16–17.

36. Bachrach, Interest, Participation, and Democratic Theory, in Participation in Politics: NOMOS XVI, at 41 (J. Pennock & J. Chapman eds. 1975).

37. Sunstein, supra note 9, at 1540.

38. Id.

39. Heavily relied upon as support for the role of "civic republicanism" is Madison's Federalist No. 10. See, e.g., G. Stone, M. Seidman, C. Sunstein & M. Tushnet, Constitutional Law 7–17 (1986). It is, of course, true that there Madison expressed significant concern over the dangers caused by factions. However, it is initially worth noting that, contrary to suggestion [id. at 16], his concern was not limited to factions motivated solely by narrow self-interest. Rather, he defined "faction" as "a number of citizens, whether amounting to a majority or minority of the whole, who are visited and actuated by some common impulse of passion, or of interest, adverse to the rights of other citizens, or to the permanent and aggregate interests of the community." Federalist No. 10, at 130 (Madison) (B. Wright ed.

1961). See D. Epstein, The Political Theory of the Federalist 68 (1984). According to this definition, then, a "faction" could as easily be motivated by an ideological conception of the public good (for example, the right-to-life or civil rights movements) as by selfish economic concerns.

More important to the modern debate about the interaction of "civic republicanism" and the judicial role is Madison's suggestion for how the problem of faction should be handled. As to the suggestion that it be controlled "by destroying the liberty which is essential to its existence," he replied that such a remedy "was worse than the disease." *Id.* at 130. In his words, "it could not be a less folly to abolish liberty, which is essential to political life, because it nourishes faction than it would be to wish the annihilation of air, which is essential to animal life, because it imparts to fire its destructive agency." Id. See also Federalist No. 51, where Madison rejected the approach of "creating a will in the community independent of the majority . . . ," finding it to be "a precarious security, because a power independent of the society may as well espouse the unjust views of the major, as the rightful interests of the minor party. . . . " Id. at 358. Thus, Madison was not of the opinion that the unrepresentative judiciary should possess power effectively to veto acts of Congress deemed to be the product of faction. Instead, he believed the governmental structure provided for in the Constitution would be adequate to deal with the problem—much the same structure under which modern federal legislation is enacted. See J. Mansbridge, supra note 34, at 16–17 (footnote omitted):

> Although James Madison believed in the existence of a "public good" and a "true interest of [the] country," he had adopted enough of the adversary logic to conclude that no government could eliminate the "causes of faction"—self-love and self-interest combined with differing economic circumstances. The task he set the framers of the Constitution was not the abolition of self-interested behavior but the "regulation of the various and interfering interests" in a way that actually "involves the spirit of party and faction in the necessary and ordinary operations of the government."

Indeed, in Federalist No. 57, Madison expressed the view that "[t]he most effectual [means of avoiding "sacrifice of the many to the aggrandizement of the few"] is such a limitation of the term of appointments as will maintain a proper responsibility to the people." The Federalist Papers, supra at 358. It was, then, accountability to the electorate, not exercise of ultimate political authority by an unrepresentative group of officials, that would best avoid the dangers of faction. Today, as Professor Mansbridge concludes, "[b]ecause interests often conflict in the modern nation-state, a fundamentally adversary system of electoral representation based on competing interests, equally weighted votes, and majority rule is probably the least dangerous method of managing these conflicting interests." J. Mansbridge, supra note 34, at 18. See also D. Truman, The Governmental Process 168 (1951), arguing that "the fact that memberships in organized and potential groups overlap in the long run imposes restraints and conformities on interest groups on pain of dissolution or of failure. . . . If [a society] maintains its stability, however, it may do so in large measure because of the fact of multiple memberships."

40. See, e,g., J. Mansbridge, supra note 34, at 16 (footnote omitted):

> Over the generations, the idea gradually gained acceptance that a democracy should weigh and come to terms with conflicting selfish interests rather than trying to reconcile them or to make them subordinate to a larger common good. John Locke,

> in the treatise that would inspire the framers of the American Constitution, borrowed more from Hobbes in this respect than he dared admit. In spite of the crucial role he sometimes gives to common interest, Locke has men unite in political society chiefly in order to protect their property against others, and he defends majority rule on the grounds that it is required by the "contrariety of interests, which unavoidably happen in all collections of men."
>
> By the next century, the framers of the American Constitution explicitly espoused a philosophy of adversary democracy built on self-interest.

Although certain modern historians have argued that republicanism did play a dominant role [see, e.g., J. Pocock, supra note 24; G. Wood, supra note 1], others have seriously questioned this assertion. Some have attacked the notion that the values of civic republicanism played any significant role at all. See, e.g., Diggins, Comrades and Citizens: New Mythologies in American Historiography, 90 Am. Hist. Rev. 614, 631 (1985), arguing that

> [a]lthough the classical idea of political virtue has become an important influence in modern historical scholarship, it had no central importance in four of the most significant documents of the revolutionary and constitutional eras: Paine's Common Sense, Jefferson's Declaration of Independence, Hamilton, Jay and Madison's Federalist, and John Adams' A Defense of the Constitutions of the United States of America.

See also Appleby, The Social Origins of American Revolutionary Ideology, 64 J. Am. Hist. 935, 951 (1977–78), contending that "[p]articularly astute observers of the American scene . . . early conceded the dominance of self-interest."

It should be noted that Professor Sunstein eventually appears to retreat somewhat from his initial assertion that civic republicanism played "a central role in the framing period" [Sunstein, supra note 9, at 1540], later asserting only that "elements of both pluralist and republican thought played a role during the period of the constitutional framing." Id. at 1558.

41. These include primarily the bicameralism and presentment requirements, U.S. Const. Art. I, sections 1, 7. It is true that the framers did insert several other republican-like provisions in the body of the Constitution, such as the electoral college and the state legislative selection of senators. However, like the bicameralism and presentment requirements, these provisions of course do not in any way constitute a vesting of a broad, discretionary veto power in the judiciary, but rather merely represent additional structural requirements.

42. See Immigration & Naturalization Service v. Chadha, 462 U.S. 919 (1983) (relying on bicameralism and presentment requirements to invalidate one-house veto).

43. See, e.g., Michelman, Law's Republic, 97 Yale L.J. 1493, 1495 (1988), acknowledging that his version of "[r]epublican constitutionalism . . . involves a kind of normative tinkering." See also Sunstein, supra note 9, at 1539: "For modern republicans, the task is not simply one of excavation. History does not supply conceptions of political life that can be applied mechanically to current problems."

44. Epstein, Modern Republicanism—Or the Flight From Substance, 97 Yale L.J. 1633, 1635 (1988). According to Professor Fallon:

> "[T]he paradigm of classical republicanism" seems a poor candidate for contemporary adoption. Too many of its central assumptions—that human nature has a uniform

> purpose or telos that can be fulfilled only through participation in political activity, that there exists an objective public good apart from individual goods, and that this objective good can be discovered through virtuous political debate—are highly uncongenial to modern ontology and epistemology.

Fallon, supra note 25, at 1698 (footnotes omitted).

Professor Fallon is no doubt correct in his assertion that classical republican philosophy is inconsistent with modern perceptions and political realities. According to Gordon Wood, "[w]hat made . . . the republican emphasis on the collective welfare of the people comprehensible was the assumption that the people, especially when set against their rulers, were a homogeneous body whose 'interests when candidly considered are one.' Since everyone in the community was linked organically to everyone else, what was good for the whole community was ultimately good for all the parts." G. Wood, supra note 1, at 57–58. Whether or not this assumption was empirically accurate at the time of the Constitution's framing, it would be absurd to suggest that it is accurate today. Respected modern political scientists have expressed substantial doubt that there can be, in our society at the national level, an ascertainable "common good" or unified "public interest." See, e.g., J. Mansbridge, supra note 34, at 17; D. Truman, supra note 39, at 51; R. MacIver, The Web of Government 416 (1947). See generally J. Schumpeter, Capitalism, Socialism, and Democracy (1962). Nevertheless, it does appear that modern neo-republican philosophy continues to adhere to at least the last two points of classical theory mentioned by Professor Fallon. See discussion supra at 13.

45. See Epstein, supra note 44, at 1636: "The transformation of classical to modern republicanism that both Michelman and Sunstein seek is not some refinement of classical doctrine. It is in large measure a new theory which borrows selectively, and seductively, from the past." See also Powell, Reviving Republicanism, 97 Yale L.J. 1703, 1707 (1988): "Professor Sunstein does not offer us historical republicanism and commend its virtues to us; he offers us a contemporary political theory and notes that at times the founders said similar things." Professor Powell asserts that "Professor Sunstein identifies only a quite attenuated relationship between his ideas and specific schools of thought in the founding era." Id. at 1711.

Neo-republicans openly reject classical republicanism's "legacy of excluding from the political community all those whose voices would—by reason of supposed defects of understanding, foreignness of outlook, subservience of position, or corruption of interest—threaten disruption of a community's normative unity. . . ." Michelman, supra note 43, at 1495. Professor Sunstein acknowledges that "[r]epublican thought has traditionally been allied with exclusionary practices" and that he is "invok[ing] republicanism as a basis for rejecting those same practices," Sunstein, supra note 9, at 1581. But see Kerber, Making Republicanism Useful, 97 Yale L.J. 1663, 1665 (1988) (emphasis in original):

> Both Sunstein and Michelman disarmingly acknowledge that they want to retrieve only some aspects of classical republicanism. The classical republican tradition assumed that deliberation was possible only in small and exclusive communities; the absence of the dependent classes—defined by race, gender, and property—was *essential* to the republican view of the world, not an easily correctable accident.

46. Sunstein, supra note 9, at 1556.

47. Cf. Macey, The Missing Element in the Republican Revival, 97 Yale L.J. 1673, 1675 (1988) (footnote omitted), noting that, though

> [e]lements of republican thought did play a role in the framing period . . . the very elements of republicanism that Sunstein identifies invariably have been jettisoned as the country has grown and become more diverse and less elitist. Senators are not chosen by state legislators, and the electoral college . . . has assumed a far more passive role than was envisioned by those who wanted it to become a fully deliberative body.
>
> These concrete examples of the modern rejection of the framers' republican aspirations do not begin to scratch the surface. . . . Through a gradual process of political evolution and adaptation, we have come to accept and even value diversity and dissent, while we no longer see such republican "virtues" as homogeneity and cooperation as particularly valuable goals to which to aspire.

48. See sources cited in notes 1, 6, 7, supra.

49. See note 39, supra.

50. See, e.g., C. MacPherson, The Life and Times of Liberal Democracy 51 (1977); Walker, A Critique of the Elitist Theory of Democracy, 60 Am. Pol. Sci. Rev. 285 288 (1966).

51. See Macey, supra note 47, at 1676–77 (footnote omitted): "Sunstein believes that deliberation will foster virtue and wisdom among our leaders, who therefore will act in our best interests, even when we are unable to discern properly for ourselves what those interests are."

52. According to Professors Farber and Frickey, "[t]o limit undue influence by special interest groups and foster legislative deliberation, several recent commentators have advocated more stringent judicial review of statutes. The purpose of such review would be to ensure that legislation reflects public values, rather than simply producing benefits for special interest groups." Farber & Frickey, supra note 17, at 908.

53. Examples include stronger legislative ethics legislation and reform of campaign spending laws, though the latter may implicate First Amendment problems. See, e.g., Buckley v. Valeo, 424 U.S. 1 (1976).

54. See, e.g., W. Riker, Liberalism vs. Populism: A Confrontation between the Theory of Democracy and the Theory of Public Choice (1982); Reiker & Weingast, Constitutional Regulation of Legislative Choice: The Political Consequences of Judicial Deference to Legislatures, 74 Va. L. Rev. 373 (1988). Cf. Sunstein, supra note 9, at 1545–46 (footnotes omitted): "[A]ccurate aggregation of preferences through politics is unlikely to be accomplished in light of the conundrums in developing a social welfare function. . . . In any representative democracy, there is simply too much slippage between legislative outcomes and constituent desires."

55. According to political scientist Robert Dahl, A Preface to Democratic Theory 131–32 (1956):

> elections are a crucial device for controlling leaders and . . . they are quite ineffective as indicators of majority preference. These statements are really not in contradiction. A good deal of traditional democratic theory leads us to expect more from national elections than they can possibly provide. We expect elections to reveal the "will" or the preferences of a majority on a set of issues. This is one thing elections rarely do, except in an almost trivial fashion. Despite this limitation the election process is one of two fundamental methods of social control which, operating together, make gov-

> ernmental leaders so responsive to non-leaders that the distinction between democracy and dictatorship still makes sense.... Elections and political competition do not make for government by majorities in any very significant way, but they vastly increase the size, number, and variety of minorities whose preferences must be taken into account by leaders in making policy choices.

See also A. Bickel, The Least Dangerous Branch: The Supreme Court at the Bar of Politics 19 (1962): "[I]f the control is exercised by 'groups of various types and sizes, all seeking in various ways to advance their goals,' so that we have 'minorities rule' rather than majority rule, it remains true nevertheless that only those minorities rule which can command the votes of a majority of individuals in the electorate."

56. The delegation doctrinc, prohibiting the delegation of congressional power to the executive branch which "ensures to the extent consistent with orderly government administration that important choices of social policy are made by Congress, the branch of our government most responsive to the popular will," [Industrial Union Dep't v. American Petroleum Inst., 448 U.S. 607 (1980) (Rehnquist, J., concurring)] was developed primarily in a series of cases during the New Deal. See, e.g., Schechter Poultry Corp. v. United States, 295 U.S. 495 (1935); Pancanco Refining Co. v. Ryan, 293 U.S. 388 (1935). Subsequent decisions approved broad delegations of legislative power. See, e.g., Yakus v. United States, 321 U.S. 414 (1944). But, more recently, issues of delegation have occasionally given the Court greater pause. See, e.g., National Cable Television Ass'n v. United States, 415 U.S. 336 (1974).

57. See note 56, supra.

58. See note 39, supra.

59. Id.

60. U.S. Const. Art. III, section 1.

61. U.S. Const. Art. III, section 2.

62. As to congressional power to control lower federal court jurisdiction, see, e.g., Clinton, A Mandatory View of Federal Court Jurisdiction: A Guided Quest for the Original Understanding of Article III, 132 U. Pa. L. Rev. 741 (1984); Sager, The Supreme Court 1980 Term, Foreword: Constitutional Limitations on Congress' Authority to Regulate the Jurisdiction of the Federal Courts, 95 Harv. L. Rev. 17 (1981); Redish, Constitutional Limitations on Congressional Power to Control Federal Jurisdiction: A Reaction to Professor Sager, 77 Nw. U. L. Rev. 143 (1982). As to Supreme Court jurisdiction, see, e.g., Van Alstyne, A Critical Guide to Ex Parte McCardle, 15 Ariz. L. Rev. 229 (1973); Rice, Congress and the Supreme Court's Jurisdiction, 27 Vill. L. Rev. 959 (1982); Ratner, Congressional Power over the Appellate Jurisdiction of the Supreme Court, 109 U. Pa. L. Rev. 157 (1960); Redish, Congressional Power to Limit Supreme Court Appellate Jurisdiction Under the Exceptions Clause: An Internal and External Examination, 27 Vill. L. Rev. 900 (1982).

63. One example is the due process clause. U.S. Const. Amend. V. See Lockerty v. Phillips, 319 U.S. 182 (1943).

64. The Supreme Court has long recognized this point in requiring state courts to exercise their jurisdiction to enforce federal rights. Testa v. Katt, 330 U.S. 386 (1947).

65. See, e.g., Sheldon v. Sill, 49 U.S. (8 How.) 441 (1850).

66. See Chapters 3 and 4, infra.

67. Fallon, The Ideologies of Federal Courts Law, 74 Va. L. Rev. 1141, 1143 (1988).

68. Id. at 1144.

69. "[T]he Federalist and Nationalist models ought to be abandoned as rhetorical structures.... [E]ach is excessively one-sided in its approach to complex questions. Needed are structures of thought and rhetoric located between the Nationalist and Federalist poles." Id. at 1151.

70.

> Implicit in my prescription of a between-the-poles approach to questions of judicial federalism is the assumption that the federal courts ... have and ought to have a large responsibility for the substance and health of judicial federalism.... I wholly agree that constitutional and statutory interpretation are precisely that—interpretation, not law-making.... But our interpretive tradition ... is not self-defining. And I do, more than some, assume that legal interpreters frequently have not only the power but also the duty to choose between plausible outcomes on the basis of normative attractiveness.... [N]o statutory or constitutional framer could ever foresee all of the problems, or the changed future circumstances, that time and experience inevitably generate.... Our system not only of interpretation but of statutory and constitutional law-making presupposes flexibility in the courts to accommodate language reflecting core historical purposes to the perceived needs of changing interpretive contexts.
>
> Id. at 1249–50.

(footnotes omitted).

71. Actually, in those instances in which Congress has not expressed a contrary view, I find the logic of the "Nationalist" model to be clearly more persuasive. See, e.g., M. Redish, Federal Jurisdiction: Tensions in the Allocation of Judicial Power 1–4 (2d ed. 1990); Redish, Judicial Parity, Litigant Choice, and Democratic Theory: A Comment on Federal Jurisdiction and Constitutional Rights, 36 U.C.L.A. L. Rev. 329, 331–38 (1988).

72. See discussion infra at 19–27.

73. See discussion supra at 9–10.

74. See discussion supra at 9–10.

75. Article I of the Constitution expressly vests the legislative power in Congress. U.S. Const. Art. I, § 1.

76. Although most of that attention has come from either the legal "deconstructionist" literature [see, e.g., Levinson, Law as Literature, 60 Tex. L. Rev. 373 (1982)] or the so-called "public choice" literature [see generally Symposium on the theory of Public Choice, 74 Va. L. Rev. 167 (1988)], it has also spilled over into federal courts scholarship. See Fallon, supra note 66, at 1248–51. See also Weinberg, Federal Common Law, 83 Nw. U. L. Rev. 846–47 (1989).

77. See discussion infra at 20–25.

78. See, e.g., S. Fish, Is There a Text in This Class? (1980); Levinson, supra note 76.

79. See id.

80. See, e.g., Hotchkiss v. National City Bank, 200 F.2d 287, 297 (S.D.N.Y. 1911) (L. Hand, J.) ("If it were proven by twenty bishops that either party, when he used the words, intended something else than the usual meaning which the law im-

poses upon them, he would still be held [to the reasonable meaning of the words], unless there was mutual mistake....")

81. For a more complete examination of this point, see Redish & Drizin, Constitutional Federalism and Judicial Review: The Role of Textual Analysis, 62 N.Y.U. L. Rev. 1, 23–28 (1987).

82. See discussion infra at 36–37.

83. According to Farber & Frickey, Legislative Intent and Public Choice, 74 Va. L. Rev. 423, 423–24 (1988):

> Justice Scalia, joined to some extent by Judge Frank Easterbrook, would ... jettison the whole idea of legislative intent as a guide to interpretation.
>
> The ultimate issue raised by these judges is the extent to which legislation reflects a coherent congressional view of the public interest.

84. See id. See also Macey, Promoting Public-Regarding Legislation Through Statutory Interpretation: An Interest Group Model, 86 Colum. L. Rev. 223 (1986); Eskridge, Politics Without Romance: Implications of Public Choice Theory for Statutory Interpretation, 74 Va. L. Rev. 275, 277 (1988) ("If public choice theory is correct, a court that sought to enforce the original 'deal' embodied in a statute could only contribute to the [Madisonian] nightmare.")

85. See sources cited in note 84, supra.

86. "Thus, when Judge Easterbrook argues that an interpreting court should enforce the bargain actually entered into by the legislature [see Easterbrook, The Supreme Court, 1983 Term—Foreword: The Court and the Economic System, 98 Harv. L. Rev. 4 (1988)], he is really suggesting that a good judge is one who interprets the law in the way the legislature *really meant* for it to be interpreted, not in the way that the legislature *says* that it is to be interpreted." Macey, supra note 84, at 235 (footnote omitted) (emphasis in original). For the purpose of the limited discussion in the text, I need take no position on the validity of Easterbrook's suggestion.

87. Perhaps the most extreme in this regard is Guido Calabresi, who urges that the judiciary openly exercise the authority to overrule statutes that have become obsolete—that do not fit within the existing "legal topography." G. Calabresi, A Common Law for the Age of Statutes (1982). Somewhat less extreme is William Eskridge, who urges use of a "dynamic" approach to statutory interpretation: Because of the passage of time, a statute may no longer fit its original purpose. However, unlike Calabresi, Eskridge believes that the more explicit the statutory language and legislative history, the more difficult it should be for a court to modify a statute. See generally Eskridge, Dynamic Statutory Interpretation, 135 U. Pa. L.Rev. 1479 (1987).

88. See generally R. Davidson & W. Oleszek, Congress and Its Members 263–85 (2d ed. 1985); W. Oleszek, Congressional Procedures and the Policy Process (2d ed. 1984).

89. See sources cited in note 87, supra.

90. See discussion supra at 9–10.

91. 462 U.S. 919 (1983).

92. U.S. Const. Art. I, § 7, cl. 2.

93. As to the presentment requirement, Hamilton wrote in Federalist No. 73 that "[i]t establishes a check upon the legislative body, calculated to guard the com-

munity against the effects of faction, precipitancy, or of any impulse unfriendly to the public good which may happen to influence a majority of that body. . . . " Federalist No. 73 (Hamilton), at 469 (B. Wright ed. 1961). As to the bicameralism requirement, the Court in *Chadha* wrote that "[t]he division of the Congress into two distinctive bodies assures that the legislative power would be exercised only after opportunity for full study and debate in separate settings." 462 U.S. at 951.

94. The classic illustration is the question of whether an ordinance rendering criminal bloodletting in the street, obviously intended to deter and punish violence, should be applied to a doctor who, in an emergency situation, bleeds a patient found in the street in order to save him. See H. Hart & A. Sacks, The Legal Process: Basic Problems in the Making and Application of Law 1202 (Tent. ed. 1958).

95. See discussion supra at 22–23.

96. See discussion supra at 10–17.

97. See, e.g., Michelman, supra note 43; Sunstein, supra note 9, at 1576–81.

98. See, e.g., Eskridge, Public Values in Statutory Interpretation, 137 U. Pa. L. Rev. 1007, 1066 (1989), suggesting that "[w]hile public values can readily be defended in those close cases where the text and legislative history are ambiguous, their invocation to trump a clear text and supportive legislative history would be inconsistent with legislative supremacy."

99. See, e.g., Sunstein, supra note 9 at 1581–89, suggesting several canons of construction that are openly designed to superimpose republican values on legislation, even where it is understood that the legislature did not so intend. See also Mashaw, As If Republican Interpretation, 97 Yale L.J. 1685, 1690 (1988), suggesting that under Sunstein's approach to statutory construction "[t]he role of judicial interpretation . . . seems to be a form of republican monitoring. Judicial interpretation and judicial review are largely congruent if not identical. In both, courts police legislative activity to avoid anti-republican results."

In his more recent work, Sunstein—though conceding that "the statutory text is the foundation for interpretation"—argues that "structure, purpose, intent, history and 'reasonableness' all play legitimate roles." Sunstein, Interpreting Statutes in the Regulatory State, 103 Harv. L. Rev. 405, 503 (1989). He expressly rejects such "generally accepted understandings about statutory construction" as the postulates that "courts must always adhere to the original meaning of the statute, or the original intent of the enacting legislature," that "courts are or can be mere agents of the Congress," and that "statutory meaning is equivalent to legislative intent." Id. at 412.

100. See Sunstein, supra note 9, at 1560: "Madisonian republicanism calls for substantial autonomy on the part of representatives." See also Fitts, Look Before You Leap: Some Cautionary Notes on Civic Republicanism, 97 Yale L. J. 165 (1988) (footnote omitted), noting that under Sunstein's theory, "representatives' relative insulation from 'pressure' by their constituents helps free them to deliberate in the public interest."

101. See Macey, supra note 47, at 1677, n. 16 (emphasis in original): "One must wonder . . . why Sunstein is so certain that deliberation will lead to *virtue*. Deliberation may lead to *rationality*, but if the deliberators do not begin their conclaves with a predisposition towards virtue, it is not obvious why the discussion necessarily will lead them in this direction."

102. See discussion supra at 13.
103. See discussion supra at 13–14.
104. See discussion supra at 20–25.
105. See discussion supra at 18–19.
106. See discussion supra at 20–22.
107. See discussion supra at 24.
108. As will be seen, this analysis logically leads to the conclusion that so-called implied statutory rights of action are in fact conceptually more properly classified as exercises in common lawmaking power, rather than statutory interpretation. See discussion infra at 39.
109. An example is the issue of the application of the doctrines of collateral estoppel and res judicata to a suit to enforce federal civil rights pursuant to 42 U.S.C. § 1983. See Allen v. McCurry, 449 U.S. 90 (1980); discussion infra at 38.

THREE

1. 304 U.S. 64 (1938).
2. See, e.g., West Virginia v. United States, 479 U.S. 305 (1987) (federal "proprietary" interests); Illinois v. City of Milwaukee, 406 U.S. 91 (1972) (control of interstate pollution); Banco Nacional de Cuba v. Sabbatino, 376 U.S. 398 (1964) (private party commercial case involving foreign relations implications); Kossick v. United Fruit Co., 365 U.S. 731 (1961) (admiralty case); Hinderlider v. La Plata River & Cherry Creek Ditch Co., 304 U.S. 92 (1938) (interstate disputes); see also Redish, Judicial Parity, Litigant Choice, and Democratic Theory: A Comment on Federal Jurisdiction and Constitutional Rights, 36 UCLA L. Rev. 329, 342–67 (1988) (judge-made law of abstention) [hereinafter Redish, A Comment on Federal Jurisdiction]; Redish, Abstention, Separation of Powers, and the Limits of the Judicial Function, 94 Yale L. J. 71 (1984) (same).

With limited exception (see discussion infra at 38–39; 42–44), this chapter will not focus on specific doctrinal elements of federal common law. Its emphasis, rather, is on the place of federal common law as a generic doctrine within the American political and constitutional framework. For a discussion of the specific legal doctrines, see M. Redish, Federal Jurisdiction: Tensions in the Allocation of Judicial Power 119–48 (2d ed. 1990) [hereinafter M. Redish, Federal Jurisdiction: Tensions].

3. See discussion supra at 3–28.
4. See, e.g., Friendly, In Praise of *Erie*—and the New Federal Common Law, 39 N.Y.U. L. Rev. 383 (1964).
5. See, e.g., Field, Sources of Law: The Scope of Federal Common Law, 99 Harv. L. Rev. 881 (1986); see discussion infra at 36–37.
6. See, e.g., Merrill, The Common Law Powers of Federal Courts, 52 U. Chi. L. Rev. 1 (1985); see discussion infra at 40.
7. In Erie R. Co. v. Tompkins, 304 U.S. 64 (1938), Justice Brandeis, speaking for the Court, concluded that it is unconstitutional for the federal courts to supplant all state common law because "Congress has no power to declare substantive rules of common law applicable to a State. . . . [a]nd no clause in the Constitution purports

to confer such a power upon the federal courts." Id. at 78. However, in light of the Supreme Court's extremely broad construction of federal constitutional power, see Garcia v. San Antonio Metro. Transit Auth., 469 U.S. 528 (1985), it might be argued that today *Erie*'s constitutional component is no longer good law. Nevertheless, on a separation-of-powers level, judicial law creation—at least on a sub-constitutional level—might be thought to violate Article I's vesting of "[a]ll legislative power" in Congress. U.S. Const. Art. I, § 1.

8. Federal Judiciary Act of September 24, 1789, § 34.

9. 28 U.S.C. 1652. The only textual difference between the Act's current version and its original 1789 form is that the Act now extends to "civil actions," rather than merely to "trials at common law." Thus, the explicit reach of the Act has been extended since its original passage.

10. See discussion infra at 35.

11. See discussion infra at 35.

12. To the extent what is today generally referred to as "federal common law" could actually be legitimately described as "statutory interpretation," it may be properly deemed not to violate the dictates of the Rules of Decision Act. As will be seen, however, relatively little current "federal common law" can legitimately be so viewed. See infra at 38.

13. It has been argued that, in cases in which there was no applicable state statute or "local" law,

> a number of different kinds of law could provide the relevant rules for decision. The general common law was by far the most important of these nonlocal and nonfederal laws.... [T]he fact that it was not mentioned [in the original version of the Rules of Decision Act] probably suggests ... that its applicability was so obvious as to go without saying.

Fletcher, The General Common Law and Section 34 of the Judiciary Act of 1789: The Example of Marine Insurance, 97 Harv. L. Rev. 1513, 1517 (1984). If Professor Fletcher is correct, then, at least as a matter of statutory construction, Justice Story in Swift v. Tyson, 41 U.S. (16 Pet.) 1 (1842), may have been more accurate than Justice Brandeis in *Erie*. But, although resolution of the issue raised by Professor Fletcher might have an impact on the practical effect of my critique of modern substantive federal common law, its theoretical impact would be negligible.

Neither Justice Story nor Professor Fletcher denied that the Rules of Decision Act was intended to prohibit federal common law in the face of an applicable state statute or "local" common law doctrine. Yet modern substantive federal common law will apply, regardless of the existence of state statutes or "local" common law. Thus, if Professor Fletcher's historical contention were accepted—a point on which I presently take no position—it would simply mean that my critique of substantive current substantive federal common law would apply only to those instances in which a state statute or "local" common law doctrine existed.

14. See discussion supra at 18–19.

15. See discussion infra at 35.

16. See discussion infra at 31–32.

17. See discussion supra at 18–19.

18. Field, supra note 5, at 924–26, 931–32.

19. See id. at 953–62.

20. See discussion supra at 26–28.

21. It would be difficult to characterize most modern Supreme Court decisions developing principles of substantive federal common law as part of a legitimate process of statutory construction. Rarely does the Court even purport to rely on the language or purpose of a particular congressional statute or statutes, either when making the initial decision to adopt a distinct federal common law standard, or in fashioning the substance of that federal standard. See generally M. Redish, Federal Jurisdiction: Tensions; supra note 2, at 124–25; see discussion infra at 45.

22. 28 U.S.C. § 1652.

23. See discussion infra at 34–42.

24. Westen, After "Life for Erie"—A Reply, 78 Mich. L. Rev. 971, 989 (1980) (emphasis in original); see generally Westen & Lehman, Is There Life for Erie After the Death of Diversity? 78 Mich. L. Rev. 311 (1980).

25. Westen & Lehman, supra note 24, at 316.

26. See discussion supra at 26–27. It has been suggested that, by including the words "in cases where they apply" in the Rules of Decision Act, the drafters rendered the Act "tautological." Weinberg, Federal Common Law, 83 Nw. U. L. Rev. 805, 816 (1990). I take Professor Weinberg to mean that, because the Act directs application of state law only in cases where that law "appl[ies]," the Act's requirements are automatically met, whether the federal court chooses to use state law or not: if the federal court chooses not to "apply" state law, then state law does not "apply," by definition. Professor Weinberg's textual analysis is reminiscent of the student who expects a perfect score on a test because he was asked to "write everything you know about the American Revolution," and the student—with perfect accuracy—answered by leaving the page completely blank.

Professor Weinberg, of course, suggests a linguistically permissible—or at least conceivable—construction of the words, "where they apply." But such a construction is permissible only when those words are viewed in a total vacuum, wholly divorced from both the remainder of the text and the political perceptions at the time of passage. If the Act were intended to mean what Professor Weinberg suggests, it would effectively amount to no restraint at all on the power of the federal courts to fashion substantive federal law. It seems highly unlikely Congress would intend such a result, purely as a practical political matter. Even if we were to assume that, as an abstract matter, Congress might choose to enact legislation that directed the federal courts to do whatever they would have chosen to do even absent the statute, when one examines the remainder of the Act's text such a construction becomes nonsensical. Preceding the Act's operative clause is an extensive *exemption* from the Act's command. If the Act truly commanded nothing, what possibly could have been the point of drawing a broad exemption from such a "non-command"?

When one acknowledges that the Rules of Decision Act, like virtually all legislation, was enacted to achieve a purpose, Professor Weinberg's construction becomes unworkable. Placed in proper textual and political context, then, the words on which she focuses must mean, simply, that state law will provide the rule of decision only for cases in which, as a substantive matter, it is found to be relevant—that is, where it "appl[ies]". Thus, the Act necessarily vests in the interpreting court the power to decide which state laws "apply" to which cases. But this power is a narrow one; it extends no further than to match particular substantive state law with the specific controversy before the federal court. It cannot, within our representational democratic structure, be construed to authorize the federal judiciary effectively to subvert the unambiguous legislative policy behind the Act.

27. Professor Westen has replied to the charge that his construction renders the Act a nullity by arguing that, if so, criticism should be directed "at the Supreme Court because it has been saying for over 150 years that the Rules of Decision Act is nothing but a truism." Westen, supra note 24, at 982 n. 45. Of course, even if that were true, it would not be responsive to a normative attack on Supreme Court precedent. But Professor Westen has clearly quoted the Court out of context. What it has actually said is that the Rules of Decision Act is "merely declaratory of what would in any event have governed the federal courts." Guaranty Trust Co. v. York, 326 U.S. 99, 103–04 (1945). This statement can hardly be taken to suggest that the Act is a "nullity," but only that what it accomplishes the courts would have chosen to accomplish in any event, even in the absence of the statute. Passage of a statute under such circumstances would hardly amount to enactment of a nullity because it would constitute a legislative guarantee of preexisting judicial self-limitation.

This point is confirmed when Justice Frankfurter's statement in *York* is placed in its original context. In that case, the Court held that the principles embodied in the Rules of Decision Act were to be applied to suits in equity, even though at the time the terms of the Act expressly applied only to suits at common law. It was as an elaboration of this holding that Justice Frankfurter made the statement relied upon by Professor Westen. Id.

28. I should acknowledge that my earlier writing on the Rules of Decision Act may be accused of the same sin. Although at no point did I suggest a construction that would render the Act a nullity, I did suggest that the decision whether to apply state or federal law to procedural issues reached by the Act be governed by standards not discernible in any way from its text or legislative history. See generally Redish & Phillips, *Erie* and the Rules of Decision Act: In Search of the Appropriate Dilemma, 91 Harv. L. Rev. 356 (1977). In light of my more recent focus on the nature and importance of textual analysis, see, e.g., Redish & Drizin, Constitutional Federalism and Judicial Review: The Role of Textual Analysis, 62 N.Y.U. L. Rev. 1 (1987), I now believe that my earlier dismissive attitude toward the importance of the text of the Rules of Decision Act is improper. See, e.g., Redish, Continuing the Erie Debate: A Response to Westen and Lehman, 78 Mich. L. Rev. 959, 968 n. 60 (1980) [hereinafter Redish, Continuing the Erie Debate]. I thus now accept the criticism leveled in Burbank, Interjurisdictional Preclusion and Federal Common Law: Toward a General Approach, 70 Cornell L. Rev. 625, 632 (1985).

Despite this rejection of my previous methodology, I adhere to the general conclusion I reached in my earlier analysis. This is because that analysis concerned solely issues that are in some sense procedural. Redish & Phillips, supra at 358. The phrase "rules of decision" is an operative textual term, and, though it is not the only conceivable construction, it is quite reasonable to construe that phrase to apply only to purely substantive matters. See Merrill, supra note 6, at 46–47. For it is on such matters, extending completely beyond the four walls of the federal courthouse, that the decision of the case will generally be made, and that the states' fear of federal judicial interference was probably at its most intense. This question of statutory construction appears to fall into that category in which even a good–faith judicial effort cannot sharply and concretely define congressional intent, and the court therefore must make its best educated guess. Interpreting the phrase "rules of decision" to be confined to purely substantive matters is at the very least a defensible outgrowth of such a process. So construed, the Act would not command use of state law on matters that are in some sense procedural. Thus, the federal courts are not constrained by the Act in such matters. Hence, my suggested standards for choosing between state and federal judge-made procedural rules, developed on grounds of normative social policy and political philosophy, could be adopted without doing violence to the text of the Rules of Decision Act. See Redish & Phillips, supra, at 378–84.

29. Westen & Lehman, supra note 24, at 332.

30. See, e.g., Grano, Prophylactic Rules in Criminal Procedure: A Question of Article III Legitimacy, 80 Nw. U. L. Rev. 100, 134, n. 208 (1985) ("If [Westen and Lehman's comment on the difference between statutory and constitutional interpretation and common law as one of degree] is intended to suggest that courts can do the latter because they can do the former, it is obvious nonsense"); see also Burbank, supra note 28, at 632. For my own critical view, see Redish, Continuing the Erie Debate, supra note 28.

31. This point applies with full force to the Supreme Court's development of federal common law. For, when the Court shapes substantive federal common law doctrine, it rarely points to the language or purpose of particular statutes as either a guide or authorization for the creation of the rules in question. See M. Redish, Federal Jurisdiction: Tensions, supra note 2, at 125–48.

32. See discussion infra at 44–45.

33. See discussion supra at 19–28.

34. See discussion supra at 19–20.

35. Merrill, supra note 6, at 40–46.

36. 15 U.S.C. § 1.

37. See, e.g., Standard Oil Co. v. United States, 221 U.S. 1, 69–70 (1911).

38. The Act provides that

> [s]uits for violations of contracts between an employer and a labor organization representing employees in an industry affecting commerce as defined in this chapter, or between any such labor organizations, may be brought in any district court of the United States having jurisdiction of the parties, without regard to the citizenship of the parties.

29 U.S.C. § 185(a).

39. In its controversial decision in Textile Workers Union v. Lincoln Mills, 353 U.S. 448 (1957), the Court construed § 301(a) to constitute a delegation of substantive lawmaking authority to the federal courts, rather than merely a jurisdictional grant. In dissent, Justice Frankfurter made a persuasive case for the view that the Act was intended to be merely jurisdictional in nature. Id. at 460 (Frankfurter, J., dissenting).

40. See M. Redish, Federal Jurisdiction: Tensions, supra note 2, at 123–24.

41. The Supreme Court should not be able to construe a statute to delegate common law-like power to the federal judiciary, without first carefully examining the statute in question to determine that Congress so intended, lest the Court effectively usurp legislative power.

If the assertion of judicial "gap-filling" is employed merely as an introductory incantation which—much like its ancient predecessor, the phrase "Open Sesame"—is invoked by the court simply in order to get to the "treasure" of unrestrained law creation, the concept is rendered worse than meaningless; it becomes nothing more than thinly disguised manipulation. For a court legitimately to engage in the gap-filling process, then, it must tie its decisions much more closely and carefully to the structure, text, and purposes of specific federal statutes.

42. See discussion supra at 31–32.

43. See discussion supra at 26–28.

44. See discussion supra at 9–10.

45. The metaphor has been employed by Professor Eskridge, who attributes it to Professor Alienkoff. Eskridge, Dynamic Statutory Interpretation, 135 U. Pa. L. Rev. 1479, 1482 n. 12 (1987).

46. Although considerable historical attention has been given to the origins of the Rules of Decision Act, it has overwhelmingly been devoted to the issue, focused on in *Swift* and *Erie*, whether the Act's use of the terms "laws" of the several states was intended to include state common law, as well as statutes. See, e.g., R. Bridwell & R. Whitten, The Constitution and the Common Law (1977). See Merrill, supra note 6, at 30.

47. It was this division that ultimately led to adoption of the so-called "Madisonian Compromise," under which Congress was to be permitted—but not obligated—to create lower federal courts. The relevant history is discussed in Redish & Woods, Congressional Power to Control the Jurisdiction of Lower Federal Courts: A Critical Review and a New Synthesis, 124 U. Pa. L. Rev. 45, 52–56 (1975).

48. As Madison argued:

> As a security of the rights and powers of the States in their individual capacities ag[ainst] an undue preponderance of the powers granted to the Government over them in their united capacity, the Constitution has relied on . . . [t]he responsibility of the Senators and Representatives in the Legislature and people of the States.

Letter of James Madison to Edward Everett (Aug. 28, 1830) in 9 The Writings of James Madison 338, 395–96 (1910).

49. The mandatory creation of lower federal courts was opposed in the Convention because it would make "an unnecessary encroachment on the jurisdiction [of the states]." 1 Records of the Federal Convention of 1787, at 124 (M. Farrand rev. ed. 1937). See also Nowak, The Scope of Congressional Power to Create Causes of Action against State Governments and the History of the Eleventh and Fourteenth Amendments, 75 Colum. L. Rev. 1413, 1440–41 (1975); Redish & Nugent, The Dormant Commerce Clause and the Constitutional Balance of Federalism, 1987 Duke L.J. 569, 596–97.

50. The relationship was relied upon by the Court in Garcia v. Metropolitan Transit Authority, 469 U.S. 528, 550–52 (1985).

51. See, e.g., J. Choper, Judicial Review and the Political Process 176–90 (1980); Wechsler, The Political Safeguards of Federalism: The Role of the States in the Composition and Selection of the National Government, 54 Colum. L. Rev. 543 (1954).

52. See supra note 1.

53. Merrill, supra note 6, at 15; Mishkin Some Further Last Words on Erie—The Thread, 87 Harv. L. Rev. 1682 (1974).

54. U.S. Const. Art. I, § 7. See discussion supra at 23.

55. See Redish & Nugent, supra note 49, at 592–94.

56. At the very least, it is difficult to discern any *textual* support for the dichotomy.

57. See discussion supra at 31–32.

58. See discussion supra at 34–35.

59. Field, supra note 5, at 887.

60. Id. (footnote omitted) ("The only limitation on courts' power to create federal common law is that the court must point to a federal enactment, constitutional or statutory, that it interprets as authorizing the federal common law rule.") Professor Field notes that "[i]f loosely interpreted, a requirement that a court point to an authorizing enactment states no limit at all." Id.

61. Although under her suggested standard "federal courts cannot make a rule unless they identify some enactment giving them power to do so," Professor Field notes that ultimately her approach "leaves judges great freedom to make federal common law where they will." Her standard, she states, is characterized by its "extreme flexibility." Id. at 929. See also Note, The Competence of Federal Courts to Formulate Rules of Decision, 77 Harv. L. Rev. 1084, 1093 (1964) ("[I]t should not be necessary for the court to point to any single statute sufficient itself to engender a decisional rule").

62. See discussion supra at 21.

63. See discussion supra at 34–35.

64. See Westen & Lehman, supra note 24, at 332–34.

65. See discussion supra at 33 (interpretation of § 1 of the Sherman Act).

66. See chapter 4, infra.

67. See, e.g., Cannon v. University of Chicago, 441 U.S. 677 (1979).

68. See, e.g., Banco Nacional de Cuba v. Sabbatino, 376 U.S. 398 (1964); Henkin, The Foreign Affairs Power of the Federal Courts: Sabbatino, 64 Colum. L. Rev. 805, 814–17 (1964).

69. See, e.g., Clearfield Trust Co. v. United States, 318 U.S. 363 (1943); M. Redish, Federal Jurisdiction: Tensions, supra note 2, at 125–35.

70. See discussion supra at 9–10.

71. Cf. Field, supra note 5, at 893.

72. See Allen v. McCurry, 449 U.S. 90 (1980).

73. See M. Redish, Federal Jurisdiction: Tensions, supra note 2, at 149–56.

74. See, e.g., J. I. Case Co. v. Borak, 377 U.S. 426 (1964).

75. See Stewart & Sunstein, Public Programs and Private Rights, 95 Harv. L. Rev. 1193, 1229 (1982).

76. This was the thrust of the decision in INS v. Chadha, 462 U.S. 919 (1983), which invalidated the one-house veto.

77. See generally Macey, Promoting Public Regarding Legislation Through Statutory Interpretation: An Interest Group Model, 86 Colum. L. Rev. 223 (1986).

78. See discussion supra at 30.

79. See discussion supra at 4–5.

80. See discussion supra at 9–10.

81. See generally chapters 5–7.

82. Merrill, supra note 6, at 48–50.

83. Id. at 40.

84. Cf. Bivens v. Six Unknown Named Agents of Federal Bureau of Narcotics, 403 U.S. 388, 404 (1971) (Harlan, J., concurring) ("[T]he presumed availability of federal equitable relief against threatened invasions of constitutional interests appears entirely to negate the contention that the status of an interest as constitutionally protected divests federal courts of the power to grant damages absent express congressional authorization").

85. See generally Easterbrook, The Supreme Court, 1983 Term—Foreword: The Court and the Economic System, 98 Harv. L. Rev. 4 (1988).

86. See generally Monaghan, The Supreme Court—1974 Term—Foreword: Constitutional Common Law, 89 Harv. L. Rev. 1 (1975).

87. See M. Redish, Federal Courts: Cases, Comments, and Questions 553–54 (2d ed. 1989).

88. Cf. Merrill, supra note 6, at 50–52.

89. U.S. Const. Amend. XIV, § 1.

90. 163 U.S. 537 (1896).

91. See. 5 K. Davis, Administrative Law Treatise 149–56, 160–66 (2d ed. 1978).

92. See discussion supra at 33–34.

93. See discussion supra at 34.

94. See discussion supra at 26–28.

95. Professor Merrill argues that there exists an additional legitimate basis for the creation of federal common law—what he refers to as "preemptive lawmaking." Merrill, supra note 6, at 35. He suggests that, pursuant to this concept, federal courts may properly fashion substantive federal common law rules in order to prevent state law from undermining existing federal statutes. Id. at 36. See, e.g., Howard v. Lyons, 360 U.S. 593 (1959).

A federal court is clearly within its jurisdictional authority to inquire whether state law has been preempted by contrary federal law. See, e.g., Pacific Gas & Electric Co. v. State Energy Resources Conservation & Development Comm'n, 461 U.S. 190 (1983). It does not inexorably follow, however, that this power to find state law preempted implies a corresponding federal power to supplant state law with its own substantive common law principle. If a particular state rule is preempted, a vacuum might be left as a result, and it is therefore conceivable that the federal court could fashion its own replacement rule pursuant to its "gap-filling" function. In light of the strict limitations that must be placed on reliance on the "gap-filling" concept, see discussion supra at 27–28; 38–39, development of a separate federal rule would be proper only if the open legal issue represents an intermediate question that must be resolved before the federal statute may be appropriately applied.

96. In re "Agent Orange" Prod. Liab. Litig., 635 F.2d 987 (2d Cir. 1980).

97. No federal statute explicitly provided a damage remedy, and the district court declined to infer a private damage remedy in any existing federal pesticide regulation statute. In re "Agent Orange" Prod. Liab. Litig., 506 F.Supp. 737, 741–42 (E.D.N.Y. 1979), rev'd, 635 F.2d 987 (2d Cir. 1980).

98. Id. at 743–49.

99. See discussion supra at 39.
100. 506 F. Supp. at 747–48.
101. 635 F.2d at 995–99 (Feinberg, C.J. dissenting).
102. Id. at 988.
103. Id. at 993–95.
104. See P. Schuck, Agent Orange on Trial: Mass Toxic Disasters In The Courts 66 (1987) (characterizing the Second Circuit's decision as "irrational on its face . . . ").
105. In re Agent Orange, 635 F.2d at 993 (footnote omitted).
106. The district court relied on the Supreme Court's decisions in Miree v. DeKalb County, 433 U.S. 25 (1977), and Wallis v. Pan Am. Petroleum Corp., 384 U.S. 63 (1966), both of which could be thought to adopt an interest analysis. See M. Redish, Federal Jurisdiction: Tensions, supra note 2, at 125, 133.
107. See discussion supra at 38–39.
108. See discussion supra at 31–41.
109. The phrase is Jefferson Powell's. See Powell, Reaching the Limits of Traditional Constitutional Scholarship, 80 Nw. U.L. Rev. 1128, 1136–37 (1986).
110. 163 U.S. 537 (1896).
111. See, e.g., Gulfstream Aerospace Corp. v. Mayacamass Corp., 485 U.S. 271 (1988) (overruling long-standing *Enelow-Ettelson* doctrine).
112. See, e.g., Monaghan, Stare Decisis and Constitutional Adjudication, 88 Colum. L. Rev. 723 (1988).
113. See, e.g., Marshall, Let Congress Do It: The Case for an Absolute Rule of Statutory Stare Decisis, 88 Mich. L. Rev. 177 (1989).
114. See D'Oench, Duhme & Co. v. Federal Deposit Ins. Corp., 315 U.S. 447, 472 (1942) (Jackson, J., concurring) ("Federal common law implements the federal Constitution and statutes, and is conditioned by them.") (footnote omitted); see also Wallis v. Pan Am. Petroleum Corp., 384 U.S. 63, 69 (1966) ("If there is a federal statute dealing with the general subject, it is a prime repository of federal policy and a starting point for federal common law").
115. 42 U.S.C. § 2000.
116. 42 U.S.C. § 4321.
117. While courts may construe ambiguous statutes in order to avoid constitutional problems, it is important to note that the mere possibility of a constitutional issue does not authorize the judiciary to overturn an unambiguous congressional judgment without first actually deciding that constitutional issue. The argument that "construing" a statute to avoid potential constitutional difficulties represents a form of judicial restraint, when applied to an unambiguous statute, ignores the key fact that, when the dust settles, the judiciary will have effectively invalidated legislative policy choices without initially determining that such action violated the Constitution. There is no legitimate place for such judicial action in a predominantly democratic society.

FOUR

1. See M. Redish, Federal Jurisdiction: Tensions in the Allocation of Judicial Power 281-308 (2d ed. 1990); C. Wright, Law of Federal Courts 302–30 (4th ed.

1983); Field, Abstention in Constitutional Cases: The Scope of the Pullman Abstention Doctrine, 122 U. Pa. L. Rev. 1071 (1974).

2. An example is the so-called Colorado River abstention in the face of parallel state proceedings.

3. See, e.g., Field, supra note 1; Fiss, Dombrowski, 86 Yale L.J. 1103 (1977); Laycock, Federal Interference with State Prosecutions: The Need for Prospective Relief, 1977 Sup. Ct. Rev. 193; Wechsler, Federal Courts, State Criminal Law, and the First Amendment, 49 N.Y.U. L. Rev. 740 (1974).

4. This is true of some of my previous writing, which questioned various judge-made abstention doctrines solely on the basis of policy considerations. E.g., Redish, The Doctrine of Younger v. Harris: Deference in Search of Rationale, 63 Cornell L. Rev. 463 (1978). At least one commentator has persuasively questioned the viability of the judge-made equitable abstention doctrine of Younger v. Harris, 401 U.S. 37 (1971), by examining the legislative history of the Civil Rights Act of 1871, ch. 22, 17 Stat. 13 (codified as amended at 42 U.S.C. § 1983). See Ziegler, A Reassessment of the Younger Doctrine in Light of the Legislative History of Reconstruction, 1983 Duke L.J. 987. However, to date no commentator has undertaken a structural separation-of-powers analysis of the entire range of judge-made abstention.

5. See generally chapter 2.

6. Chief Justice Rehnquist is the foremost advocate of this view, though former Chief Justice Burger was of the same school. See discussion infra at 68–71.

7. 42 U.S.C. § 1983 provides:

> Every person who, under color of any statue, ordinance, regulation, custom, or usage, of any State of Territory or the District of Columbia, subjects, or causes to be subjected, any citizen of the United States or other person within the jurisdiction thereof to the deprivation of any rights, privileges, or immunities secured by the Constitution and laws, shall be liable to the party injured in an action at law, suit in equity, or other proper proceeding for redress. . . .

8. 28 U.S.C. § 1343(a) provides:

> The district courts shall have original jurisdiction of any civil action authorized by law to be commenced by any person: . . . (3) To redress the deprivation, under color of any State law, statute, ordinance, regulation, custom or usage, of any right, privilege or immunity secured by the Constitution of the United States or by any Act of Congress providing for equal rights of citizens or of all persons within the jurisdiction of the United States. . . .

9. See discussion infra at 68–71.

10. See discussion infra at 68–70; 72–73.

11. See discussion infra at 72–73.

12. See discussion infra at 49.

13. See e.g., Laycock, supra note 3; Neuborne, The Myth of Parity, 90 Harv. L. Rev. 1105 (1977); Redish, supra note 4.

14. These arguments are the following:

> [T]he dramatic changes in the philosophy of federalism, culminating in the Civil War and enactment of the post-Civil War constitutional amendments and statutes limiting state power to interfere with federal rights, dictated a corresponding shift in the bal-

> ance of judicial power between state and federal courts. Post-Civil War Congresses expressed grave mistrust of state court willingness to protect federal rights and to further federal interests. While of course state court ability or willingness to protect federal rights cannot be absolutely measured by the realities present over a hundred years ago, the changes in federal jurisdiction introduced at that time have had a far-reaching effect, both practically and philosophically, on the relative capabilities of state and federal courts in the modern federal system. Since that time federal courts have developed a vast expertise in dealing with the intricacies of federal law, while the state judiciary has, quite naturally, devoted the bulk of its efforts to the evolution and refinement of state law and policy. It would be unreasonable to expect state judiciaries to possess a facility equal to that of the federal courts in adjudicating federal law. Moreover, because federal judges are guaranteed the independence protections of Article III, while many state judges are forced to stand for election, we can generally be assured of a greater degree of independence of the federal judiciary from external political forces. When the issue is which court system is better able to protect minority rights from majoritarian infringement, this is not an insignificant factor. Finally, because of the process of presidential selection and Senate confirmation, we can usually be assured of a floor of competence on the federal judiciary.

M. Redish, supra note 1, at 2 (footnotes omitted). See also Redish, supra note 4 (suggesting superiority of federal courts as protectors of federal rights).

15. Because the various forms of abstention have been described in detail elsewhere, this section will provide only their essential elements. For more detailed analysis, see the sources cited supra in note 1.

16. 312 U.S. 496 (1941).

17. See England v. Louisiana State Bd. of Medical Examiners, 375 U.S. 411, 415–17 (1964).

18. See Redish, supra note 1, at 304–08.

19. 401 U.S. 37 (1971).

20. See Samuels v. Mackell, 401 U.S. 66, 73 (1971).

21. See e.g., Trainor v. Hernandez, 431 U.S. 434, 444 (1977) (state interest in preventing welfare fraud); Juidice v. Vail, 430 U.S. 327, 335 (1977) (state contempt power).

22. 319 U.S. 315, 332 (1943). See also Alabama Pub. Serv. Comm'n v. Southern Ry., 341 U.S. 341, 349–50 (1951) (federal court will abstain in suit challenging constitutionality of commission order requiring railroad to continue in operation).

23. 360 U.S. 25, 30 (1959).

24. 424 U.S. 800, 818–20 (1976).

25. See Merrill, The Common Law Powers of Federal Courts, 52 U. Chi. L. Rev. 1 (1985).

26. See discussion supra at 9–10.

27. This has been accepted at least since the decision in Marbury v. Madison, 5 U.S. (1 Cranch) 137 (1803). See discussion infra at 75–85.

28. See , e.g., California v. Sierra Club, 451 U.S. 287, 298 (1981); Touche Ross & Co. v. Redington, 442 U.S. 560, 576 (1979).

29. 437 U.S. 153 (1978).

30. Id. at 194, quoting Marbury v. Madison, 5 U.S. (1 Cranch) 137, 177 (1803).

31. U.S. Const. Amend. XIV, § 5, provides: "The Congress shall have power to enforce, by appropriate legislation, the provisions of this article."

32. By way of analogy, if Congress enacted a substantive federal right of libel and slander in interstate commerce, a federal court would violate separation of powers if it ignored the legislatively dictated jurisdiction to enforce the statute simply because the court disagreed with its merits. The court would depart no less from accepted institutional norms if it were instead to "modify" the statute by ignoring the cause of action for slander and enforcing only the cause of action for libel. Although such judicial action leaves intact a portion of the congressional scheme, the decision to ignore another portion of that scheme clearly usurps legislative authority.

33. One might argue that, even if such a delegation had been clearly intended, it would violate the principle of separation of powers because it would amount to an abdication of authority by the representative branches of government.

34. For example, in the face of silence in the legislative history, the Court will not infer a congressional intent to allow the federal judiciary to develop a private cause of action not expressly authorized in the statute. In making a determination of whether to infer a private cause of action in the face of congressional silence, the courts must examine, inter alia, whether "there [is] any indication of legislative intent, explicit or implicit, either to create such a remedy or to deny one" and whether such an inference is "consistent with the underlying purposes of the legislative scheme to imply such a remedy for the plaintiff. . . . " Cort v. Ash, 422 U.S. 66, 78 (1975). The Court has stated that in making this determination, "our task is limited solely to determining whether Congress intended to create the private right of action. . . . And as with any case involving the interpretation of a statute, our analysis must begin with the language of the statute itself." Touche Ross & Co. v. Redington, 442 U.S. 560, 568 (1979). In California v. Sierra Club, 451 U.S. 287 (1981), holding that §10 of the Rivers and Harbors Appropriation Act of 1899 did not imply a private cause of action, the Court noted that "there is no 'indication of legislative intent, explicit or implicit, either to create such a remedy or to deny one'" (citing Cort v. Ash, 422 U.S. at 78) and therefore that "[t]his silence on the remedy question serves to confirm that in enacting the Act, Congress was concerned not with private rights but with the Federal Government's ability to respond to obstructions on navigable waterways." 451 U.S. at 295–96 (footnote omitted).

It should be noted that, even with these limitations, the concept of implied statutory remedies appears inconsistent with the dictates of the Representational principle. See the discussion in chapter 3, supra at 39. The point to be emphasized here, however, is that, as limited, it does not represent as flagrant a violation of that principle as does judge-made abstention.

35. See discussion infra at 55–60.

36. Pursuant to England v. Louisiana State Bd. of Medical Examiners, 375 U.S. 411 (1964), the federal court may reserve jurisdiction, and decide the federal issue once the state courts have definitively interpreted the state law. However, several commentators have urged that Pullman abstention be modified so that the entire case could be shifted to the state court, instead of returning to the federal court for an adjudication of the federal issue after the state court has decided the meaning of the state law. See, e.g., American Law Institute, Study of the Division of Jurisdiction between State and Federal Courts 49, 285-86 (1969) (proposed statutory rejection

of *England*); Kurland, Toward a Co-Operative Judicial Federalism: The Federal Court Abstention Doctrine, 24 F.R.D. 481, 489 (1959) (urging that state court be allowed to decide both federal and state questions).

37. Steffel v. Thompson, 415 U.S. 452, 461 (1974).

38. See generally 28 U.S.C. § 2283 (prohibiting injunctions against state court proceedings except when authorized by Act of Congress or necessary to aid federal court's jurisdiction or enforcement of judgments); Redish, The Anti-Injunction Statute Reconsidered, 44 U. Chi. L. Rev. 717 (1977).

39. 353 U.S. 448 (1957).

40. The relevant statute was § 301(a) of the Labor Management Relations Act of 1947, ch. 120, 61 Stat. 136, 156 (codified as amended at 29 U.S.C. § 185).

41. 15 U.S.C. § 1 provides in relevant part: "Every contract, combination in the form of trust or otherwise, or conspiracy, in restraint of trade or commerce among the several States, or with foreign nations, is declared to be illegal. . . ."

42. See, e.g., Standard Oil v. United States, 221 U.S. 1, 50–62 (1911); Northern Sec. v. United States, 193 U.S. 197, 404 (1904) (Holmes, J., dissenting); see also National Soc'y of Professional Eng'rs v. United States, 435 U.S. 679, 688 (1978) (It is "perfectly clear" that Congress "expected the courts to give shape to . . . [the Sherman Act's] broad mandate by drawing on common-law tradition").

43. The most recent recodification came in 1948. Act of June 25, 1948, Pub. L. No. 773, ch. 646, 62 Stat. 932.

44. 28 U.S.C. § 2283.

45. 28 U.S.C. § 2284.

46. 28 U.S.C. § 2254(b).

47. 28 U.S.C. § 1341.

48. 28 U.S.C. § 1342.

49. The House report made only brief reference to § 1343, and the Senate report made no reference to it. H.R. Rep. No. 308, 80th Cong., 1st Sess. 1, A121 (1947); S. Rep. No. 1559, 80th Cong., 2d Sess. 1 (1948).

50. It is in part on this basis that the decision in Merrill Lynch, Pierce, Fenner & Smith v. Curran, 456 U.S. 353 (1982), may be distinguished from my separation-of-powers critique of judge-made abstention. In *Merrill Lynch*, the Court inferred a private cause of action from the Commodity Exchange Act, 7 U.S.C. § 1, which was silent on the question. The Court noted that

> [p]rior to the comprehensive amendments to the CEA enacted in 1974, the federal courts routinely and consistently had recognized an implied private cause of action on behalf of plaintiffs seeking to enforce and to collect damages for violation of provisions of the CEA on rules and regulations promulgated pursuant to the statute. . . . [T]he fact that a comprehensive reexamination and significant amendment of the CEA left intact the statutory provisions under which the federal courts had implied a cause of action is itself evidence that Congress affirmatively intended to preserve that remedy.

456 U.S. at 353, 381–82 (footnote omitted). Thus, at least in part, the Court based its finding of an implied private cause of action on Congress' failure to revoke the judicially recognized cause of action. If this were the only evidence available to the Court, I would have to reject its analysis as a violation of separation of powers. However, the Court also referred to various direct congressional actions and to specific legislative history manifesting congressional awareness of—and desire not to alter—

the judicially recognized private cause of action. Such evidence, never cited in support of judge-made abstention, at least presents a closer question in terms of separation of powers. But see the discussion in chapter 3, supra at 38–39. Even if one accepts in principle the concept of implied statutory remedies, the two situations can also be distinguished because the private cause of action recognized in *Merrill Lynch* could only strengthen the congressional scheme to prevent violations of the CEA. Judge-made abstention, on the other hand, can serve only to undermine achievement of Congress's goals. This factor alone may legitimately dictate the need for a considerably stronger showing of legislative acquiescence before the judiciary should be deemed authorized to depart from the explicit statutory structure.

In any event, it is worthy of note that Chief Justice Burger and Justices Powell, Rehnquist, and O'Connor—generally the leading advocates of judge-made abstention—dissented in *Merrill Lynch*. Justice Powell's dissent, in which the others joined, argued that the majority's "theory is incompatible with our constitutional separation of powers, and in my view it is without support in logic or in law." 456 U.S. at 395. If the four Justices applied the same rigorous analysis to the issue of judge-made abstention, they would be required to alter drastically their support of such judicial power.

51. Merrill, supra note 25, at 28 (footnotes omitted).

52. 451 U.S. 304 (1981).

53. Id. at 313.

54. See discussion supra at note 34.

55. See discussion supra at 39.

56. Bator, The State Courts and Federal Constitutional Litigation, 22 Wm. & Mary L. Rev. 605, 622 n. 49 (1981).

57. See 28 U.S.C. § 1343; 42 U.S.C. § 1983.

58. See sources cited supra note 4.

59. Bator, supra note 56, at 622 n. 49.

60. 42 U.S.C. § 1983 (emphasis added).

61. Professor Bator's earlier work acknowledged this fact. P. Bator, P. Mishkin, D. Shapiro & H. Wechsler, Hart & Wechsler's The Federal Courts and The Federal System 1009 (2d ed. 1973). See also Whitten, Federal Declaratory and Injunctive Interference with State Court Proceedings: The Supreme Court and the Limits of Judicial Discretion, 53 N.C.L. Rev. 591, 637–38 (1975).

Justice Black in *Younger* also conceded this limitation. After acknowledging the equitable basis for the doctrine of federal court restraint, he noted that "[t]he doctrine may originally have grown out of circumstances peculiar to the English judicial system and not applicable in this country. . . ." 401 U.S. at 44. It is true that he completed the sentence by stating, "but its fundamental purpose of restraining equity jurisdiction within narrow limits is equally important under our Constitution, in order to prevent erosion of the role of the jury and avoid a duplication of legal proceedings and legal sanctions where a single suit would be adequate to protect the rights asserted." Id. However, such a response fails to consider the issue from the perspective and understanding of the Congress that originally authorized equitable relief for violations of federal rights.

62. See Soifer & Macgill, The *Younger* Doctrine: Reconstructing Reconstruction, 55 Tex. L. Rev. 1141, 1189 (1977) ("The systemic emphasis of the *Younger* doctrine deletes the individual concern of equity from the calculus.").

63. 28 U.S.C. § 2283.

64. 407 U.S. 225 (1972).

65. In an earlier article, I argued that the *Mitchum* analysis is illogical and inconsistent with both *Younger* and the statutory language. Redish, supra note 38, at 733–39.

66. 407 U.S. at 243.

67. Proponents of the Civil Rights Act of 1871, the predecessor of § 1983, believed "that state courts were being used to harass and injure individuals. . . ." Id. at 240.

68. For example, in explicating *Younger*, the Court has emphasized the need to avoid the "unseemly failure to give effect to the principle that state courts have the solemn responsibility, equally with the federal courts 'to guard, enforce, and protect every right granted or secured by the Constitution of the United States. . . .' " Steffel v. Thompson, 415 U.S. 452, 460–61 (1974) (quoting Robb v. Connolly, 111 U.S. 624, 637 (1884)). See also Huffman v. Pursue, Ltd., 420 U.S. 592, 604 (1975) (federal judicial interference with state court nuisance litigation would be "an offense to the State's interest"). Professor Bator has urged that "we should devote serious and sustained attention to protecting and improving the conditions which determine whether constitutional claims are hospitably adjudicated in state courts. This is a more fruitful enterprise than the channeling of more and more cases from the state courts to the federal courts." Bator, supra note 56, at 629.

69. Several commentators have urged that *Younger* be extended to situations in which a state enforcement proceeding is merely contemplated. See Bator, supra note 56, at 616–21; Whitten, supra note 61. The Anti-Injunction Act, however, is applicable only when there is an ongoing state proceeding. Dombrowski v. Pfister, 380 U.S. 479, 484 n. 2 (1965).

70. These exceptions include prosecutions filed in bad faith, multiple prosecutions for purposes of harassment, and blatantly unconstitutional state statutes. For a discussion of these exceptions, see M. Redish, supra note 1, at 351–55.

71. In my earlier writing on the Anti-Injunction Act, I argued that the "in-aid-of-jurisdiction exception should receive a broader construction than the courts have given it. Properly construed, the exception would vest in the federal district court discretion to enjoin a parallel state proceeding, the outcome of which might significantly interfere with the federal court's meaningful exercise of its jurisdiction. Redish, supra note 38, at 743–60. Thus,

> [i]f, in addition to seeking an injunction, the federal complaint [under § 1983] also seeks a declaration of the federal rights being adjudicated in the state proceeding, the requirement that the federal court possess jurisdiction to be aided is met so long as the declaratory judgment request is cognizable in federal court. The free exercise of jurisdiction to render the declaratory judgment might be impeded substantially by the operation of collateral estoppel if the state proceeding concludes first.

Id. at 759 (footnote omitted). If courts were to adopt my approach, the "in-aid-of-jurisdiction" exception might achieve many of the results reached by the *Mitchum* approach . . . while avoiding many of the problems generated by the *Mitchum* approach." Id. (footnote omitted).

72. See, e.g., Pennzoil v. Texaco, Inc., 481 U.S. 1 (1987); Moore v. Sims, 442 U.S. 415 (1979) (pending civil proceeding); Trainor v. Hernandez, 431 U.S. 434 (1977) (ongoing civil enforcement action).

73. See Hale v. Bimco Trading, Inc., 306 U.S. 375, 378 (1939) (Frankfurter, J.) (The statute "is an historical mechanism . . . for achieving harmony in one phase of our complicated federalism by avoiding needless friction between two systems of courts having potential jurisdiction over the same subject-matter"); Redish, supra note 38, at 718.

74. See Redish, supra note 4, at 473–74.

75. As Soifer and Macgill have observed:

> The considerations of equity and comity developed through decades by the Court to accommodate the tensions among state power, federal power, and individual rights, have been turned into a single, rigid commandment of federal judicial inaction that violates even such rules as equity and comity could be said to have contained. As the Court declared recently, "where a case is properly within [the scope of the *Younger* doctrine], there is no discretion to grant injunctive relief." [quoting Colorado River Water Conserv. Dist. v. United States, 424 U.S. 800, 816 n.22 (1976).] This rigidity has eliminated the discretionary balancing at the heart of equity.

Soifer & Macgill, supra note 62, at 1143 (footnote omitted) (brackets in original).

76. It is interesting to note that the Supreme Court itself does not believe that equity alone supports most forms of judicial abstention. In Younger v. Harris, the Court instead relied on the principles of "equity, comity and federalism"—clearly demonstrating its own view that the values of comity and federalism are distinct from principles of equity. Indeed, in *Younger* the Court conceded that the equity doctrine "may originally have grown out of circumstances peculiar to the English judicial system and not applicable in this country," and viewed the comity precept as "an even more vital consideration." 401 U.S. at 43–44.

77. 312 U.S. at 500–01.

78. See, e.g., Fornaris v. Ridge Tool Co., 400 U.S. 41 (1970) (per curiam); United Gas Pipe Line Co. v. Ideal Cement Co., 369 U.S. 134 (1962) (per curiam).

79. See discussion supra at 56.

80. 312 U.S. at 501.

81. Justice Frankfurter's comment is even more puzzling in light of the fact that his statement was followed by a citation to the then-existing form of the Anti-Injunction Act. Id.

82. See England v. Louisiana State Bd. of Medical Examiners, 375 U.S. 411, 418 (1964).

83. The Supreme Court recognized this fact in rejecting the requirement of exhaustion of state administrative remedies for 1983 suits in Patsy v. Board of Regents, 457 U.S. 496 (1982).

84. See Field, supra note 1, at 1087.

85. Wells, Why Professor Redish is Wrong about Abstention, 19 Ga. L. Rev. 1097, 1097 (1985).

86. Id. at 1097–98.

87. Id. at 1098.

88. 365 U.S. 167 (1961).

89. Wells, supra note 85, at 1098.

90. Id

91. 42 U.S.C. § 1983.

92. See, e.g., id., §§ 1981–1982.

93. Professor Wells criticized Justice Douglas's use in Monroe v. Pape, 365 U.S. 167 (1961), of statements by the opponents of § 1983. Wells, supra note 85, at 1105. However, Professor Wells ignored the clear statement by Representative Shellabarger, the principal drafter and sponsor of the bill on the floor of the House, concerning the intended scope of the Act. Shellabarger introduced the bill as a measure "which does affect the foundations of the Government itself, which goes to every part of it, and touches the liberties and the rights of all the people." He further stated that § 1983 provides a civil remedy not only for "person[s] who may have been . . . slaves, but also to all people where, under color of State law, they . . . may be deprived of rights to which they are entitled under the Constitution." Cong. Globc, 42d Cong., 1st Sess., app. 67–68 (1871).

Shellabarger did not have to be clairvoyant to realize that a bill so controversial as the 1871 Act was likely to be tampered with by the courts. He therefore provided instruction on how § 1983 should be judicially construed. "This act is remedial, and in aid of the preservation of human liberty and human rights . . . the largest latitude consistent with the words employed is [to be] uniformly given in construing such statutes." Id. at 68; see also Shapo, Constitutional Tort: *Monroe v. Pape* and Beyond, 60 Nw. U. L. Rev. 277, 282 (1965) ("It is obvious from the words spoken on both sides that the framers contemplated a bill of great scope").

94. Professor Wells acknowledges that the claim that abstention is an exercise in equitable discretion, rather than judicial lawmaking, is "untenable." Wells, supra note 85, at 1097.

95. See generally Merrill, supra note 25.

96. The Court has expressed its willingness to undertake this practice. See Patterson v. McLean Credit Union, 108 S. Ct. 1419 (1988) (authorizing reconsideration of the interpretation of 42 U.S.C. § 1981 in Runyon v. McCrary, 427 U.S. 160 (1976)).

97. Shapiro, Jurisdiction and Discretion, 60 N.Y.U. L. Rev. 543 (1985).

98. Id. at 545.

99. Id.

100. A similar argument against reliance on descriptive tradition is fashioned in Redish & Nugent, The Dormant Commerce Clause and the Constitutional Balance of Federalism, 1987 Duke L.J. 569, 604–05.

101. See Korematsu v. United States, 323 U.S. 214 (1944).

102. But see discussion infra at 64–67.

103. See id.

104. Shapiro, supra note 97, at 552–74.

105. See generally Monaghan, Constitutional Adjudication: The Who and When, 82 Yale L.J. 1363 (1973).

106. Whether or not such doctrines violate the Representational principle, I believe that in many instances they violate the Counter-Majoritarian principle. See chapter 6, infra at 88–108.

107. I refer here to the argument that § 1983's textual authorization of equitable relief inherently implies judicial discretion not to act. See discussion supra at 55–60.

108. See discussion supra at 52–55.

109. 330 U.S. 386 (1947).

110. See also Mondou v. New York, N.H. & H.R.R., 223 U.S. 1 (1912).

111. Gulf Oil Co. v. Gilbert, 330 U.S. 501, 507 (1947).

112. Id. at 508.

113. 28 U.S.C. § 1404(a).

114. 457 U.S. 496 (1982).

115. Id. at 511–12.

116. Shapiro, supra note 97, at 560.

117. See generally Freer, A Principled Statutory Approach to Supplemental Jurisdiction, 1987 Duke L.J. 34; Schenkier, Ensuring Access to Federal Courts: A Revised Rationale for Pendent Jurisdiction, 75 Nw. U. L. Rev. 245 (1980).

118. See discussion supra at 63.

119. 22 U.S. (9 Wheat.) 738 (1824).

120. Basically, these decisions represent interpretations of the phrase "arising under" in the general federal question statute, 28 U.S.C. § 1331. See, e.g., Merrell Dow Pharmaceuticals, Inc., v. Thompson, 478 U.S. 804 (1986); Smith v. Kansas City Title & Trust Co., 255 U.S. 180 (1921).

121. 28 U.S.C. 1254, 1257; see generally Kurland, Jurisdiction of the United States Supreme Court: Time for a Change?, 59 Cornell L. Rev. 616 (1974).

122. See Pub. L. No. 100–352, 102 Stat. 662 (1988).

123. See, e.g., Hicks v. Miranda, 422 U.S. 332 (1975).

124. Shapiro, supra note 97, at 572–73.

125. See discussion supra at 55–60.

126. Shapiro, supra note 97, at 579.

127. The congressional grant is codified at 28 U.S.C. § 1343 (a)(3); 42 U.S.C. § 1983.

128. 365 U.S. 167 (1961).

129. Id. at 170.

130. See generally Shapo, supra note 93.

131. 365 U.S. at 183.

132. Id. at 173.

133. Id. at 174.

134. City of Columbus v. Leonard, 443 U.S. 905, 911 (1979) (Rehnquist, J., dissenting from denial of certiorari).

135. 365 U.S. at 183.

136. The administrative exhaustion requirement for § 1983 suits was firmly rejected by the Supreme Court in Patsy v. Board of Regents, 457 U.S. 496 (1982).

137. See 28 U.S.C. § 2254(b).

138. 28 U.S.C. § 2254.

139. Cover, The Uses of Jurisdictional Redundancy: Interest, Ideology, and Innovation, 22 Wm. & Mary L. Rev. 639, 646 (1981).

140. 449 U.S. 90 (1980).

141. 28 U.S.C. § 1738.

142. See Restatement (Second) Of Judgments § 18 (1982).

143. See Allen v. McCurry, 449 U.S. 90, 96 (1980).

144. See, e.g., Bator, supra note 56, at 616.

145. Professor Bator wrote:

> The participation of the state courts in the formulation and application of federal constitutional principles is, after all, the explicit premise of the supremacy clause, and has been deeply engrained in our institutional structures since the beginning. Its legitimacy and desirability are buttressed by an enormous tradition of federalistic rhetoric, running in an unbroken line from the Federalist Papers down to today's Supreme Court opinions.

Id. at 606 (footnotes omitted).

146. One clear indication that Chief Justice Rehnquist's "adequacy" analysis of available state remedies would be something less than fully rigorous appeared in his opinion for the Court in Parratt v. Taylor, 451 U.S. 527 (1981). There, by means of substantive constitutional analysis, he effectively adopted his state exhaustion requirement, at least in certain cases. See Redish, Abstention, Separation of Powers, and the Limits of the Judicial Function, 94 Yale L.J. 71, 98–101 (1984). He found the state tort remedy adequate in that case, even though it failed to afford all the substantive advantages of a section 1983 suit. 451 U.S. at 543–44.

147. 28 U.S.C. § 1443 provides in relevant part:

> Any of the following civil actions or criminal prosecutions, commenced in a State court may be removed by the defendant to the district court of the United States for the district and division embracing the place wherein it is pending:
>
> (1) Against any person who is denied or cannot enforce in the courts of such State a right under any law providing for the equal civil rights of citizens of the United States, or of all persons within the jurisdiction thereof. . . .

The statute finds its origins in § 3 of the Civil Rights Act of 1866, ch. 31, 3, 14 Stat. 27.

148. See City of Greenwood v. Peacock, 384 U.S. 808 (1966); Virginia v. Rives, 100 U.S. 313 (1879); see also Redish, Revitalizing Civil Rights Removal Jurisdiction, 64 Minn. L. Rev. 523. 524–26 (1980) (courts should permit removal where a state defendant is unable to enforce his federal right to equality in state court).

149. Bator, supra note 56, at 626–27 (footnotes omitted). Professor Bator purported to consider, "at least directly," only those cases "where state enforcement courts must and will adjudicate federal constitutional defenses unless some affirmative intervention occurs to 'reroute' the federal question into a federal district court." Id. at 611 n. 16.

150. Id. at 626–27.

151. For Chief Justice Rehnquist's views, see Moore v. Sims, 442 U.S. 415, 430–31 (1979) (state proceedings offer adequate opportunity to raise constitutional claims). For Professor Bator's view, see generally Bator, supra note 56.

152. 400 U.S. at 433, 439–43 (1971) (Burger, C.J., dissenting).

153. See Reetz v. Bozanich, 397 U.S. 82 (1970).

154. 400 U.S. at 433.

155. Although Chief Justice Burger acknowledged that the state law was probably unconstitutional, he contended that it was "a very odd business to strike down a state statute, on the books for almost 40 years, without any opportunity for the state courts to dispose of the problem either under the Wisconsin Constitution or the U.S. Constitution." 400 U.S. at 440.

156. In the context of this discussion, one must recall the applicability of the principles of res judicata and collateral estoppel. See discussion supra at 69.

157. Moore v. Sims, 442 U.S. 415 (1979).

158. Id. at 429–30.

159. *Moore* ultimately relied on *Younger* because the federal court action sought to interfere with an ongoing state proceeding. Therefore, the Court did not have to consider the broader abstention issue.

160 See discussion supra at 52–55.

161. See Zeigler, supra note 4. Cf. H. Hyman, A More Perfect Union: The Impact Of The Civil War and Reconstruction on the Constitution 528–42 (1973) (comprehensive discussion of Reconstruction legislation); S. Kutler, Judicial Power and Reconstruction Politics 143–59 (1968) (discussion of removal statutes and congressional expansion of federal court jurisdiction); Wiecek, The Reconstruction of Federal Judicial Power, 1863–1875. 13 Am. J. Legal Hist. 333 (1969) (discussing expansion of federal jurisdiction during Reconstruction).

162. According to the Court's decision in Mitchum v. Foster:

> The predecessor of § 1983 was . . . an important part of the basic alteration in our federal system wrought in the Reconstruction era through federal legislation and constitutional amendment. As a result of the new structure of law that emerged in the post-Civil War era—and especially of the Fourteenth Amendment, which was its centerpiece—the role of the Federal Government as a guarantor of basic federal rights against state power was clearly established.

407 U.S. 225, 238–39 (1972) (footnote omitted). The Court observed that "[p]roponents of the legislation noted that state courts were being used to harass and injure individuals, either because the state courts were powerless to stop deprivations or were in league with those who were bent upon abrogation of federally protected rights." Id. at 240. See also Patsy v. Board of Regents, 457 U.S. 496, 503 (1982).

163. 365 U.S. at 183. See discussion supra at 68.

164. See discussion supra at 70.

165. For example, in Aldinger v. Howard, 427 U.S. 1 (1976), Justice Rehnquist, speaking for the Court, held that a federal court could not assert pendent party jurisdiction over a state claim against a municipality in a § 1983 suit, in part because Congress had not intended that municipalities be subject to liability under § 1983. Id. at 16–17.

166. Cf. Testa v. Katt, 330 U.S. 386 (1947) (state cannot refuse to enforce federal policies); M. Redish, supra note 1, at 169–78 (state court refusal to adjudicate federal causes of action frustrates federal policy that case load created by a federal statute be shared by the two judicial systems).

167. Jurisdictional statutes generally provide that "[t]he district courts shall have original jurisdiction of. . . . " Although one might suggest that this language is not inherently mandatory, the use of the term "shall" arguably tends to undermine such an argument.

FIVE

1. 5 U.S. (1 Cranch) 137 (1803).
2. See generally chapter 7.

3. See discussion infra at 122; 125.
4. See discussion infra at 76–78.
5. See chapter 1, supra at 4–6.
6. A. Bickel, The Least Dangerous Branch: The Supreme Court at the Bar of Politics 16 (1962).
7. Id. at 17.
8. See id. at 23–28.
9. Id. at 18.
10. Id. at 19.
11. See discussion supra at 76.
12. See J. Pennock, Democratic Political Theory 307–308 (1979): "[C]onstitutionalism provides a useful, if not an essential, framework and set of constraints for the operation of social pluralism for democratic ends." Because the Constitution is subject to amendment by a super-majoritarian process, in effect a constitutional democracy imposes what Professor Pennock refers to as a "qualified majority" rule for those issues resolved by the Constitution. Such issues, in Professor Pennock's words, about which "the (generic) rational individual at the constitution-making stage would feel that the chances for relatively high external costs from such action were great. Accordingly, he would favor a restrictive voting rule (qualified majority) for [those] subject[s]." Id. at 395–95 (footnote omitted). See also D. Held, Models of Democracy 65 (1987). According to Professor Held, "[t]he 'tyranny of the majority,' as it has often been called, can only be forestalled by particular constitutional arrangements." Id. at 64.
13. According to one historian, the framers were concerned with avoiding "a democratic despotism. . . . " R. Wiebe, the Opening of American Society 12 (1984). As Madison argued in Federalist No. 10, "pure democracies . . . have always been intolerant, unjust and unstable. . . . " He noted that "they have in general been as short in their lives as they have been violent in their deaths." Id. See D. Held, supra note 12, at 61–62.
14. See the discussion in chapter 2, supra at 9–10.
15. See note 13, supra.
16. See U.S. Const. Arts. I, II, III.
17. These include primarily the bicameralism [U.S. Const. Art. I, sections 1, 7] and presentment [U.S. Const. Art. I, section 7, cls. 2, 3] requirements. See Immigration & Naturalization Service v. Chadha, 462 U.S. 919 (1983).
18. See U.S. Const. Art. I, § 3, providing for selection of U.S. senators by the state legislatures, later altered by the Seventeenth Amendment, which provided for direct senatorial election.
19. U.S. Const. Art. III, § 1.
20. U.S. Const. Amends. I-IX.
21. See chapter 2, supra at 10–17; 24–25.
22. A. Bickel, supra note 6, at 24.
23. Id. at 25.
24. See id. at 24: "[M]any actions of government have two aspects: their immediate, necessarily intended, practical effects, and their perhaps unintended or unappreciated bearing on values we hold to have more general and permanent interest."
25. Id. at 7.

26. Van Alstyne, A Critical Guide to Marbury v. Madison, 1969 Duke L.J. 1, 17.

27. See J. Barron, C. Dienes, W. McCormack & M. Redish, Constitutional Law: Principles and Policy 14–15 (3d ed. 1987).

28. See discussion supra at 77.

29. See discussion supra at 77.

30. Bickel, it should be ultimately rationalized the exercise of judicial review on the ability of the courts to ascertain long-range guiding principles. See discussion supra at 78.

31. Dr. Bonham's Case, 77 Eng. Rep. 646, 8 Coke 114(a) (C.P. 1610). See generally Redish & Marshall, Adjudicatory Independence and the Values of Procedural Due Process, 95 Yale L.J. 455 (1986).

32. See U.S. Const. Art. III.

33. See United States v. Will, 449 U.S. 200 (1980).

34. U.S. Const. Art. VI, cl. 2. See Wechsler, Toward Neutral Principles of Constitutional Law, 73 Harv. L. Rev. 1, 6 (1959).

35. See A. Bickel, supra note 6, at 124–27.

36. U.S. Const. Art. III, § 1, cl. 1.

37. See, e.g., J. Goebel, I The History of the Supreme Court of the United States—Antecedents and Beginnings to 1801 (1971); R. Berger, Congress v. The Supreme Court (1969); G. Haskins & H. Johnson, II The History of the Supreme Court of the United States—Foundations of Power: John Marshall, 1801–15, 186 (1981). According to Professor Bickel, "although the Framers of the Constitution had failed to be explicit about the function of judicial review, the evidence of their deliberations demonstrates that they foresaw—indeed, invited it." A. Bickel, supra note 6, at 15.

38. In Federalist No. 78, Hamilton wrote:

> The complete independence of the courts of justice is peculiarly essential in a limited Constitution.... Limitations [on legislative authority] can be preserved in practice no other way than through the medium of courts of justice; whose duty it must be to declare all acts contrary to the manifest tenor of the Constitution void. Without this, all the reservations of particular rights or privileges would amount to nothing.

Federalist No. 78, at 505 (Edward Mead Earle ed. 1976). Hamilton transformed the Constitution's textual silence on the necessity of judicial review from a problem into an asset by shifting the burden of production, reasoning that "[i]f it be said that the Legislative body are themselves the Constitutional judges of their own powers... it may be answered, that this cannot be the natural presumption, where it is not to be collected from any particular provisions in the Constitution.... It is far more rational to suppose, that the courts were designed to be an intermediate body between the people and the Legislature, in order, among other things, to keep the latter within the limits assigned to their authority." Id. at 506.

39. To the extent that majoritarian action deprives an individual of life, liberty, or property, the exclusion of judicial review could arguably constitute a violation of the Fifth Amendment's due process clause by depriving the individual of a constitutionally protected interest without a sufficiently independent adjudicator. See generally Redish & Marshall, supra note 31; Bartlett v. Bowen, 816 F.2d 695 (D.C.

Cir. 1987). However, it is generally assumed that such a requirement may be satisfied by the availability of a state judicial forum, or possibly an administrative process.

40. See note 39, supra.

41. E. Rostow, The Sovereign Prerogative: The Supreme Court and the Quest for Law 149 (1962).

42. J. Choper, Judicial Review and the National Political Process 263, 275 (1980).

43. See generally Redish, The Value of Free Speech, 130 U. Pa. L. Rev. 591 (1982).

44. These include the protection of habeas corpus [U.S. Const. Art. I, section 9, cl. 2] and the prohibitions on bill of attainder and ex post facto laws [id. cl. 3].

45. See R. Nagel, Constitutional Cultures: The Mentality and Consequences of Judicial Review 73 (1989).

46. See Ins v. Chadha, 462 U.S. 919 (1983).

47. See discussion supra at 78–81.

48. See discussion supra at 6–7.

49. See discussion supra at 75.

SIX

1. Bickel, The Supreme Court, 1960 Term—Foreword: The Passive Virtues, 75 Harv. L. Rev. 40, 42 (1961).

2. See generally id. See also A. Bickel, The Least Dangerous Branch: The Supreme Court at the Bar of Politics 111–98 (1962).

3. See sources cited in note 2.

4. See discussion supra at 5–7, 78–81.

5. See, e.g., Warth v. Seldin, 422 U.S. 490 (1975).

6. See id. at 498–500.

7. Compare Flast v. Cohen, 392 U.S. 83 (1968) (recognition of "taxpayer standing" in certain cases) with Valley Forge Christian College v. Americans United for Separation of Church and State, Inc., 454 U.S. 464 (1982) (restrictive view of "taxpayer standing").

8. See id. at 472 (footnote omitted): "[A]t an irreducible minimum, Art. III requires the party who invokes the court's authority to 'show that he personally has suffered some actual or threatened injury as a result of the particularly illegal conduct of the defendant,' Gladstone Realtors v. Village of Bellwood, 441 U.S. 91, 99 (1979), and that the injury 'fairly can be traced to the challenged action' and 'is likely to be redressed by a favorable decision.' Simon v. Eastern Kentucky Welfare Rights Org., 426 U.S. 26, 38 (1976)." See also Sierra Club v. Morton, 405 U.S. 727 (1972).

9. See, e.g., United States v. SCRAP, 412 U.S. 669 (1973) (rejection of argument that standing should be limited to only those who have been "significantly" affected by the challenged action). But see Lujan v. Nat'l Wildlife Fed., 110 S. Ct. 3177 (1990).

10. See cases cited in note 8.

11. E.g., A. Bickel, supra note 2, at 114; Scalia, The Doctrine of Standing As an Essential Element of the Separation of Powers, 17 Suffolk L. Rev. 835 (1983).

12. 5 U.S. (1 Cranch) 137 (1803).

13. See, e.g., Valley Forge Christian College v. Americans United for Separation of Church and State, Inc., 454 U.S. 464 (1982); Frothingham v. Mellon, 262 U.S. 447 (1923); Scalia, supra note 11.

14. See Brilmayer, The Jurisprudence of Article III: Perspectives on the "Case or Controversy" Requirement, 93 Harv. L. Rev. 297 (1979).

15. See discussion infra at 90–92.

16. See discussion infra at 92–97.

17. See discussion infra at 100–03.

18. See discussion supra at 75–85.

19. See discussion infra at 90–94.

20. See discussion infra at 103–05.

21. It should be noted that by no means am I the first commentator to suggest rejection of the injury-in-fact requirement for standing. See, e.g., Tushnet, The Sociology of Article III: A Response to Professor Brilmayer, 93 Harv. L. Rev. 1698 (1980); Albert, Justiciability and Theories of Judicial Review: A Remote Relationship, 50 S. Cal. L. Rev. 1139 (1977). Other scholars have suggested substantial modifications or expansions of the concept of the injury required for standing. See, e.g., Monaghan, Constitutional Adjudication: The Who and When, 82 Yale L.J. 1363 (1979); Nichol, Rethinking Standing, 72 Cal. L. Rev. 68 (1984). However, my alternative to the injury-in-fact requirement [see discussion infra at 102], my rationale for rejection of that requirement [see discussion supra at 89] and my response to the defenses of the requirement [see discussion infra at 92–103], I believe, provide a new theoretical framework from which to examine the issue.

22. 5 U.S. (1 Cranch) 137 (1803).

23. See sources cited in notes 1, 11, supra.

24. Monaghan, supra note 21, at 1365.

25. 5 U.S. (1 Cranch) at 177–78.

26. Id. at 170.

27. Frothingham v. Mellon, 262 U.S. 447 (1923).

28. Monaghan, supra note 21, at 1365.

29. Cf. 3 A. Beveridge, The Life of John Marshall 107–10, 125–27 (1919), commenting on *Marbury*:

> Marshall resolved to make use of this unimportant litigation to assert, at the critical hour ... the power of the Constitution.... So far... as practical results were concerned, the case of *Marbury v. Madison* had now come to the point where it was of no consequence whatever to anyone. It presented only theoretical questions, and, on the face of the record, even these were as simple as they were unimportant. This controversy, in fact, had degenerated into little more than a "moot case" as Jefferson termed it twenty years later.... [H]e made the decision of this insignificant case—about which the applicants themselves no longer cared—the occasion for asserting [the] principle [of judicial review].

30. See discussion supra at 78–85.

31. 5 U.S. (1 Cranch) at 176.

32. Id.

33. See discussion supra at 79–80.

34. Scalia, supra note 11, at 881 (footnote omitted).

35. 262 U.S. 447 (1923).
36. Id. at 488.
37. See discussion supra at 90–91.
38. Scalia, supra note 11, at 895.
39. Id. at 894.
40. See discussion supra at 89.
41. See discussion supra at 79–85.
42. See Sup. Ct. Rule 17.
43. 410 U.S. 113 (1973).
44. See, e.g., Adkins v. Children's Hospital, 261 U.S. 525 (1923); Adair v. United States, 208 U.S. 161 (1908); Lochner v. New York, 198 U.S. 45 (1905).
45. See Nebbia v. New York, 291 U.S. 502 (1934); Strong, The Economic Philosophy of *Lochner*: Emergence, Embrasure, and Emasculation, 15 Ariz. L. Rev. 419 (1973).
46. See discussion supra at 84–85.
47. See discussion supra at 90–92.
48. See discussion infra at 103–05.
49. See Schlesinger v. Reservists Committee to Stop the War, 418 U.S. 208 (1974), rejecting standing for five individuals and an association of current and former members of the Armed Forces Reserves opposing United States involvement in Vietnam, challenging the membership of members of Congress in the Reserves as a violation of the Incompatibility Clause, Art. I, § 6, cl. 2 of the Constitution, providing that "no Person holding any Office under the United States, shall be a Member of either House during his Continuance in Office."
50. See Valley Forge Christian College v. Americans United for Separation of Church and State, Inc., 454 U.S. 464 (1982), viewing restrictively the standing of taxpayers to challenge governmental expenditures alleged to violate the establishment clause, U.S. Const. Amend. I, cl. 1.
51. See cases cited in notes 49 and 50.
52. 461 U.S. 95 (1983).
53. The Court acknowledged that Lyons had standing to pursue his damage remedy. Id. at 105.
54. Lyons alleged that the chokehold procedure violated the First Amendment's protection of speech and assembly, the Fourth Amendment's prohibition of unreasonable search and seizure, and the Eighth Amendment's prohibition of cruel and unusual punishment, as applied to the states through the Fourteenth Amendment. Id. at 98.
55. Id. at 105, 108, 111.
56. Id. at 113 (Marshall, J., dissenting). Justices Brennan, Blackmun, and Stevens joined Justice Marshall's dissent.
57. See Scalia, supra note 11, at 894–95; discussion supra at 83–84.
58. J. Choper, Judicial Review and the National Political Process (1980).
59. See the discussion, in chapter 5, supra at 83–84.
60. 458 U.S. 50 (1982).
61. Id. at 56–57.
62. See, e.g., Perez v. United States, 402 U.S. 146 (1971).
63. U.S. Const. Amend. I, cl. 1.

64. See e.g., Valley Forge Christian College v. Americans United for Separation of Church and State, Inc., 454 U.S. 464 (1982).

65. See Bickel, supra note 1; A. Bickel, supra note 2.

66. A. Bickel, supra note 2, at 132.

67. See discussion supra at 78.

68. A. Bickel, supra note 2, at 30–31.

69. Id. at 129.

70. Id.

71. Gunther, The Subtle Vices of the "Passive Virtues"—A Comment on Principle and Expediency in Judicial Review, 64 Colum. L. Rev. 1, 7 (1964).

72. Id.

73. A. Bickel, supra note 2, at 129–33.

74. Pub. L. 100–352, 102 Stat. 662 (1988).

75. Bickel himself placed reliance on the discretionary nature of the certiorari jurisdiction, see A. Bickel, supra note 2, at 126–27, though his use of the writ has been criticized. See Gunther, supra note 71, at 13–14.

76. Cf. id. at 5: "[T]he inferences Bickel draws ultimately fail to satisfy: they rest on faulty perceptions of the adjudicatory process; and they yield guidelines which invite not accommodation but surrender of principle to expediency."

77. See id. at 6: "With so rigorous a standard of principled adjudication, it follows for Bickel that there will be many 'bad' laws that the Court cannot with propriety strike down."

78. See, e.g., Whitney v. California, 274 U.S., 357, 375 (Brandeis, J., concurring) ("Those who won our independence believed that . . . with [the right of free speech], discussion affords ordinarily adequate protection against the dissemination of noxious doctrine").

79. See discussion supra at 98.

80. See, e.g., Posadas de Puerto Rico Associates v. Tourism Co. of Puerto Rico, 478 U.S. 328 (1986).

81. Texas v. Johnson, 109 S. Ct. 2533 (1989).

82. A. Bickel, supra note 2, at 116.

83. Id. at 115.

84. See, e.g., Village of Schaumburg v. Citizens for a Better Environment, 444 U.S. 620 (1980); United States v. Robel, 389 U.S. 258 (1967). See generally Redish, The Warren Court, the Burger Court and the First Amendment Overbreadth Doctrine, 78 Nw. U. L. Rev. 1031 (1983).

85. Broadrick v. Oklahoma, 413 U.S. 601, 615 (1973) (adopting the position that a statute will be declared unconstitutional on its face only when the statute's overbreadth is "not only" . . . real, but substantial as well, judged in relation to the statute's plainly legitimate sweep"). See also New York v. Ferber, 458 U.S. 747 (1982), extending *Broadrick*, which had been applied to cases in which speech and conduct were involved, to cases of pure speech.

86. Traditionally, under the overbreadth doctrine, one whose conduct could constitutionally be regulated may, under certain circumstances, object to the constitutionality of the statute's applicability to a third party. See, e.g., Kunz v. New York, 340 U.S. 290 (1951). Thus, although the doctrine does not abandon the requirement of injury-in-fact, it does establish that at least on occasion the Court will

decide a case on its constitutional merits, untied to the specific facts of the case before it.

87. Brilmayer, supra note 14, at 302 (footnotes omitted).

88. Id.

89. Id.

90. Id. at 304.

91. Id. at 306.

92. See discussion supra at 99–100.

93. Brilmayer, supra note 14, at 306.

94. Id.

95. Res judicata is a "*prohibition* in relitigating a claim which has already been litigated and gone to judgment." R. Marcus, M. Redish & E. Sherman, Civil Procedure: A Modern Approach 947 (1989) (emphasis added). Stare decisis, on the other hand, imposes something less than an absolute prohibition.

96. See Scalia, supra note 11, at 891: "[I]f the purpose of standing is 'to assure that concrete adverseness which sharpens the presentation of issues,' the doctrine is remarkably ill designed for its end. Often the very best adversaries are national organizations such as the NAACP or the American Civil Liberties Union that have a keen interest in the abstract question at issue in the case, but no 'concrete injury in fact' whatever."

97. Texas v. Johnson, 109 S. Ct. 2533 (1989).

98. See United States v. SCRAP, 412 U.S. 669 (1973).

99. See discussion supra at 89.

100. Fed. R. Civ. P. 23 (a)(4).

101. See C. Wright, A. Miller & M. Kane, Federal Practice and Procedure § 1765 (2d ed. 1986).

102. 28 U.S.C. § 1359 provides that "[a] district court shall not have jurisdiction of a civil action in which any party, by assignment or otherwise, has been improperly or collusively made or joined to invoke the jurisdiction of such court." See Kramer v. Caribbean Mills, Inc., 394 U.S. 823 (1969).

103. Brilmayer, supra note 14, at 310–15.

104. See note 50, supra.

105. See note 49, supra.

106. See discussion supra at 95–97.

107. See discussion supra at 102.

108. See discussion supra at 78–85.

109. Valley Forge Christian College v. Americans United for Separation of Church and State, Inc., 454 U.S. 464, 472 (1982).

110. In light of the Supreme Court's rigid demand for injury-in-fact in order to preserve the federal courts' "judicial" nature, it is ironic that the Court recently upheld the statutorily dictated use of Article III federal judges as members of the United States Sentencing Commission, which was empowered to issue binding sentencing guidelines in a purely legislative manner. Mistretta v. United States, 109 S. Ct. 647 (1989). See also Morrison v. Olsen, 108 S. Ct. 2597 (1988). For a critique of these decisions, see Redish, Separation of Powers, Judicial Authority, and the Scope of Article III: The Troubling Cases of *Morrison* and *Mistretta*, 39 DePaul L. Rev. 299 (1989).

111. See generally Bickel, supra note 1.

112. See, e.g., Honig v. Doe, 108 S. Ct. 592 (1988), discussed infra at 106–07.

113. 416 U.S. 312 (1974) (per curiam).

114. 108 S. Ct. 592 (1988).

115. 416 U.S. at 317.

116. Id.

117. See discussion supra at 90–92.

118. 416 U.S. at 349 (Brennan, J., dissenting).

119. Id. at 350 (Brennan, J., dissenting).

120. See discussion supra at 78–85.

121. Although one might reasonably argue that the "private rights" model should also be inapplicable when disputed questions of federal statutory interpretation are involved, I have confined my rejection of that model to cases that call for the judiciary's performance of its fundamental political role as constitutional expositor and enforcer.

122. 20 U.S.C. § 1400 et seq.

123. 108 S. Ct. at 601–02 (footnotes omitted).

124. See id. at 611 (Scalia, J., dissenting):

> If our established mode of analysis were followed, the conclusion that a live controversy exists in the present case would require a demonstrated probability that *all* of the following events will occur: (1) [the student] will return to public school; (2) he will be placed in an educational setting that is unable to tolerate his dangerous behavior; (3) he will again engage in dangerous behavior; and (4) local school officials will again attempt unilaterally to change his placement and the state defendants will fail to prevent such action. The Court spends considerable time establishing that the last two of these events are likely to recur, but relegates to a footnote its discussion of the first event, upon which all others depend, and only briefly alludes to the second. Neither the facts in the record, nor even the extra-record assurances of counsel, establish a demonstrated probability of either of them.

125. See discussion supra at 102.

126. United Public Workers of America v. Mitchell, 330 U.S. 75, 89–90 (1947).

127. See id.

128. See discussion supra at 99–100.

129. See discussion supra at 100.

SEVEN

1. The Supreme Court has held that the political question doctrine is inapplicable to constitutional challenges to actions of state governments. Baker v. Carr, 369 U.S. 186, 226 (1962). However, one leading commentator has argued that the doctrine has not historically been limited in this manner. Scharpf, Judicial Review and the Political Question: A Functional Analysis, 75 Yale L.J. 517, 538–39 (1966).

2. Crockett v. Reagan, 720 F.2d 1355 (D.C. Cir. 1983) (per curiam), cert denied, 467 U.S. 1251 (1984).

3. Cf. Wechsler, Toward Neutral Principles of Constitutional Law, 73 Harv. L. Rev. 1, 6–9 (1959), with A. Bickel, The Least Dangerous Branch: The Supreme Court at the Bar of Politics 183–98 (1962). See discussion infra at 116–21.

4. See Henkin, Is There a "Political Question" Doctrine?, 85 Yale L.J. 597 (1976). See also discussion infra at 112–16.

5. See discussion infra at 117–19.

6. A. Bickel, supra note 3, at 183–98. See discussion infra at 119–21.

7. This label was coined in Scharpf, supra note 1, at 548.

8. Wechsler, supra note 3.

9. Henkin, supra note 4.

10. Id. at 600–01.

11. Professor Henkin correctly notes that much of what is considered the classical version of the political question doctrine is nothing more than the application of traditional principles of judicial review. I believe he is incorrect, however, when he suggests that all applications of the doctrine—even in its classical form—can be explained without resort to exceptional doctrines of judicial deference. See discussion infra at 116–19.

12. See discussion infra at 113–14.

13. See discussion infra at 114–16.

14. See Redish, Judicial Review and the "Political Question," 79 Nw. U. L. Rev. 1031, 1037–39 (1985).

15. The most perceptive policy attack on many of the underlying assumptions of the political question doctrine appears in Tigar, The Judicial Power, The "Political Question Doctrine" and Foreign Relations, 17 UCLA L. Rev. 1135, 1141–52 (1970). However, much of Tigar's critique extends beyond the political question doctrine, to include all of the possible grounds for judicial abdication of the review function. Although there is a slight overlap between Tigar's arguments and those made here, I have attempted to emphasize and elaborate upon points not mentioned, or not emphasized, by Tigar.

16. I should emphasize that in arguing that the political question doctrine should have no relevance to the exercise of judicial review, I take no position on the numerous controversies over how the power of judicial review should be exercised.

17. 369 U.S. 186 (1962).

18. Id. at 209.

19. Id. at 217.

20. The case was Powell v. McCormack, 395 U.S. 486 (1969), where the Court refused to invoke the doctrine to prevent its review of the constitutionality of the exclusion of Congressman Adam Clayton Powell by the House of Representatives.

21. 413 U.S. 1 (1973).

22. 444 U.S. 996 (1979).

23. Mora v. McNamara, 387 F.2d 862 (D.C. Cir.), cert. denied, 389 U.S. 934 (1967).

24. Crockett v. Reagan, 720 F.2d 1355 (D.C. Cir. 1983) (per curiam), cert. denied, 467 U.S. 1251 (1984).

25. In Cousins v. Wigoda, 419 U.S. 477, 484 n. 4 (1975), the Court expressly left unresolved the question "whether or to what extent national political parties and their nominating conventions are regulable by, or only by, Congress." See also

O'Brien v. Brown, 409 U.S. 1 (1972) (per curiam). However, on a number of occasions the Court has reviewed the constitutionality of racial discrimination by political parties. See, e.g., Terry v. Adams, 345 U.S. 461 (1953); Smith v. Allwright, 321 U.S. 649 (1944). For an excellent discussion of the issue, see Rotunda, Constitutional and Statutory Restrictions on Political Parties in the Wake of Cousins v. Wigoda, 53 Tex. L. Rev. 935 (1975).

26. Henkin, supra note 4, at 620–21.

27. See id. at 622; Tigar, supra note 15, at 1163.

28. As already noted, I ultimately reject the doctrine as a normative matter. See discussion supra at 112; infra at 121–30.

29. See, e.g., Georgia v. Stanton, 73 U.S. (6 Wall.) 50 (1867); Luther v. Borden, 48 U.S. (7 How.) 1 (1849).

30. Finkelstein, Judicial Self-Limitation, 37 Harv. L. Rev. 338, 344–45 (1924) (citations omitted). See Scharpf, supra note 1, at 548–49.

31. See Field, The Doctrine of Political Questions in the Federal Courts, 87 Minn. L. Rev. 485 (1924).

32. 48 U.S. (7 How.) 1 (1849).

33. Baker v. Carr, 369 U.S. 186, 222 (1962).

34. Henkin, supra note 4, at 608.

35. Id. See also Tigar, supra note 15, at 1160–62.

36. See discussion infra at 117.

37. This point takes on special importance in the critique of the classical version of the political question doctrine. See discussion infra at 116–19. Ironically, perhaps the only constitutional provision that actually may be thought to provide a textual basis for excluding judicial review is Article I, section 5, which provides that "[e]ach House shall be the Judge of the Elections, Returns and Qualifications of its own Members. . . ." The irony derives from the fact that in Powell v. McCormack, 395 U.S. 486 (1969), the Supreme Court held the political question doctrine inapplicable to a case in which Congress sought to invoke its authority under this provision.

38. 48 U.S. (7 How.) at 38–39.

39. Henkin, supra note 4, at 606.

40. See discussion infra at 119–30.

41. Wechsler, supra note 3, at 7–8.

42. Henkin, supra note 4, at 606.

43. Id. at 611.

44. Id. at 610.

45. Id. at 611.

46. U.S. Const. Art. IV, § 4: "The United States shall guarantee to every State in this Union a Republican Form of Government, and shall protect each of them against Invasion. . . ."

47. Henkin, supra note 4, at 609.

48. See generally Bonfield, The Guarantee Clause of Article IV, Section 4: A Study in Constitutional Desuetude, 46 Minn. L. Rev. 513 (1962).

49. 285 U.S. 22 (1932).

50. Wechsler, supra note 3, at 8–9 (footnotes omitted). Professor Wechsler noted, however, that "there are arguments the other way. . . ." Id. at 8 (footnote omitted).

51. U.S. Const. Amend. XIV.

52. See, e.g., Reynolds v. Sims, 377 U.S. 533 (1964).

53. It is arguable that application of the political question doctrine in *Gilligan* could be justified on more prudential grounds. See discussion infra at 119–27.

54. 413 U.S. 1 (1973).

55. U.S. Const. Amend. XIV.

56. Gilligan, 413 U.S. at 6.

57. U.S. Const. Art. I, § 8, cl. 16: "The Congress shall have Power . . . [t]o provide for organizing, arming, and disciplining, the Militia . . . reserving to the States respectively, the . . . Authority of training the Militia according to the discipline prescribed by Congress. . . ."

58. Justices Douglas, Brennan, Stewart, and Marshall dissented, urging that the case should have been deemed moot. *Gilligan*, 413 U.S. at 12. Professor Henkin suggests that the inherent limitations on the nature of equitable relief could have justified the Court's refusal to have the judiciary supervise the weaponry and training of the National Guard. Henkin, supra note 4, at 621. See discussion infra at 132–34.

59. In a certain sense, of course, my critique of the classical version of the political question doctrine does not constitute a rejection of the doctrine's theoretical underpinnings. Rather, I accept the fundamental postulate underlying the classical doctrine that on occasion the Constitution is neutral to the particular exercises of constitutional power. As to these provisions, Professor Henkin is surely correct in suggesting that no special deference of judicial review is involved. But it is in the specific application of this valid abstract principle that serious conceptual and practical difficulties arise. In these applications, the Court and commentators have effectively distorted the concept of judicial review into a form of special judicial deference, absent any distinguishing principle to reconcile these abstentions from traditional exercises of judicial review. Although this difference may appear simply to be one of degree, then, it is of such an enormous magnitude that it effectively leads to a practical rejection of the classical version, as it has been described.

60. Scharpf, supra note 1, at 566.

61. Scharpf includes as rationales under this heading such factors as difficulties of access to information and the need for uniformity of governmental decision. Id. at 567–77.

62. A. Bickel, supra note 3, at 184.

63. U.S. Const. Art. VI, cl. 2: "This Constitution, and the Laws of the United States which shall be made in Pursuance thereof; and all Treaties made, or which shall be made, under the Authority of the United States, shall be the supreme Law of the Land; and the Judges in every State shall be bound thereby, any Thing in the Constitution or Laws of any State to the Contrary notwithstanding."

64. 5 U.S. (1 Cranch) 137 (1803). Marshall reasoned that it was the judiciary's duty to interpret the law, that the power included the authority to resolve a conflict between two conflicting laws, and that therefore the courts could resolve a conflict between a statute and the Constitution. Id. at 173–74. See the discussion of *Marbury* in chapters 5 and 6, supra at 79–80; 90–92.

65. Wechsler, supra note 3, at 6.

66. Id.

67. See generally M. Perry, The Constitution, the Courts and Human Rights (1982); J. Ely, Democracy and Distrust (1980).

68. In chapter 4, I argue that doctrines of judge-made abstention generally violate separation of powers because they conflict with the congressional grant of jurisdiction to adjudicate the cases in which the courts choose to abstain. See discussion supra at 47–74. Theoretically, the same argument could be made against the political question doctrine. Thus, this doctrine can be seen as a violation of the Representational principle, as well as the Counter-Majoritarian principle, illustrating that the two precepts are not mutually exclusive. This point is examined in chapter 8, infra at 137–38. However, if one accepts the concept of implied congressional delegation, a stronger case can be made for the political question doctrine than for judge-made abstention because the political question doctrine prevents the courts from interfering with the activities of the political branches. Judge-Made abstention, on the other hand, undermines the achievement of the congressional goals contained in the relevant substantive and jurisdictional statutes. See supra at 47–74.

69. See M. Perry, supra note 67; J. Ely, supra note 67.

70. A. Bickel, supra note 3, at 184.

71. See generally M. Perry, supra note 77; J. Ely, supra note 77.

72. See chapter 5, supra at 75–85.

73. See discussion infra at 122–23.

74. Scharpf, supra note 1, at 555.

75. Field, supra note 31, at 511.

76. See Scharpf, supra note 1, at 556–57.

77. See, e.g., World-Wide Volkswagen Corp. v. Woodson, 444 U.S. 286 (1980); International Shoe Co. v. Washington, 326 U.S. 310 (1945). See generally Redish, Due Process, Federalism, and Personal Jurisdiction: A Theoretical Evaluation, 75 Nw. U. L. Rev. 1112 (1981).

78. See, e.g., Mathews v. Eldridge, 424 U.S. 319 (1976).

79. See generally Gunther, The Supreme Court, 1971 Term—Foreword: In Search of Evolving Doctrine on a Changing Court: A Model for a Newer Equal Protection, 86 Harv. L. Rev. 1 (1972).

80. 369 U.S. 186 (1962).

81. Id. at 210–11.

82. Jaffe, Standing to Secure Judicial Review: Public Actions, 74 Harv. L. Rev. 1265, 1303 (1961).

83. A. Bickel, supra note 3, at 186.

84. Jaffe, supra note 82, at 1302.

85. Compare Banco Nacional de Cuba v. Sabbatino, 376 U.S. 398 (1964), with First National City Bank v. Banco Nacional de Cuba, 406 U.S. 759 (1972).

86. U.S. Const. Art. 1, § 8, cl. 10.

87. I have drawn this distinction in a discussion of federal judicial deference to state executive and legislative policies. Redish, The Doctrine of Younger v. Harris: Deference in Search of a Rationale, 63 Cornell L. Rev. 463, 477–80 (1978).

It might be argued that authorizing the judiciary to engage in "substantive" deference effectively allows the legislative and executive branches the same freedom of operation that I have opposed in rejecting the total "procedural" deference of the political question doctrine. But, although in a sense the difference may be only one of degree, it is nevertheless one of vital importance. For, so long as the judiciary is available to maintain a floor of protection by providing an independent and objective review of the necessity of the legislative or executive actions when they threaten to violate a constitutional protection, the fundamental purposes of judicial review in a democracy will be achieved.

88. "The role of the Court and its raison d'etre are to evolve, 'to preserve, protect and defend' principle." A. Bickel, supra note 3, at 188. See the discussion of Bickel's theory supra at 78; 97–100.

89. For example, Bickel argues that, even in cases in which the judicial process has been invoked defensively, i.e., as a defense to a criminal action,

> outright dismissal of the suit is the solution, after all other devices have been exhausted. In the congressional-investigation cases, where the criminal process is invoked, the solution, all else failing, is to deny the process to Congress and require it to use its own, at the bar of each House.

Id. at 189. Bickel noted that in such a case "[i]ntervention by the Court would still be possible on habeas corpus." Id. However, such judicial action would seem to defeat his goal of not enmeshing the Court in this type of controversy in the first place. Perhaps he meant, as he suggested earlier, that in such a case the Court could use the opportunity to "exert immense influence," even though "[i]t may be unable to wield its ultimate power as an organ of government charged with translating principle into positive law" by speaking to the government and to the people through its opinions. Id. at 188. One may question why this procedure would not amount to an impermissible advisory opinion, however.

90. See discussion supra at 124.

91. A. Bickel, supra note 3, at 184.

92. Scharpf, supra note 1, at 566–67.

93. Id. at 567.

94. Cf. New York Times Co. v. United States, 403 U.S. 713 (1971).

95. Scharpf, supra note 1, at 567.

96. United States v. New York Times Co., 444 F.2d 544 (2d Cir. 1971).

97. Scharpf, supra note 1, at 577.

98. See cases cited supra note 85.

99. Finkelstein, supra note 30, at 344.

100. A. Bickel, supra note 3, at 184.

101. Scharpf, supra note 1, at 549–50.

102. Id. at 550.

103. See, e.g., Crockett v. Reagan, 720 F.2d 1355 (D.C. Cir. 1983) (per curiam), cert. denied, 467 U.S. 1251 (1984).

104. 323 U.S. 214, 244 (1944) (Jackson, J., dissenting).

105. See United States v. Nixon, 418 U.S. 683 (1974).

106. See generally Redish, Congressional Power to Regulate Supreme Court Appellate Jurisdiction under the Exceptions Clause: An Internal and External Examination, 27 Vill. L. Rev. 900 (1982).

107. Id. at 902.

108. Mulhern, In Defense of the Political Question Doctrine, 137 U. Pa. L. Rev. 97 (1988).

109. Id. at 119–23.
110. Id. at 127–28 (footnote omitted).
111. Id. at 133.
112. Id. at 134.
113. Id. at 141 (footnote omitted).
114. Id. at 164.
115. Id. at 164.
116. Id. at 165 (footnote omitted).
117. Id. (footnote omitted).
118. See discussion supra at 113; 116–21.
119. See id.
120. Mulhern, supra note 108, at 122–23.
121. Although the Supreme Court has not spoken definitively on the issue, the lower courts seem to be in agreement on the point. See, e.g., Bartlett v. Bowen, 816 F.2d 695 (D.C. Cir. 1987); Battaglia v. General Motors Corp., 169 F.2d 254 (2d cir.), cert. denied, 335 U.S. 887 (1948). For a discussion of this line of cases, see M. Redish, Federal Jurisdiction: Tensions in the Allocation of Judicial Power 44–47 (2d ed. 1990).
122. It should be noted that state courts, as well as federal courts, may—at least in theory—provide a valid constitutional check on congressional action. As Professor Hart has argued, "[i]n the scheme of the Constitution, [the state courts] are the primary guarantors of constitutional rights, and in many cases they may be the ultimate ones." Hart, The Power of Congress to Limit the Jurisdiction of Federal Courts: An Exercise in Dialectic, 66 Harv. L. Rev. 1362, 1401 (1953).
123. See generally chapter 5.
124. See discussion supra at 78–85.
125. See discussion supra at 115–16; 126.
126. See generally Wechsler, supra note 3.
127. Mulhern, supra note 108, at 141.
128. Henkin, supra note 4, at 617. "When federal courts deny a remedy for want of equity, they do not declare an issue nonjusticiable, whether on textual or prudential grounds; they make no extra-ordinary exception to judicial review. Rather, they review, and they may even declare invalid, though they deny all or some equitable remedies." Id. at 618.
129. Id. (footnote omitted).
130. Id. at 618–19 (footnote omitted).
131. "It was something closer to denying an equitable remedy, than to abstaining from judicial review and dismissing for nonjusticiability, that the Supreme Court may have been (and should have been) about in [*Gilligan*]." Id. at 619.
132. *Gilligan*, 413 U.S. at 10 (emphasis in original), quoted in Henkin, supra note 4, at 621.
133. *Gilligan*, 413 U.S. at 10, 11.

EIGHT

1. See, e.g., Younger v. Harris, 401 U.S. 37 (1971). Cf. Hart, The Power of Congress to Limit the Jurisdiction of Federal Courts: An Exercise in Dialectic, 66 Harv. L. Rev. 1362, 1401 (1953) ["In the scheme of the Constitution, [the state courts] are the primary guarantors of constitutional rights. . . . "

2. See, e.g., Neuborne, The Myth of Parity, 90 Harv. L. Rev. 1105 (1977). Much of my previous writing has also questioned the notion of state-federal court parity. See, e.g., M. Redish, Federal Jurisdiction: Tensions in the Allocation of Judicial Power 1–4 (2d ed. 1990).

3. Compare Chemerinsky, Parity Reconsidered: Defining a Role for the Federal Judiciary, 36 UCLA L. Rev. 233 (1988) (arguing that it is, as a practical matter, impossible to resolve definitively the state-federal court "parity" debate), with Redish, Judicial Parity, Litigant Choice, and Democratic Theory: A Comment on Federal Jurisdiction and Constitutional Rights, 36 UCLA L. Rev. 329 (1988) (institutional factors demonstrate superiority of federal courts).

4. 28 U.S.C. § 1332(a) provides that, in cases in which jurisdiction is premised on diversity of citizenship, "the matter in controversy [must] exceed[] the sum or value of $50,000, exclusive of interest and costs. . . . "

5. In Snyder v. Harris, 394 U.S. 332 (1969), the Court adhered to its long-held position that plaintiffs could aggregate their claims in order to meet the jurisdictional amount requirement only in the relatively rare situation where the claims were deemed to be "joint." The Court reasoned that "[i]f there is a present need to expand the jurisdiction of [the federal] courts we cannot overlook the fact that the Constitution specifically vests the power in the Congress, not in the courts." 394 U.S. at 341–42. The Court so held, even though the language of the statute said nothing directly about the issue of aggregation, and the drafters of the Federal Rules of Civil Procedure had recently modified the multi-party procedures in order to abandon the concept of "joint" and "several" rights as antiquated and unworkable. See Kaplan, Continuing Work of the Civil Committee: 1966 Amendments of the Federal Rules of Civil Procedure (I), 81 Harv. L. Rev. 356, 380–86 (1967).

Congress recently increased the jurisdictional minimum from $10,000 to $50,000, and in so doing did nothing to alter the Court's aggregation rules. Pub. L. 100–702, 102 Stat. 46467 (Nov. 19, 1988). Arguably, such congressional action could be taken to imply congressional approval of those rules. However, such action could just as easily be explained by a congressional willingness to defer to the Court's judgments on such issues. Moreover, the fact remains that such an analysis would effectively transform a failure to legislate into the equivalent of legislation, an unacceptable practice as a matter of political theory. See chapter 4, supra at 53–55. In any event, the Court in *Snyder* obviously did not have the benefit of this legislative data when it made its decision.

6. See note 5, supra.

7. United Steelworkers of America, AFL-CIO, v. R.H. Bouligny, Inc., 382 U.S. 145 (1965). See also Carden v. Arkoma Associates, 110 S. Ct. 1015 (1990).

8. See chapter 4, supra at 47–74.

9. See chapter 3, supra at 31–46.

INDEX